MASTERY IN 7 STEPS

UNDERSTANDING MASTERY, SUCCESS, AND MIND

Dennis E. Bradford, Ph.D.

Copyright

ISBN 978-1-940487-12-0

This electronic book is copyright @ 2014 by Ironox Works, Inc., P.O. Box 80267, Las Vegas, Nevada, 89180, U.S.A.

Second edition. (This is a slightly revised version of The 7 Steps to Mastery, which appeared in 2007.)

All rights are reserved. No part of this book shall be reproduced or transmitted in any form or by any means, such as electronic, mechanical, magnetic, photographic including photocopying, or recording by any information storage or retrieval system, without the prior written permission of the publisher. In other words, it is illegal to copy, distribute, or create derivative works from this book in whole or in part, and it is also illegal to contribute to the copying, distribution, or creating of derivative works of this book.

By the Same Author

The Fundamental Ideas

The Three Things the Rest of Us Should Know about Zen Training

The Meditative Approach to Philosophy

How to Survive College Emotionally

Personal Transformation

How to Eat Less – Easily!

Compulsive Overeating Help

Getting Things Done

How to Become Happily Published

With Anna Wright: Belly Fat Blast

Emotional Eating

Love and Respect

12 Publicity Mistakes that Keep Marketers Poor

It's Not Just About the Money!

To

Anna

Acknowledgements

I thank Ethel Bradford, Panayot Butchvarov, Megan Dreisbach, Bill Edgar, Stacey Edgar, Art Spring, and Annabella Walker-Wright for their comments on drafts of this manuscript.

Though they saved me from many mistakes, I alone, of course, am responsible for any remaining errors.

Foreword

If there is insufficient excellence in your life to suit you, this book is for you. It explains how to master any activity—including living itself.

I committed myself to mastering life when I was seventeen, which was about fifty years ago. It's taken me a long time to figure out what you are about to learn.

Even if you enjoy it, if you read this book and then put it forever on a shelf it won't have worked for you the way that I intend. What I'd like you to do is to read it, select an area for greater excellence, and then consult it again and again as you practice applying its ideas to that area until you achieve the excellence you want.

There's a critical difference between merely understanding the theory of excellence and being excellent. Understanding has to do with absorbing the abstract ideas about some activity, whereas excellence has to do with living those ideas, making them concrete. It's rather like the difference between understanding sex and doing it. You can read all you want to about sex, but experiencing it is radically different.

It's fun to learn new ideas; being an intellectual adventurer provides lots of insights, lots of wonderful "Aha!" moments. It's also a lasting joy to master an important activity.

What's not initially fun, however, is doing what it takes to become excellent, in other words, relentlessly practicing well. The trick, then, to mastery, if there is one, is to make the practicing as enjoyable as possible. It's to let go of focusing on the goal and enjoy doing—not just understanding—what it takes to become excellent. **Masters master practicing.**

The purpose of this book is to shorten your learning curve. Disciplined persistent practicing is required for excellence. Since it's much better to be excellent than merely to practice to become excellent, shortening your learning curve is extremely valuable. Life is short. Why not become excellent as quickly as possible? Depending in part upon which activity you select, it may take years of practicing properly to master it--even after you have understood the theory, selected an activity, and begun practicing. Well, better years than decades!

My hope is that this book will prove to be the most useful book you've ever read.

I'd love to receive your feedback. I value your opinion. You may email me at by commenting on any blog post at: http://dennis-bradford.com/

Let's get started!

"I'm not a teacher: only a fellow-traveler of whom you asked the way. I pointed ahead—ahead of myself as well as you."
George Bernard Shaw

Preface

We get one shot at life: why not become excellent at something important to you?

But how? After all, we weren't given instructions at birth on how to live well.

Trial and error may work, but it's slow, ineffective, and sometimes dangerous.

Imitation works. It's our basic way of learning. However, especially for adults who choose to learn new activities, imitation + understanding works better than imitation alone. Understanding a process enables us to become excellent at it more quickly and easily.

This book is about how to increase excellence in your life. *Its purpose is to help you become excellent at whatever activity you select more quickly and easily* than would otherwise have been possible. By way of contrast, its purpose is not to entice you into getting stuck merely thinking about excellence.

Which activity interests you? Here's a partial list of possibilities:

    A spiritual practice (such as zazen meditation)
    Making and keeping friends
    Writing (fiction or nonfiction)
    A physical discipline (such as strength training)
    An academic domain (to a terminal degree and beyond)
    Being a successful entrepreneur
    Parenting
    A martial art
    Dating
    Real estate investing

Establishing your own profitable business (such as network marketing)
A sport (such as tennis or hockey)
A fine art (such as painting)
Selling
Public speaking
Another language
An outdoor pastime (such as camping or fishing)
A game (such as chess)
A performing art (such as ballet)
Cooking
A craft or hobby (such as needlepoint or woodworking)

I encourage you to do much better than you are already doing.

This book organizes a vast welter of sometimes confusing and conflicting ideas. It offers *a coherent system for understanding how to become excellent at an activity of your choice*. It will help you find an activity that suits you well and provide a clear blueprint of what to do to begin mastering it.

The **good news** is that becoming excellent at an activity is the result of taking a sequence of steps and this sequence is the same in all successful cases. This book contains the method that, once you learn it and use it, will shorten your learning curve and lead you to mastery.

You are very valuable. In my judgment, you are infinitely important. Each of us is.

You are also unique. There's nobody else exactly like you. You are an original. Nobody else has a brain that is just like yours. Nobody else has been blessed with your genetic endowment and your experiences. Because of your uniqueness, what works well for someone else may not work well for you.

You may also be a lot more creative than you give yourself credit for being. Many people have too low an opinion of their own creativity. Though you may not yet have found your niche, in some way or other you are enormously gifted. I know that you have what it takes for excellence, and I explain in what follows how I know that.

You are seriously interested in doing better, which is why you purchased this book. If you are like me, you've read many dozens of self-help books, listened to dozens of self-improvement audio programs, watched many training DVD's or videotapes, and even attended lots of seminars and courses. It can all seem as intimidating as it is confusing. Most of it makes at least superficial sense, but perhaps nothing so far has worked excellently for you.

Since you are unique, nobody knows exactly what you should do to become excellent at something. However, what you are about to learn is (i) the way to excellence that has been successfully used by many others and (ii) how to tailor that way best to suit your unique abilities. It involves a set of skills that can be learned in a simple, step-by-step manner.

Just because it is simple, it doesn't follow that excellence is easy. It also doesn't follow that you will be able to become excellent at any particular activity; there may be some activities that are not a good match for your talents.

You'll learn[1] how to select the best activity for you to master. Rest assured: you not only have the aptitude for becoming excellent at an activity of your choice, you have the aptitude for becoming excellent at more than one. Just learning how to pick the best one could save you a lot of money and years of frustrated effort.

It might be that you are not very motivated at the moment. It might be that you are not feeling particularly good about your life right now. You might even be feeling discouraged and frustrated. Why not turn these thoughts around? Imagine how much better you'd feel about your life if you became excellent at some activity that was important to you. Just imagine how glorious each day could be!

Would you like to feel a lot better about your life? Unless you are already fully engaged in mastering a valuable activity (in which case, except perhaps for reinforcement, you don't need it), this book will teach you how.

Furthermore, amazingly and more importantly, **everyone has the aptitude for mastering life itself.** Doing that involves mastering our most important asset, namely, the mind. Once you grasp the method for mastering a particular activity, you'll be able to understand how mastering life itself is possible and how, in principle, to do it.[2] This is the most important mastery of all.

As quickly as you understand the ideas contained in this book, you should just as quickly become a lot more hopeful that your life will improve. You'll understand not only how mastering a specific kind of activity occurs, but also you'll understand how mastering life itself occurs. In effect, you'll have **a clear blueprint for living better**.

By the end of Chapter 3, you'll already have begun to understand the critical difference between the standard success model of excellence and the mastery model of excellence.

I do not promise that you will become excellent at an important activity. Since nobody else can live your life for you, that would be foolish. You may do nothing with the powerful information contained in this book. What you will learn is a coherent plan of action that, *if you use it*, will enable you to begin mastering an activity of your choice.

Ideally, after a while, others will notice the improvements in your life. You'll be showing them how to live better. (If they happen to ask how it is that you are doing so much better, perhaps you'd be kind enough to mention this book.)

Mastery is not a zero-sum game. There's no benefit to keeping excellent ideas about living better to yourself. The more mastery we can promote, the better all our lives will be.

What's the best way to get the most value for your money?

The best way is simply to read it once from beginning to end very quickly. This view from 30,000 feet will enable you to grasp the big picture. Then proceed at whatever pace suits you best to reread it at your leisure. This will enable you really to absorb all its ideas—and to notice those you missed on the initial reading. Then, of course, begin to install the relevant ideas in your daily activities. Check back with it occasionally after that to ensure that you aren't missing the forest for the trees.

However you read it, please approach it with **an open mind**. It's good to be skeptical and questioning, but it's foolish to be automatically negative about new ideas and stuck on old ideas. How could your life improve unless you improve your thinking? How could your thinking improve unless you permit yourself to try new thoughts? The time to evaluate the contents of this (or any other) book is *after* you have understood and absorbed them.

In terms of the quality of your life, if you are unwilling to improve how you think, you have already reached your maximum potential.

The ideas expressed here are neither new nor original. Some thinkers have understood the basic ideas at least since the Axial Age (about 2500 years ago) and probably for centuries before that. The structure of the presentation is original, but the coherence and efficacy of the method have stood the test of time.

By reading this book, you are trying to understand how to live better. Though you may not have realized it before, that's exactly what philosophers do. Philosophers are just people who are serious about living wisely.

If this is an initial or early exposure to philosophy, welcome! This book is packed with interesting and useful ideas. You'll find some of them exciting.

Furthermore, there's nothing to fear. Please don't be intimidated. Permit me to explain why you cannot lose anything valuable by reading this book or, in general, by doing philosophy.

To be a philosopher is to attempt to live better by leading an examined life. To examine is to question. Unless one makes the false assumption that it is possible to live well accidentally, it is beneficial frequently to question what we think, say, and do.

Though it is not easy to live an examined life, the alternative is much worse. Why? Anyone who does not examine life will fail to learn its lessons, and anyone who fails to learn its lessons is doomed to suffer their repetition. For a philosopher, inappropriate or false judgments, unkind words, and actions that cause harm are all opportunities to improve. Without noticing the feedback life is giving us, how could we learn from our errors? Everyone who practices philosophy benefits from it.

It may be initially uncomfortable to examine your own ideas, but you'll quickly find that it's only beneficial. *Intellectual progress comes about only when there's a clash of ideas.* What could happen if you were to question your own ideas by clashing alien ideas against them?

There can be only one of two outcomes in a given case. (i) If your idea withstands scrutiny, if it stands up to the challenge, then you can have even more confidence in it. It's good to have confidence in your own ideas. It's good to know that they have been tested. (ii) If your idea doesn't withstand scrutiny and you replace it with a better idea, then you'll benefit forever from your improved understanding. It's good to have better ideas.

Therefore, examining your own ideas can only have a beneficial outcome. There are only two possible outcomes, and both are beneficial. So you have nothing to lose. Fear is unjustifiable.

A word of caution: even if they appeal to you, please do not get attached to the ideas advocated in this book. In other words, even if you adopt them temporarily, please don't fail to continue the process of examining them. Of course, it's good to detach from bad ideas in favor of better ones, but use those better ones only to provide some additional traction and continue to advance by continuing to examine. **Excellence is dynamic**; it's not static.

Thank you for purchasing this book. I want you to benefit greatly from having done so.

However wonderful they may be, the ideas from this (or any other) book won't serve you well until they are used. My hope for you is that you will quickly understand them and then make them concrete in your own life. I hope that your life becomes more and more excellent. If you don't already, may you soon realize that **happiness is a by-product of excellence.** May you enjoy the journey!

Conesus, New York　　　　　Dennis E. Bradford, Ph.D.
14 May 2014

Contents

FOREWORD VII
PREFACE IX
PART I: THE WAY OF THE WORLD 1
   CHAPTER 1: WHERE WE ARE 3
      1.1 The Existential Questions 3
      1.2 Living Better 6
      1.3 The Human Condition 13
      1.4 Improving Life 18
   CHAPTER 2: THE WAY OF THE WORLD 23
      2.1 Minds as Gardens 24
      2.2 Understanding Understanding 28
      2.3 Increasing Understanding 30
      2.4 Accounts of Human Nature 36
      2.5 A Worldly Account of Being Human 38
      2.6 Getting Ahead 44
   CHAPTER 3: SUCCESS AND MASTERY 49
      3.1 The Living and the Dead 49
      3.2. Abstract Goods 57
      3.3. The Time of Our Lives 63
      3.4 Desire 68
      3.5 The Success Model and the Mastery Model 71
PART II: THE 7 STEPS TO MASTERY 77
   CHAPTER 4: WHAT-IS 79
      4.1.   Transition 79
      4.2 Confidence 82
      4.3 Coming To Our Senses 87
      4.4 Awareness 94
      4.5 The Obstructed Obvious 98
   CHAPTER 5: CREATING YOUR REALITY 105
      5.1 Worldmaking 106
      5.2 Interbeing 112
      5.3 Identity 117
      5.4 Mastering and Conceptualizing 119

CHAPTER 6: UNDERSTANDING YOURSELF 123
- 6.1 Nothing, Everything, or In Between? 125
- 6.2 Our Sort 132
- 6.3 Mind 134
- 6.4 Selflessness 140

CHAPTER 7: ADJUSTING YOUR ATTITUDE 149
- 7.1 Detachment 153
- 7.2 Gratitude 157
- 7.3 Responsibility 161
- 7.4 Humility 165
- 7.5 Philosophical Courage 167
- 7.6 Compassion 170
- 7.7 Abundance 174
- 7.8 Cheerfulness 176

CHAPTER 8: ORGANIZING YOUR VALUES 179
- 8.1 Personality 184
- 8.2 Eliciting Value 189
- 8.3 Physical 191
- 8.4 Mental 194
- 8.5 Perceptual 198
- 8.6 Emotional 200
- 8.7 Activity 202

CHAPTER 9: HABITS 207
- 9.1 I's and Me's 208
- 9.2 System 211
- 9.3 Physical 218
- 9.4 Mental 228
- 9.5 Perceptual 232
- 9.6 Emotional 234
- 9.7 Activity 235
- 9.8 Daily Habits 237

CHAPTER 10: TECHNIQUES 243
- 10.1 Behold 243
- 10.2 Beware 245
- 10.3 Practicing With a Job 251
- 10.4 One Kind of Freedom 257
- 10.5 Reaction 266

PART III: MAKING MASTERY CONCRETE 269
    CHAPTER 11: SELECTING AN ACTIVITY TO MASTER 271
        11.1 Flow 272
        11.2 Heritage 275
        11.3 Strategy 279
        11.4 Entrapment 281
        11.5 Identifying Talents 289
        11.6 Selecting a Talent 293
        11.7 Strengths 300
    CHAPTER 12: THE MOST IMPORTANT ACTIVITY 307
        12.1 Sages 307
        12.2 Zen Buddhism 312
        12.3 Ego Reduction 316
        12.4 The Greatest Advantage 318
        12.5 A Natural Koan 319
        12.5 Falling In Love 323

ENDNOTES 329

SELECTED BIBLIOGRAPHY 343

ABOUT THE AUTHOR 361

Part I:
The Way of the World

Chapter 1: Where We Are

1.1 The Existential Questions

There are no more important questions than questions such as: *Who am I?* (Let that question sink from your head to your gut and percolate for a few years.)

Somehow or other I came to be living in the world. How did it happen that I just found myself living?

What should I do now that I am here? What should my life be like? How ought I to arrange it? *What should I do?*

What will become of me? What may I hope for?

How can I make the best of this strange, occasionally dreadful, situation I just find myself in? If I am going to live, might I be able to live better or, even, well? Might there be a way to master life?

Wondering about the answers to such questions comes easily to children. It's natural when we are youngsters to ask existential questions like these.

[*Sidebar quotation* from Socrates: "This sense of wonder is the mark of the philosopher. Philosophy indeed has no other origin..."[3]]

Many teens wonder hard about them. They can lead to an identity crisis, or to numbness, or to death by a thousand distractions.

We adults have a tendency to try to ignore them when they arise; after all, we're older and have more urgent and practical business to attend to. The problem with this tactic, though, is that it doesn't really work well. Unanswered existential questions don't magically answer themselves or vaporize; they remain unanswered beneath the surface.

At least in this one respect, it's beneficial to be like children. It's good to ask ourselves the existential questions. Their answers are important. They are questions about ourselves. Why shouldn't adults, too, ask an individual's most important questions? How do we fit into the world?

[*Sidebar quotation* from Aristotle: "For it is owing to their wonder that men both now begin and at first began to philosophize."]

It's instructive to note a recent controversy from the modern tradition of western philosophy.

Hegel was the last thinker in that tradition who is universally recognized as great. (There may have been great thinkers since Hegel and there may even be great thinkers alive today, but it's difficult to recognize them because we are too close to them. It'll be easier in a hundred or a thousand years.) Even though he's been dead less than two centuries, there's already agreement that Hegel was a great thinker and as yet no agreement that anyone since him has been a great thinker.

Hegel recommends that we forget ourselves.

At the end of a long Preface to the book that he thought of as introducing his system of ideas, Hegel wrote that, although of course the individual "must make of himself and achieve what he can," since his contribution "can only be very small . . . the individual must all the more forget himself."[4]

This, as I attempt to make clear in what follows, is excellent advice for those relatively few of us who have satisfactorily answered the existential questions for themselves. In other words, though "Forget yourself" is excellent advice for mature mastery, it is wholly useless advice with respect to children or for those of us who are older and who have not yet answered the existential questions.

Kierkegaard vehemently objected to what he considered Hegel's ignoring the importance of the individual self. Though Kierkegaard had predecessors such as Pascal in the tradition, we now understand that western philosophy took an important turn with Kierkegaard. It was a **turn away from conceptualizing toward existing.**

Here's how Kierkegaard once put it: "One sticks one's finger into the soil to tell by the smell in what land one is: I stick my finger into existence—it smells of nothing. Where am I? Who am I? How came I here? What is this thing called the world? What does this world mean? Who is it that has lured me into this thing and now leaves me there? . . . How did I come into the world? Why was I not consulted . . . but was thrust into the ranks as though I had been bought of a kidnapper, a dealer in souls? How did I obtain an interest in this big enterprise they call reality? Why should I have an interest in it? It is not a voluntary concern? And if I am compelled to take part in it, where is the director? . . .Whither shall I turn with my complaint?"

Who's right?

Is Hegel right that I should forget myself (and, presumably, focus on what is other), or is Kierkegaard right that I should focus on myself and answer the existential questions?

On the one hand, if I want to forget myself, is that even possible? If so, how? On the other hand, how can I genuinely help others without helping myself first?

These, too, are important questions. Aren't they questions that, in one way or another, we confront every day? If you happen to be a parent, it will be obvious to you that you do.

By the time you have finished this book, it's my intention that you'll have come to terms with all these questions. You won't find all the answers here, but that's because in the process of thinking them through carefully some of the questions will transform and, perhaps, dissolve. It's a fascinating process. Coming to terms with them is an important achievement.

Let us begin by being honest about our human condition. We must begin where we are.

What are our lives actually like?

Do you have all the answers? Is your life going as well as you would wish? Is it going as you planned it? Is there sufficient excellence in it?

If not, then you are dissatisfied. **Being dissatisfied is an excellent place to begin.** Instead of feeling guilty that you haven't yet mastered life or wallowing in the idea that you are an irredeemable failure, it's important simply to admit honestly to being dissatisfied in order to use that dissatisfaction to motivate significant improvements. Let's think about how your life is and how it could be.

1.2 Living Better

How are you doing?

The dull, the complacent, the immature, and some others never reach this level of reflection. They don't step back from their lives and ask themselves how they are doing. Whatever happens, some seem resolutely to remain attached to their favorite distractions and trivial engagements. (At least in the first part of the story, Meursault, the protagonist in Camus's *The Stranger*, is a literary example of someone like this.)

Therefore, I congratulate you. Really. You have already separated yourself from many people who never permit themselves to reflect on their lives.

Why don't they ever reach this point? I don't know. Your guess is as good as mine. Perhaps they are afraid. Because we fear the answers we may get, *it takes courage to question ourselves.*[5]

Fear is natural. Everyone has fears. The hero is not someone without fear; the hero is someone who has overcome fear.

Some fears are justifiable, and some aren't.

One way to overcome unjustifiable fear is to practice doing whatever one fears. At first, we have to force ourselves to practice, but the more we do it the easier it gets. The more we practice confronting whatever it is that we fear, the more the fear recedes.

[*Sidebar quotations*:

The Bible [Proverbs 12:1]: "He who loves correction loves knowledge; / he who hates reproof is a mere brute."

Johann W. von Goethe: ". . . nobody wants to grow."

Ralph Waldo Emerson: "Do the thing you fear and the death of fear is certain."

Henry David Thoreau: "It is never too late to give up your prejudices.

Winston Churchill: "Remember the story of the Spanish prisoner. For many years he was confined in a dungeon . . . One day it occurred to him to push the door of his cell. It was open; and it had never been locked."]

Let's assume that you're in the process of overcoming your fear of questioning. The more you practice questioning, the less fear will impede you.

It'd be a good idea to take a moment to remember actually doing that sometime in your life. Think of an episode that paralyzed you with fear. Think of how, for whatever reason, you forced yourself, or someone else such as a parent or teacher forced you, to proceed. Think of how you kept doing whatever it was until the fear receded into the background. Remember how good that freedom felt?

There's a word for people who question: "philosopher." If you have been questioning for years, if you have been seriously asking the existential questions for a while now, whether you realized it or not, you already are a philosopher.

Philosophy begins when we seriously wonder how we can do better.

The fact that you purchased this book demonstrates concretely that you are seriously interested in improving your life. You wouldn't have been seriously interested in doing that if you had not been dissatisfied with your life.

I taught philosophy full-time for 32 years, and during the first couple of classes of every semester some undergraduates realize that they had already become philosophers without realizing it. They were already at home questioning life, putting it to the test. You may be the same way. Even if it doesn't yet feel comfortable, if you persist in practicing questioning, it soon will.

If you just continue to think your way through this book, you'll feel better about your life. If you then were to reread it and actually begin to practice some of its ideas, you may be astounded at how much better you begin to feel.

Please, though, let go of any expectation you may have that your life will immediately start getting better and better. It never works that way. *With respect to excellence, things have to unravel and get worse before they begin to get better and better.*

Think of a young eagle flying from its nest for the first time. It must require courage to step forth into the void, because that always initially results in falling rapidly toward the ground; then the eaglet frantically struggles with all its might to get its wings working to stabilize itself and begin mastering the air. Soon the eaglet begins flying upward and, even, soaring. That's the natural way the process works.

My task in this book is to encourage you until you don't need encouraging any more, until you begin soaring.

This explains why being dissatisfied is an excellent place to begin. Where else is there to begin? Why would someone who is wholly satisfied question anything? Without dissatisfaction, why would any eaglet ever step forth into the unknown? There is never opportunity without risk. Everything has a price. **There's no soaring without letting go**. Mastering a new way of life requires releasing an old way of life.

I'm not the only one who thinks this way. All philosophers do. If you select any experienced philosopher at random, that person will confirm this. Here, for example, is just one example among thousands. Julia Annas writes, "most of us are dissatisfied with both our achievement and our promise, and it is only the dissatisfied who have the urge to live differently, and hence the need to find out what ways of living differently would be improvements."[6] She's right, of course.

Furthermore, it's been this way for thousands of years. You may previously have picked up the idea that philosophy is some esoteric subject studied at universities by eager-faced undergraduates. Well, it is an academic subject, but essentially, and centuries before there were ever universities, it was **a way of life.**

One reason I picked Julia Annas as an example is that she quotes Arius Didymus who wrote over two millennia ago: "It is not the person who listens eagerly and takes notes at philosophy lectures who is ready for philosophizing, rather the person whose state is ready for transferring the lessons of philosophy into action, and for living accordingly."[7]

I also assume that you are ready to use philosophy to improve your life (and improving your life will automatically improve the lives of those others around you who you love).

Has the importance of this begun to sink in?

By being a philosopher you make yourself part of a venerable tradition that stretches back thousands of years. Far from being alone, you are already in the select company of some of the most outstanding human beings who have ever lived. Unless you are already practicing excellence, you are on the threshold of creating a much more wonderful life for yourself.

The meaning of our word 'philosopher' comes from the ancient Greek for 'lover of wisdom'. Etymologically, then, a philosopher is someone who seeks wisdom.

There's no sense seeking what one already has. The purpose of philosophy is to succeed in one's search, in other words, to become wise. A successful philosopher, someone who is wise, is a sage. A sage is someone who lives well, someone who is excellent at living.

So, anyone who seriously wants to live well is a philosopher, and anyone who succeeds is a sage.

Living better is the purpose of philosophy. Its goal is living well. Despite what you may have picked up elsewhere, it's that simple.

In other words, **living well is the purpose of philosophizing**, of reflecting about life. The point is not to get stuck questioning or seeking or merely reflecting; the point is to live excellently.

That's the subject of this book. You didn't purchase it just to own it or even read it; you purchased it as a tool to live better. Unless acted upon, even the greatest ideas are useless. Now that we've become clear about the goal, where should we begin?

[*Sidebar quotation* from Master Chinul: "Obviously, if you are going to make a journey of a thousand miles, the first step has to be right; if the first step is mistaken, the whole thousand miles is mistaken . . . if the initial belief is mistaken, then all virtues fall away."]

There is no ideal starting point. If you are serious about improving your life, you've no choice but to begin wherever you are. It's like that for everyone.

Suppose that I'm in New York and would like to travel to Iceland. Where should I begin my journey? London? Cairo? Los Angeles? Of course not. I've no choice but to begin from New York, from where I am. *We must all begin from wherever we are.*

This is why philosophy always begins with **self-examination**. It cannot begin elsewhere.

Though we are all unique individuals, though we are all different, we are all similar in that we are all human beings.

In fundamental ways, your life is similar to mine. We share the human condition, which is the subject of the next section. Once pointed out, this is an obvious point.

Nevertheless, it is also an important one. Because we are different, we may have different values. Where's the best place to live? What's the most delicious dessert? Who was the greatest composer? Which political view is the best? Which football team do you want to win the championship? And so on and on. We all have lots of different preferences and opinions, and there is so much disagreement that it can seem as if we've little in common. That's not true.

Plato and Aristotle were the first two great philosophers in the western tradition. As Aristotle emphasized, since we are all of the same kind, since we are all human beings, what is good for us will be of the same kind. What is really good for one human being will be good for another human being.

11

What is good for a human being may not be the same as what is good for, say, a star or for an ocean or for a spider. Nevertheless, fundamentally, what is good for you is also good for me.

It would be good to understand what is good for human beings. If we knew what was best for us, we could arrange our lives to favor it. So, let's ask:

What is good for a human being? In other words, what is an excellent human being? When a human being lives well, what's that like?

It's important to notice that these questions cannot be coherently answered until a logically more fundamental question is answered, namely, "What is a human being?" Unless one understands what a human being is, one cannot sort human beings into those who live excellently (the wise, those who are sages) and those who don't (the foolish, those who are not sages).

There's no issue here. Nobody disagrees. The question, "What is good for a human being?" is less fundamental than the question, "What is a human being?" This is why we should consider the nature of human being.

Permit me to push this one step further. The question, "What is a human being?" is less fundamental than the question, "What is a being?" Unless one understands what a being is, one cannot sort beings into those who are human and those who aren't.

Does the question, "What is a being?" take your intellectual breath away? It should. It may make you dizzy. If you think about it too much, it may give you a headache. Initially, one has no idea even how to begin answering it. Nobody said this was going to be easy.

What is an excellent human being?
What is a human being?

What is a being?

As philosophers, though, we must have the courage to ask such difficult questions. Why? It's logically simple: unless I understand what a being is, I cannot understand what a human being is, and, unless I understand what a human being is, I cannot understand what an excellent human being is. If I don't understand what an excellent human being is, how, except by accident, could I be one?[8]

Whew! We've actually made a lot of progress already. The key point is that we have focused our attention on the importance of having a clear understanding about what it means to be a human being.

Let's discuss human nature in the next chapter; instead, let's now zero in on its most critical feature. Ready to focus on your life? If not, take a break and come back when you are refreshed and ready. If so, let's go.

1.3 The Human Condition

What's **the human condition**? It's the way we are.

We are dissatisfied. Life is difficult, imperfect, flawed. Sometimes we suffer acutely; sometimes we are on fire. Usually, though, for most North Americans at least, such misery as we experience is often routine. Life is often merely boring. Moments of intense happiness are fleeting. We experience snatches of happiness sometimes for minutes, occasionally for days, and almost never for weeks or months. Episodes of unadulterated joy are few and far between. We adults realize that, which always makes them bittersweet and makes us inclined to cling to them.

They are not our normal condition, which is why we priz nger. It's not as if our lives are constantly and smoothly transitioning from one joyful experience to the next, is it?

Though we may usually prefer to avoid thinking about it, **life humbles us**. Humiliation awaits each of us. We pretend that it is otherwise, but, even when we smile confidently to the outside world, we may feel hollow or frightened.

Who among us is exempt from decay and illness? Only those who die too young will escape the infirmities of aging. Who among us won't die? Who among us has established permanent loving relationships? Who among us has contributed great achievements that will last forever?

We would like it to be otherwise. We greatly value our destinies, but we are humbled and frustrated by being unable to control them. We keep asking of life what it cannot give.

We are human animals. We were born, and we shall die. We have grown and matured, but our inexorable fate was inherent in our conception. We breed and raise our young only to be replaced by them. We think of ourselves as having a normal temporal duration of some five or ten decades. The biological cycle is unforgiving.

What, we occasionally wonder, does it all mean? Does it mean anything at all? Is there a way to make it meaningful if it isn't or to make it more meaningful if it is?

We find ourselves in quite a muddle. We've thought ourselves into quite a fix. We want to do better, but we're unsure what to do to enjoy better outcomes. We want the consequences of our decisions to be good, but we are unable to tell which decisions will have the best consequences.

Neither returning to maximum thoughtlessness nor just more thoughtfulness is sufficient to cure what ails us. Some clear-headed thinking can point the way toward more excellent living, which is what this book is all about, but fixing our problems will actually require more than just thinking better. However, that's not really surprising. Though it is initially helpful in deciding what to select, merely thinking about a menu will not cure hunger.

We do not create reality, but we do create our individual surrealities. Your thinking does not create the world, but your thinking does create your world, how you understand your relation to the world. This is the subject matter of Chapters 4 and 5. For now, begin to try out the idea that this is why good thinking is important for living well, but it is also why, by itself, it is insufficient.

This is a critical point about the human condition: **we are not born understanding ourselves.** In fact, we weren't born understanding anything.

How did we get into this fix? We cannot remember. We cannot remember because we didn't understand anything, and we can only remember what we can understand. If so, we somehow managed to go from existing without any understanding to existing with understanding. That's a miracle.

Furthermore, somehow we managed to become aware of ourselves (our egos, our personal identities). We found ourselves existing separately from other beings. We learned to appreciate the difference, for example, between our own bodies and other bodies around us. We came to understand ourselves by discerning our relations to those other, separate beings.[9]

Eventually, this initial separation gives rise to the problem identified above, the great problem of self and other. Assuming that we understand the difference between self and other, what, if anything, should we do about it? Should we, <u>a la Hegel,</u> forget self and focus on other, or should we, <u>a la Kierkegaard,</u> forget other and focus on self?

We struggle for years and years with this problem. There is no mastering life without solving it.

Living is a process of relating to other beings. This relating is never stationary; it's always moving. Living is an incessant flux, a continual process of falling away from the past toward the future. Daily we must reposition ourselves with respect to others.

It is not possible to think about oneself, one's own life, without thinking about the process of relating to other beings. In fact, we may say that the ongoing **work** of life is nothing other than this process of relating to other beings.

This is essentially why Aristotle pointed out that we understand other individuals when we understand their work. For him, to be real is to be at work.[10] Reality is not an abstraction; it's a process of working. For example, consider some particular acorn. What's its work? Well, its work is the work of nutrition and growth. If it is successful at its work, it will become an oak tree that reproduces.

Not all individuals succeed. Not all individuals do their work well. If a squirrel eats this acorn, although it may succeed in helping to nourish the squirrel, it won't ever become an oak tree.

So Aristotle suggests that we understand individuals in terms of their functions.[11] If so, what's the function of a human being? What's being human for? What's a human being who lives well like?

Notice, again, that it is impossible to answer these questions coherently until we become clear about the nature of human being. To claim that something is an example of a successful human being presupposes understanding what human being is (and also presupposes understanding what being is).

Is this clear? Did you notice it yourself? If so and you are a beginner, very good. This demonstrates an aptitude for thinking better, more clearly.

We want to understand what it is for a human being to live well (to master life, to work successfully). To do that, we must first understand what a human being is. To do that, we must first understand what a being is.

Thinking better isn't easy. One is occasionally tempted to stomp off angrily and say it's all useless rubbish. At times, practicing philosophy can seem useless. It can certainly be frustrating.

However, whenever it gets frustrating, please remind yourself that *the only alternative* to thinking better is not thinking better. Since your life won't improve until you think better, why would you want to do that to yourself? Why not be kinder to yourself than that? Since it's not possible to improve life without it, thinking better is too important to let yourself be deterred by occasional frustration.

Life never gets magically better. It's true that it's wonderful when good fortune smiles on us, but good fortune is as unstable as it is unpredictable. It can be here one day and gone the next. Living well is not an accident. **Nobody lives well accidentally.** Nobody ever accidentally becomes excellent at any deliberate activity.

(If you have the slightest doubt about that, please review the list of activities provided in the Preface and try to think of a single person you've encountered who ever mastered any one of them accidentally. Come back when you fail.)

Though it's important not to confuse thinking well with living well, it's nevertheless true that at least some good thinking is necessary for living well.

Fortunately, we don't have to solve all the problems that arise in philosophy or in life to live well. We do, though, have to think well enough to solve some of them; unless we can at least figure out what living well is, we'll fail to live well.

It's important to resolve not to get stuck theorizing. *Theorizing is endless.* Sadly, there are many professors of philosophy who have gotten stuck doing just that. They are the ones who give philosophy a bad name. This book isn't written for professors of philosophy. It's written for philosophers, especially those philosophers with a beginner's mind who are serious about living well.

1.4 Improving Life

Is one of your projects improving your life, improving the work you are doing? Are you serious about becoming an excellent human being? Are you ready to do whatever it takes to live well?

If so, keep reading. If so and you are serious about it, then you already are a philosopher and the first critical step is behind you. If so and you are not serious about it, then we have already identified your problem and this book will teach you how to solve it. It's fine just to absorb its ideas and let them gestate. That's typically the first step in making permanent improvements. Eventually, though, for your sake, I hope that you make the decision to get serious and make use of them.

If not, stop reading and set it aside until you are ready for it. It's O.K. if you are not yet ready for it; that, too, will change when you have suffered more. It often requires experiencing a great loss to break the inertia. Your degree of dissatisfaction simply hasn't yet reached the critical threshold.

[*Sidebar quotation* from Ed Courtney: "When it becomes more difficult to suffer than to change, you'll change."]

The work of our lives should include improving them. My judgment is that life is worth living. Since suicide is an option and you are still alive, evidently you agree with me. If life is worth living, it's worth living well. If you are going to live it anyway, why not live it well? *Practicing philosophy is a very clever way of enjoying life.*

Would you like the choice of learning how to use mastery to improve your life? Once you understand the *how* of mastering, it's only a matter of *why*. If your *why*, your purpose, is strong enough, you'll figure out how to get better. So let's ask: Why would anyone want to live well?

Living well is a process of being in harmonious relation to other beings. More accurately, it's a process of continual becoming in a balanced, mutually beneficial relation to other beings.

Life sometimes knocks us down. A beloved parent or friend dies. Your career is ruined through no fault of your own. You are diagnosed with cancer. Your lover dumps you. A child runs away and is missing for months. Your house burns to the ground. And so on.

Have you been on a run of good luck? Excellent. Please don't, though, start taking it for granted. Luck is changeable.

Those who live well don't stay down when life knocks them down. Like one of those bottom-heavy, air-filled toys for infants, masters bounce up again immediately whenever they are knocked off balance. Furthermore, however many times they keep getting knocked down, they keep bouncing up. It's impossible to keep them down. Living excellently doesn't mean never getting knocked down; it means bouncing up again quickly after being knocked down, as many times as it takes.

Masters live centered (balanced, stabilized) lives. Occasionally, one finds them out-of-balance or off-center, but not for long.

This is why it's better to be a sage than not. Anyone who isn't busy living excellently is busy living an unbalanced, off-centered life. Why would you want to do that to yourself?

What's the only alternative? *The only alternative to living excellently is living less than excellently.* Living less than excellently is much more difficult than living well. It's true that, though perhaps simple, it's not easy to master life. However, the only alternative is much, much worse.

It's good if you practice philosophy. Everyone should practice philosophy. Why? I've yet to meet anyone who was perfectly balanced. We can all do better. You should practice philosophy as a way of mastering life. Everyone should. It would be best if we all became sages.

To begin to philosophize is simply to begin to examine your own life with the intention of improving it. If you are a fellow philosopher, the teachings in this book are just for you.

If you have made it this far into this book, my guess is that you are already a philosopher. You may not have taken any steps yet, but you are already pointed in the right direction. Good for you! Especially if you maintain the open, inquisitive mind of a beginner, I'll do my best to encourage you.

As you begin to examine your own life and the lives of others more seriously, you will notice certain similarities and differences. You'll notice qualities that are present in some lives and absent in others. This is natural. Qualities are nothing but commonalities, and individuals are nothing but clusters of qualities.

What qualities do we ordinarily take ourselves to have? In other words, how do we ordinarily think of ourselves? That is the topic of the next chapter.

Why discuss it? Think of it as a study in gap recognition. There is a difference between where we are and where we'd like to be. There's a difference between an ordinary life and a master's life. In order to bridge the chasm between the two, it's important to identify it clearly. Let's begin by identifying how we ordinarily live.

That will eventually lead us to understanding what not to do to live well. Learning how not to live well puts us closer to understanding how to live well. By noticing and learning from our own mistakes as well as those of others, we'll be able to understand how to improve how we are doing. By the end of Chapter 3, you'll already have a much clearer idea how excellence occurs.

Chapter 2: The Way of the World

The way of the world is seeking to gain what we want and to avoid or lose what we don't want. The purpose and work of life is to get whatever we prefer and to avoid or lose whatever we prefer to avoid. Living is a process of ceaselessly striving to obtain what we desire and to avoid what we desire to avoid.

Getting ahead is having more successes than failures. Anyone who has more gains than losses has been successful at getting ahead. Greater **success** is enjoying a higher ratio of gains to losses.

So the idea of **gaining** (getting ahead, acquiring success) is rooted in the way of the world. The way of the world is rooted in thinking that I'm over here and everything else is over there.

Am I, though, what I think I am?

What do I think I am?

Is gaining really the best way to live?

As counterintuitive as it may appear, I argue in what follows that (a certain kind of) **losing, not gaining, is living well** (mastering life). This thesis won't even begin to appear plausible until we exhaust the idea that gaining is living well. If the argument is sound, success isn't what it's cracked up to be; it doesn't result in living well.

Although being successful is preferable to being unsuccessful, it makes no difference with respect to living well whether you are successful or unsuccessful. An important, popular mistake is valuing being successful too highly. The strange truth is that *being successful is irrelevant to living well*.

The way to work into a position to understand this is to begin where we are, to begin with self-examination. Self-examination is inherently difficult. Since I'm the one doing the understanding, understanding myself is tricky. I lack perspective. The same goes for you and everyone else.

In this chapter, let's become clearer about how the process of understanding works, apply that process to understanding ourselves as human beings, and sketch an initially plausible account of what success is, in other words, what gaining means in terms of the way of the world.

2.1 Minds as Gardens

To attempt to **understand understanding** is to attempt to understand how our minds work.

I don't know how our minds work. Even if I did, this would not be the place for a thorough discussion.

Permit me, however, to point out one helpful analogy: our minds are like bountiful gardens. Our minds incessantly bring forth thoughts.

In his motivational classic <u>As A Man Thinketh</u>, James Allen wrote:

"A man's mind may be likened to a garden, which may be intelligently cultivated or allowed to run wild; but whether cultivated or neglected, it must, and will, *bring forth*. . . Just as a gardener cultivates his plot, keeping it free from weeds, and growing the flowers and fruits which he requires, so may a man tend the garden of his mind, weeding out all the wrong, useless, and impure thoughts, and cultivating toward perfection the flowers and fruits of right, useful, and pure thoughts. By pursuing this process, a man sooner or later discovers that he is the master-gardener of his soul, the director of his life . . . shaping . . . his character, circumstances, and destiny."[12]

Minds constantly produce thoughts (judgments, beliefs, propositions). That's an essential aspect of our human condition.

If you don't happen to like that, is there anything you could do to change it? Well, you could try various tactics (such as using intoxicating substances to dull or alter thoughts), but none of them will work well. The work of the mind is constantly to produce thoughts. As long as you are conscious with a healthy brain, the mind will keep producing thoughts.

Thoughts are divisible into useful and useless. Useful thoughts are, like flowers and fruits, beneficial and beautiful; useless thoughts are, like weeds in a garden, harmful and ugly.

The ongoing process of pruning the mind is the process of letting go of useless thoughts. This, as I attempt to explain in what follows, is the key to living wisely. Losing useless thoughts is the right kind of losing, and it's infinitely more valuable than any kind of gaining.

Whether you engage in this pruning process or not, your thoughts will determine the quality of your life. Why? It is your decisions that determine the quality of your life. Your decisions determine how you understand and what you do or fail to do.

[*Sidebar quotations:*

The Buddha: "Our life is shaped by our mind; we become what we think."

Lance Secretan: "[W]e are suffering from truth decay."]

It's true that life humbles us, that we are not in full control of our destinies, of *what* happens to us. On the other hand, we are in full control of *how* we understand what happens to us, which does enable us to control the quality of our lives.[13] We do control whether and how we act with respect to our understanding of our circumstances.

Where do acts come from? Thoughts! As Allen writes, "every act of a man springs from the hidden seeds of thought, and could not have appeared without them. This applies equally to those acts called 'spontaneous' and 'unpremeditated' as to those which are deliberately executed."[14]

The reason that this applies even to acts (actions, behaviors, doings) that are supposedly spontaneous or unpremeditated is that there are no spontaneous or unpremeditated acts. All that we mean by so classifying some acts that way is that we haven't noticed or cared about the thoughts that spawned them.

It's true that there are bodily motions that are purely reflexive such as when a physician taps my relaxed knee with a hammer and causes my lower leg to jerk. However, the physical motion of my leg isn't my act—nor is the beating of my heart or the peristaltic action of my colon. It's just an automatic reaction. Distinguish reactions from responses. Anything *I* do occurs in the context of my thinking. I may, for example, tie my shoe while deciding what to eat for breakfast, but that doesn't mean that I wasn't also noticing my shoe. I may, for example, instantly spin around if I didn't sense you behind me and you tap me on the shoulder, but that doesn't mean that I spun around mindlessly. Usually, I'm aware of what I'm doing but I'm not paying attention to it.

In fact, most of my acts are so habitual that I rarely deliberate about what to do.[15] That doesn't mean that my acts are only occasionally thoughtful.

It's terrific that all our acts come from our thoughts. Why? We control what we notice and how we understand (interpret, think about) what we notice; we control our thoughts. *Since we control our thoughts, since our thoughts determine the quality of our decisions, since our decisions determine the quality of our lives, then we control the quality of our lives.* **If so and you want a better life, take charge of your thoughts.**

[*Sidebar quotations:*

Charles Darwin: "[T]he highest possible stage in moral culture is when we recognize that we ought to control our thoughts."

Mihaly Csikszentmihalyi: "To control attention means to control experience, and therefore the quality of life."

John-Roger and Peter McWilliams: "Whenever he thought about it he felt terrible. And so, at last, he came to a fateful decision. He decided not to think about it."]

Most of my thoughts, perhaps a minimum of 80% of them, are useless. Assuming that you are the same way, let's ask: why should we squander such an enormous amount of our attention on what is useless?

There's an alternative: don't. Stop. Instead, engage in the ongoing process of pruning our thoughts. Notice them, let the useless ones go, and pay attention to the beneficial ones.

(Is this what your life is like? Are you working to control your thoughts? If so, again, you are living an examined life, which is the life of a philosopher. If you have begun pruning successfully, you are already pointed towards mastery.)

If we want to ensure that we are pruning correctly, it's important to take a self-conscious look at some relevant themes among our thoughts, namely, *understanding, being human, and living well.* Let's resolve to do this intellectual work carefully and patiently so that we don't have to repeat it. Let's examine these ideas, perhaps with more thoroughness than is familiar or even comfortable for you, in order to create a firm foundation for proceeding toward understanding excellence.

2.2 Understanding Understanding

In order to reduce vagueness and facilitate clear communication, it's important to define our terms. It's also important that any technical terms, or technical uses of ordinary terms, be defined in nontechnical language.

There may be paragraphs or even occasional sections in this book that you'll be tempted to scan rather than read carefully. Please don't. Here's why:

You want to use these ideas to make improvements. However, you cannot use them without understanding them, and you cannot understand them without understanding my words. That means that it's critical to understand my terminology. So, though it may be sometimes tedious, it is important to proceed carefully through sections where terminology is being explained.

There's no substitute for accurate thinking.

Since we must begin from where we are, I invite you to pay attention to **noticing**. Right now you may be able to notice, say, a desk or a tree or your right hand or hunger or a call from an unseen bird. These objects (things) are all very familiar.

[*Sidebar quotations:*

William James: "My experience is what I agree to attend to. Only those items I notice shape my mind."

Friedrich Nietzsche: "your thoughts are not your experiences, they are the echo and after-effect of your experiences: as when your room trembles after a carriage goes past. I however am sitting in the carriage, and often I am the carriage itself."]

You are free to notice (pay attention to, single out, attend to) objects or not. This freedom of noticing that we enjoy is quite marvelous and extremely important. Objects are what we notice; they are the stuff to be understood.

[*Sidebar quotation* from Aldous Huxley: "Experience is not what happens to a man; it is what a man does with what happens to him."]

There's nothing particularly puzzling any ordinary objects; you already understand them. As a matter of fact, and this is also an important point, *the way that you understand objects affects how you notice them.* Believing is seeing. This is true for all of us.

[*Sidebar quotation* from Gary Hoy: "There is a popular expression, 'I'll believe it when I see it.' Talk with any successful person, and they will tell you the opposite is true, 'You will see it when you believe it.'"]

Suppose we could magically transport a human from 50,000 years ago to your room: would he notice the desk the same way we do? How would a lion or an octopus notice it? Instead of perceiving it, wondering about it, and then classifying it, it's such a familiar object to us that we simply perceive it as a desk (a piece of office furniture, a human artifact), but would they? Hardly.

How would objects appear if we were able to notice them without presupposing any understanding? Excellent question! I don't know. Like yours, my perceivings are guided by my understandings. The point is that our everyday noticings are governed by our everyday way of understanding.

Although it's ambiguous, it's traditional to use the word *'concept'* with respect to understanding. To understand is to conceptualize. A concept is a principle of understanding (classifying, sorting, dividing). Think of it as the meaning of a descriptive word.

If you are able to sort red objects from objects that are not red, then you have the concept of redness, which is a quality. You are able to use the word 'red' correctly. People who are blind lack the concept of redness and are unable to use 'red' correctly. (This, of course, doesn't mean they are stupid; all it means is that they are ignorant in a certain way.) Similarly, if you are able to sort robins from other kinds of animals, you have the concept of being a robin, which is a combination of qualities. It used to be true that you were ignorant of what it was for an object to count as a robin, but you learned what it was.

Borderline cases are always possible: is this an orangish red or is it a reddish orange? Such vagueness isn't ordinarily bad, because everyday concepts like redness wouldn't be as useful as they are if they were too precise. Vagueness can be useful. Notice, too, that, though we use our minds to classify objects into red or not, there's nothing mental about being red or being a robin.

Understanding comes in degrees. It can be increased (by learning) or decreased (by, for example, forgetting). An ornithologist has a much better concept of what counts as a robin than I do.

Misunderstanding is always possible. Concepts may be applied to objects incorrectly. If a child categorizes this desk as an elephant, then the child has misunderstood it. Objects are what they are and not other things. It's always possible that we misunderstand the way that they are. If so, it's best to resolve never to get stuck to a favorite way of understanding. Always be flexible.

2.3 Increasing Understanding

What happens when you increase your understanding? What happens when you come to understand something new, something that you have never before understood? How do you do that? How is learning possible?

Please notice how the mind works the next time you learn something new, the next time you increase (expand) your understanding.

Does the increase occur in a vacuum? Well, no. What will happen, at least if your mind works like mine, is that you will relate the new object to objects that you have already understood.

How will you relate the new object to your preexisting understanding?

You will notice relevant **similarities and differences**. Sometimes the process may occur so quickly that it's difficult to notice, but that's how it always works.

Suppose, for example, that you are an entomologist who is excited because you think you may have discovered a new kind of insect. What would you do? Surely you'd study the new insect carefully, describing its appearance, behavior, and, perhaps, its structure. In effect, you'd examine (question, test) it. You'd note its similarities and differences to other insects, and eventually submit your findings to your colleagues to have them check your results. You'd either force a revision in the conceptual space of taxonomy or not. If it were an insect new to science, you'd get to name it.

If you want to learn more efficiently, if you want to make yourself a better student, **practice paying attention to analogies.** Why? Teachers, speakers, and authors *always* rely on them. They don't always articulate them clearly, but they are always behind the words. By deliberately watching for key analogies, you'll pick up the important ideas more quickly. Once you've grasped the analogies, evaluate them by thinking through for yourself the similarities and differences they embody.

There's a close and interesting connection between conceptual systems and systems of words. When we learn a natural language, we learn to categorize objects in accordance with the semantic categories appropriate to that language. This is why it's difficult to learn another language. It's not just that we have to learn different words; we have to learn a different way of categorizing (conceptualizing, understanding) things.

There are many different languages. *There are many different ways of conceptualizing.* This is an important point. There is not just one way to understand the real objects that are the world: there are many.

Just as a certain language may be better for a certain purpose than another language, so a certain conceptual system may be better for a certain purpose than another conceptual system. Whenever the need arises, we simply revise our languages or conceptual systems to work better for us. This is why different activities naturally spawn different jargons.

Is your way of understanding the world the best possible way? Is mine? Is anyone's?

[*Sidebar quotation* from Steve Hagan: "Whenever we conceptualize, we create contradictions that we can't escape . . . A concept is anything with a skin around it, some sort of boundary dividing something from something else . . . anything put into speech is never completely reliable."]

Suppose that someone were fanatically attached to his way of understanding. What would he have to do to prove that his way was the best way? Wouldn't he have to understand all the possible ways of understanding and then argue that they are all defective except his? Wouldn't that be impossible?

In the previous chapter I introduce the concept of being a philosopher. I now introduce its contrast: a "**fanatic**." A pure philosopher is always willing to question anything; a pure philosopher will always examine or re-examine something. A pure fanatic is never willing to examine anything. In practice, it's difficult to find pure philosophers or pure fanatics; nearly all of us are somewhere on the continuum between the two extremes.

[*Sidebar quotation* from Roger von Oech: "Avoid falling in love with ideas."]

The closer we are to pure fanaticism, the more danger we are in.

Why? The world is like a river.[16] (Notice the analogy!) *Like life itself, water in a river is incessantly moving.* The world consists of moving individuals. Individuals are never motionless. A set of concepts is like a stiffly frozen fishing net. Putting the net into the river won't catch any water. (By way of contrast, putting a flexible fishing net into the river can, at least, be useful for other purposes such as catching fish.) Never mistake a net for the water (or a map for a territory). Nevertheless, nets (like maps) can be useful for certain purposes.

Fanatics seem to think that conceptual systems (nets) are reality (water). Reality is what-is[17]; thoughts are nothing in themselves because they are always about other things. Thoughts are only useful or not for certain purposes. This is why getting stuck on one way of thinking is counterproductive. In fact, the danger increases over time. As the world turns (as time goes by), there's a greater gap between the way it is and the way the fanatic is still thinking it is.

[*Sidebar quotation* from John Kenneth Galbraith: "Faced with the choice between changing one's mind and proving that there is no need to do so, almost everyone gets busy on the proof."]

Fanatics confuse their thoughts about reality, their "surrealities"[18], with reality. This is why fanatics locate truth in the wrong place. Fanatics locate truth in thoughts about reality; they think that this belief (thought, judgment, view) or creed (set of beliefs) is true or that that belief or creed is false. No: what is true is what is real. **Truth is in our lives, not in our thinking about our lives.** A truthful life is one that is continually in balance, one that continues to be perfectly in tune with reality. Living truthfully isn't a matter of being attached to a set of beliefs; it's a matter of living in harmony with what-is.

[*Sidebar quotations:*

Bertrand Russell: "In all affairs it's a healthy thing now and then to hang a question mark on the things you have long taken for granted."

Martin Seligman: "It is perilously easy to live our lives noticing only evidence in favor of our deep beliefs and to shun testing whether those beliefs are false."]

If so, whenever you notice that you are stuck to some important belief, please relax, examine it carefully, and, if necessary, let it go.

[*Sidebar quotation* from Henry David Thoreau: "It is never too late to give up your prejudices."]

Try this: stop thinking of beliefs as true or false and begin thinking of them as lily pads. (Notice the analogy!) Suppose I'm living an unbalanced life on this side of the river and that to live a balanced life I need to cross the river. A belief is useful if it helps me to cross the river and it isn't useful if it doesn't. Beliefs are useful when they work and not useful otherwise. So, a good belief is like a lily pad: think of those huge lily pads in the Amazon rain forest. Perhaps if I run fast enough, I could run across them and use them to get to the other shore! If so, those are useful lily pads. My focus should be on the other shore (on what-is, on living well, on mastering life), not on the lily pads, which are, at best, only means to an end.

Like all analogies, this one isn't perfect. However, it's acceptable for making one key point: in terms of reaching the other shore, getting attached to a lily pad is counter-productive. Please assiduously **avoid getting stuck** on any beliefs. It's impossible to become a sage, in other words, to live wisely, without seriously examining thoughts and being willing to let some go. It is *not* necessary to let them all go. What would be the point of letting useful ones go? What is necessary is being *willing* to examine all of them and to let go of all those that are unable to withstand examination.

Even just in principle fanatics are unwilling to do this. They simply quarantine the ones they are attached to from examination. As a result, they "see" the world in black and white, in clear contours, as either/or. There are no colors, even just primary colors. There are no shades and shades of grey. Their simpler surrealities, however, are purchased at a terrible price, namely, living in separation from what-is. (I discuss this important idea of separation in what follows.)

[*Sidebar quotation* from William James: "A great many people think they are thinking when they are merely rearranging their prejudices."]

Concepts are arranged systematically in *hierarchies*. Some concepts are more general than others. For example, suppose that there are 200 shades of red and that your shirt is a particular shade (call it number 7) of crimson. I notice it as being crimson 7. I also notice it as being crimson. I also notice it as being red. I also notice it as being colored. I also notice it as being qualitied. Of course, there are different kinds of qualities than colors, there are different kinds of colors than reds, there are different kinds of reds than crimsons, and there are different kinds of crimsons than shade 7. Combining similarities and differences with generality yields hierarchies.

Because there are different similarities and differences, there are different ways of understanding something, even something as simple as the color of your shirt. There are different conceptual hierarchies. There is no one conceptual hierarchy that is best for all purposes; there is no one best way to understand the world. There never has been, and there never will be. This is because understanding, like using language, has different purposes. There isn't just one purpose; there are many. Furthermore, the world is in incessant flux.

If so, in general, **there is no best way to understand anything.** If, therefore, you expect me to provide you with THE account of human nature, you'll be disappointed. Similarly, please do not expect THE account of mastery. There is no one best way to understand human nature, mastery, or anything else.

[*Sidebar quotation* from Tor Norrestranders: "In science, philosophy, and thought, it has become clear that the world cannot be captured in the net of thought or language."]

Anyone who understands that has made enormous progress toward understanding understanding.

[*Sidebar quotations:*

Peter Abelard: "The first key to wisdom is this—constant and frequent questioning. . . "

Anthony Robbins: "Successful people ask better questions, and as a result, they get better answers."]

2.4 Accounts of Human Nature

Who am I? The difficulty of answering this question is matched by its importance.[19]

Let's begin to tackle this question indirectly by asking instead, "What kind am I?" The answer is that I am a human being. So, what is a human being?

This is a fruitful move to make because it shifts our attention from individuals to qualities. Individuals are composed of non-individual parts, namely, qualities. A quality is a commonality, anything two or more individuals may have in common or share or anything that may be true of two or more individuals. Since two or more individuals may be red or rectangular, redness and rectangularity are qualities (properties, features, characteristics).

Redness and rectangularity are examples of "monadic" qualities, which are qualities that are characteristic of one individual. For example, an individual may be red or not red, rectangular or not rectangular. Not all qualities are monadic. For example, being to the left of or being between are examples of "relational" qualities, which are qualities that are characteristic of two or more individuals together. One individual cannot be to the left of itself; two individuals are required to have leftness, and three individuals are required to have betweenness. So relational qualities relate two or more individuals.

All qualities are useful as concepts. Again, a concept is a principle of classification. We may use any quality to classify individuals into those that have that quality and those that lack it, and we may use qualities of greater generality to sort qualities of lesser generality.

Any adequate account of the world (what-is, reality) must include an account of qualities. Without qualities, there'd be no intelligibility. While qualities make the world boring (for example, the shape of my right hand is the same day after day after day), they also make it intelligible. Go ahead: try to think of the world without qualities. Conceiving the world without recurrences is impossible.

If you have understood this, you are ripe to understand why it is so difficult to answer the question, "Who am I?"

Since I am an individual, I am composed of qualities. Since qualities are commonalities, listing my qualities cannot specify what is irreducibly unique or individual about me. *In trying to understand an individual, we inevitably wind up thinking about qualities,* which are paradigmatic cases of non-uniqueness (commonality). This is extremely important to understand.

A theory of **human nature** is a list of qualities that an individual has in order to be a human being.

Because there are many relevant similarities and differences between human and nonhuman beings, it should not be surprising that there are many different theories of human nature. Many different thinkers have provided different theories of human nature, thinkers such as the authors of the Upanishads, the Buddha, Confucius, Plato, Paul, Plotinus, Aquinas, Descartes, Spinoza, Rousseau, Kant, Hegel, Marx, Kierkegaard, Darwin, Nietzsche, Freud, Skinner, Sartre, Lorenz, Maslow, and Butchvarov.

Any adequate theory of human flourishing must be based on an adequate theory of human nature. Any adequate ethics or political philosophy must be based on an adequate theory of human nature. Again, there is no way to answer the question "What is an excellent human being?" without depending upon an answer to "What is a human being?"

There are many different ways of answering these important questions. Critically reviewing just the major alternatives is a massive undertaking. Is it required for an account of excellence?

2.5 A Worldly Account of Being Human

Whether it is or not, I'm not here attempting it. (However, feel free to pursue it on your own.)

Instead, let's focus just on the important question about self and other.[20] I believe you'll come to agree with me that getting clear about that is sufficient for getting clear about excellence.

Let's begin from what has become our commonsense standpoint, namely, that we are continuing selves separated from everything else. Like you, I am a continuing individual separate from the rest of the world. If so, what would it be to get ahead in life? What is it to become successful?

It would be to obtain everything I want and to avoid everything I don't want at minimal cost. It would be ideal if I could get whatever I desire at no cost. In other words, the ideal with respect to the way of the world is *something for nothing*, getting what I want and avoiding what I don't want and doing so at no cost to me. Doing that would be living well according to the success model. If so, a successful human being gains whatever is valued, avoids whatever is disvalued, and does so at minimal cost. That's one understanding of living well.

What's the best advice for success? **Get real.**

In other words, be realistic in your appraisals and decisions. Jack Welch was a successful businessman; he was a very successful CEO of General Electric. This is what he recommends: "Practice the Reality Principle; deal with the world as it is, not as you wish it would be."

Dealing with the world as it is includes dealing with other human beings as they are. How are they? How are we?

Brian Tracy provides a fruitful account of how, in reality, they take themselves to be.[21] To understand how they take themselves to be, just ask yourself the following seven questions. Why? How you take yourself to be is the same as how other people take themselves to be.

Imagine this situation: you are out of work desperately looking for a job and someone offers you a choice between two jobs. In each case, simply pick the job that you prefer.

One: The jobs you are offered are identical in terms of work and wages except that the first job requires you to be on the job forty hours weekly and the second job requires you to be on the job twenty hours weekly. Which job would you select?

Of course, you'd prefer to make the same wages for less time and effort. Why? You are lazy. It's natural to be lazy. Please let go of evaluating laziness. There's no need to think of it as being good or evil. It's just the way we all naturally are. It's the rational alternative.

Two: The jobs are identical in terms of work; however, the first job pays $75,000 annually and the second pays first job pays $100,000 annually. Which would you take?

Like everyone else, you'd take the one that pays more for the same work. Why? You are greedy. It's natural to be greedy. Again, and so for the other five qualities that follow, let go of evaluating greediness. There's no need to think of greediness as being good or evil. Unless we are irrational, it's just the way we all naturally are.

Three: The jobs are identical except for one feature: the first job lacks any opportunities for personal development and advancement and the second job has marvelous opportunities for personal development and advancement. Which would you take?

Like everyone else, you'd take the one that has opportunities for growth and advancement. Why? You are ambitious. You'd like the conditions of your life to improve. You understand that that will happen when you grow. It's natural to be ambitious.

Four: The jobs are identical with respect to their work; furthermore, their wages are the same, and each job begins at the beginning of the calendar year. The only difference is that the first job pays you one-twelfth of your annual salary every month and the other job pays you your whole annual salary at the end of January. Which would you take?

Like everyone else, you'd choose to receive your whole reward sooner rather than later. Why? You are impatient. It's natural to be impatient.

Five: Again, with one exception, everything about the two jobs is identical. The exception is that the first job will not increase your personal happiness and the second job will. Which would you take?

Like everyone else, you'd take the one that increases your personal happiness. Why? You are selfish. It's natural to be selfish.

Six: Again, with one exception, everything about the two jobs is identical. The exception is that the first job will cause you to look foolish in front of other people whereas the second job will cause you to look good in front of other people. Which would you take?

Like everyone else, you'd choose the one that makes you look better. Why? You are vain. It's natural to be vain.

Seven: Finally, with one exception, everything about the two jobs is identical. The exception is that the first job creates conditions such that your decisions will have life or death consequences for many other people and the second job doesn't. Which would you take?

Like everyone else, you'd choose the one that did not make you responsible for the lives of other people. Why? You are ignorant. You realize that you would be responsible for making very important decisions without being able to know how to make them so that their consequences would be wholly beneficial. Talk about stress! As Tracy puts it, "We live in an *uncertain* world. . . There are no guarantees that any act will achieve its aim."[22] Being ignorant is an important part of the human condition.

[*Sidebar quotations:*

Soren Kierkegaard: "Life . . . can only be understood backwards . . . "

Richard A. Fumerton: "the consequences of our actions go on and on (far beyond any point we can foresee) . . . we cannot know all, or even very many, of the consequences of our actions . . . in life we are *forced* to make choices—even inaction is a de facto decision with consequences."]

You are normal. Everyone else would answer these seven questions just as you have. I did. If you doubt that, try the test on some others. It's quite realistic.

What are the qualities of a normal human being? What is our human nature that we all share? **We are lazy, greedy, ambitious, impatient, selfish, vain, and ignorant.** That's a realistic appraisal of human nature. Expediency is essential.

[*Sidebar quotation* from Tony Parsons: "There are few things in this world more reassuring than an unhappy lottery winner."]

These are not the only qualities of human beings; this is an incomplete theory of human nature. Nor are these the most fundamental qualities of human beings; for example, these qualities presuppose that human beings are social animals. They are, though, qualities that characterize contemporary, literate human beings.

[*Sidebar quotation* from Thomas Jefferson: "The worst day of a man's life is when he sits down and begins thinking about how he can get something for nothing."]

Someone may object that this is too one-sidedly economic. Permit me three points in reply.

(i) Economies operate on the reality of scarcity. An economy distributes goods and services among its participants. Since there is not an abundance of goods and services, since it's impossible for everyone to get as much of everything as desired, a system for dividing goods and services is required. Different kinds of economies are possible.

In capitalism, for example, the means of production such as companies and land are privately owned and, unless one happens to be an owner, in theory one receives benefits in proportion to one's labor, one's energetic contributions. Its chief justification (see, for example, John Locke) is that, since labor creates economic value, it's fair that the laborer who creates it receive benefits in exchange for the labor.

So, in a capitalistic economy, it's actually good to be greedy, ambitious, impatient, and selfish. Why? The more I want to gain as many benefits as I am able to gain as soon as I am able to gain them, the more motivation I have to labor intensely. The more successful I am at working hard, the more economic value will be created. The more economic value I create, the more benefits I will accumulate *and* the more economic value there will be for the economy to distribute. So I'll be helping others by helping myself.

There is no generally agreed-upon principle for distributing scarce goods and services. There's lots of disagreement about whether we should be capitalists or socialists or communists, in other words, there are different possible ways to distribute scarce goods.

The first reply is that, even though it is an economic conception, that doesn't necessarily mean it's a negative conception. An argument frequently made by capitalists is that capitalism is a good fit with human nature. (On the other hand, an argument frequently made by the opponents of capitalism is that it fosters human vices instead of virtues.)

(ii) The second reply is that we are here practicing the Reality Principle. The reality is that, on a typical day, most adult human beings spend most of their time as employees.

More waking hours are devoted to preparing to be on the job, being on the job, and recovering from being on the job than to anything else. We might wish it were otherwise, but that's the reality all across the globe.

It's interesting to note that it didn't used to be this way. According to the scientists who investigate the lives of prehistoric humans, on average they probably had more leisure time than contemporary humans. If so, perhaps we are not doing as well as we often like to think we are.

(iii) Having these seven qualities does not entail that we lack other qualities or that we always act only on the basis of these qualities.

Perhaps the best and most obvious exception is laziness. We are not always lazy; sometimes we are not lazy. Consider some sport or hobby that you enjoy doing even though there are no economic benefits involved and you have no motivation to be doing it other than personal enjoyment. Perhaps you practice the piano for an hour every day simply because you enjoy it. Suppose that you don't have to and that you could instead be lying on the sofa watching television. This doesn't mean that you are not naturally lazy; it simply means that you are not always lazy.

Let's take this idea a bit farther. Why? When expanded, it yields an understanding of a successful life.

2.6 Getting Ahead

Have you noticed what always happens when you get into a fight with reality? You lose. Each of us learns this lesson growing up: *reality is much more powerful than I am*. This is why it is better to make decisions that are realistic rather than unrealistic.

To live better, then, practice making realistic decisions.

Given that we are lazy, greedy, ambitious, impatient, selfish, vain, and ignorant, what do we want? What do we think would make us live well?

If you enjoy playing the piano simply for the sake of playing the piano (as opposed to playing the piano for the sake of accumulating economic benefits), you would naturally like to be able to arrange your life so that you are able to play the piano whenever you feel like it. You won't play it when you don't feel like it, and you naturally wouldn't want anyone to be in a position to force you to play it. It's just that you would like a life so that, whenever you had the desire to play the piano, you were able to play it instead of, say, having to go to a job or do something else that you found relatively distasteful at that moment.

Of course, you may have other things you enjoy doing instead of playing the piano. Furthermore, even if you enjoy playing the piano regularly, you may also have different things you enjoy doing such as dining in a fine restaurant or going fishing or shopping in Manhattan.

All that is required in order to understand a successful human being is to generalize this way of thinking. If your passions happen to be playing the piano, dining out, fishing, and shopping, you will think that, for you, success at getting ahead is being able to indulge yourself whenever you want, which includes the idea of avoiding experiences (such as having a stroke or being broke) that would prevent such indulgence. You'll have become successful (gained success).

In other words, in terms of getting ahead in life a successful human being is one who is able to be, do, or have whatever one wants whenever one wants it. Ideally, there should be no serious obstacles between where one is and where one wants to be; one's getting what one wants should be as frictionless as possible. There should be no gap between one's condition and what one wants to be one's condition. The closer one comes to this ideal, the more successful one is.

Many people actually have this as their ideal human life. They assume that, by becoming successful, they will be happy. They believe that there are no successful, unhappy people.

That's a delusion. There are happy, unsuccessful people, and there are unhappy, successful people. There's nothing intrinsically wrong with being successful. It's simply irrelevant to living well.

However, there is something extrinsically wrong with being successful. If you want to live well and mistakenly believe that being successful is the same as living well, you may waste a lot of life chasing a dream that cannot yield what you think it will. If you were to put that same amount of time and effort into mastering life instead of into becoming successful, you could live well without wasting any time and effort.

[*Sidebar quotation* from The Buddha: "Don't follow the way of the world."]

It's logically possible both to live well and to be successful.[23] That's certainly a much more powerful idea than mere success. However, in practice, the attachment required for success conflicts with the nonattachment required for living well.

If you were given the choice that would be binding for the rest of your life and you could only choose one, would you choose to be successful or to live well? Are you really confident that your choice is more valuable than the other?

For the moment, please notice how far we have come. We have looked at our fecund minds. We became self-conscious about understanding. We noticed how we increase our understanding. We developed a realistic account of human nature as well as an account of being successful. It's been a quick, productive start.

It's important to savor our journey. Right now, please give yourself permission to enjoy your progress. Please take a break while you review and absorb these ideas. Notice how far you've already come. Let yourself wonder: if being successful isn't mastery, what is?

The distinction between success and mastery is the topic of the next chapter.

Chapter 3: Success and Mastery

What are your dreams? What would you really like to happen in your life? If you had ample time and money, what would you be, do, or have? What would it be for you to live excellently?

You are a unique individual, yet you are made of qualities (commonalities, properties, features, "non-individual" parts). So, you are a unique unity (togetherness, cluster, congeries) of qualities. Which qualities that you lack would you like to make part of you in order to live better?

Which qualities do you value? Which qualities should you value if you want to live better or even well?

To understand living well, it's critical to examine answers to these questions. The answers are not just important: they may surprise you.

3.1 The Living and the Dead

Concrete individuals are made of qualities. This desktop is hard. That carpet is grey. The sun is hot. She is beautiful.

We notice qualities because concrete individuals have them. Our ability to understand depends upon our ability to notice and compare individualized qualities. The hardness of this desktop may be indistinguishable from the hardness of that wall. The color of the carpet in this room is the same as the color of the carpet in the hallway. The sun feels hotter today than yesterday. She is even more beautiful than her sister.

We are able to abstract (isolate, separate) qualities from the concrete individuals that embody them. We use a relatively static hierarchical web of qualities as concepts to order the ever-changing flux we experience. Conception and perception are inter-dependent.

Though we take this ability to abstract for granted, it actually developed relatively recently with Plato.[24] His philosophy was possible only after the advent of phonetic writing by the ancient Greek scribes who severed the connection between the common language and the shared perceptual field.

Phonetic scripts were developed in the ancient Middle East. From more ancient rebuses (pictographic puns), Semitic scribes established characters (letters) for each of the consonants of their oral language, which created an "aleph-beth." This widened the gap between the human world and the more-than-human (other-than-human) world. "*A direct association is established between the pictorial sign and the vocal gesture for the first time, completely bypassing the thing pictured.*" [25] The life of the more-than-human world became no longer necessary with respect to the world of human language, the world of human-made signs.

The ancient Greek scribes severed the connection completely. They modified both the shapes and the names of the Semitic letters, which completely cut them off from all non-grammatological meanings and sensorial references. By introducing written vowels, they greatly increased the abstractive power of the writing system. Language came to be seen as an exclusively human power. *Letters and written words are unlike all the other individuals we perceive: whereas other individuals are constantly in flux, they are not.* This had many important consequences such as reducing the need for remembering and story telling.

For oral, indigenous people, the world speaks. Nature speaks. Human languages are only loosely distinguished from the languages of ravens and wolves, lakes and mountains.

Shamans interpret between human and nonhuman languages. When a human being from such a culture encounters a raven, wolf, lake, or mountain, the human understands the interaction to be one between two speaking, living beings. In fact, such humans directly take the most profound teachings in life to be from the more-than-human world. They take their lives to be intimately interconnected with everything else.

[S*idebar quotation* from the Flower Ornament Scripture: "Beings teach, lands teach, all things in all times teach, constantly, without interruption."]

By way of contrast, for literate people, only humans speak. Language speaks, but the nonhuman world lacks language. Nature doesn't speak; ravens, wolves, lakes, and mountains aren't articulate. A formal writing system seals the border between the human domain of language and the more-than-human domain without language. A human being from such a culture thinks of his or her self (I, ego, ego/I) as hermetically sealed within the domain of language. *Our self-concepts become prisoners of human language.*

The importance of this **epochal shift in understanding the world and ourselves** cannot be overemphasized. Let's briefly note its effects on the way we understand (i) ourselves and (ii) qualities.

(i) For oral, indigenous people, to be a human individual is to be a process of continually interacting with the more-than-human. Specifically, there is a breathing interaction with the air, which is invisible. Humans feel themselves enveloped by the mysteriousness of the atmosphere. The awesome air is ubiquitous and yet unseen; it is both always here and yet not here. It is the magic of blended immanence and transcendence.

It's not like that for us literate people. "*[T]he Greek scribes effectively dissolved the primordial power of the air.*" [26] Much to the detriment of both the human and the more-than-human worlds, the consequences of this momentous bifurcation are still unfolding. It's as if we are still alive but the rest of nature, the more-than-human, is dead. Instead of living movements, the movements of nonhuman animals and lakes and mountains are merely mechanical. Only we are alive.

Only we have the power of language. Since letters are unchanging, we must be unchanging. Phonetic literacy enables us to think about ourselves in isolation from the more-than-human. This new reflexive ability profoundly changes how we think of ourselves. **To be a literate human being is to be an unchanging self who is separate from the more-than-human.** We think of ourselves as separate continuants.[27]

Please mull this over. Begin really thinking about it. Who am I? Who, really, am I?

(ii) For the first time in human thought, Plato divorces individuals from their qualities. Plato is the first great thinker in the western philosophic tradition; he is the first western philosopher to ask all the right questions. Western philosophers ever since Plato have been discussing answers to the questions he asks.

One of the marks of Plato's genius is that he questions his own ideas. Plato is a great philosopher; he is not a fanatic. He isn't slavishly attached to his own views. This is why he writes dialogues rather than monologues; he not only wants to present his ideas, he wants to encourage us to think for ourselves and dialogues do that better than monologues.

It's no accident that the first great western philosopher appears just after the development of phonetic literacy. Plato himself understands that his thinking had been impacted by the development of this new linguistic technology, and he himself has reservations about it.[28]

In effect, he separates what-is into "Forms" (Ideas, *eidos*) and individuals. What's a Form? Forms are abstract qualities, in other words, qualities considered apart from their concrete embodiments. Plato is willing to consider hardness, greyness, heat, and beauty apart from the individuals that have them.

Why? Why separate qualities from individuals?

Plato distinguishes sharply between *knowing and believing*.[29] What's the difference? When I believe something, what I believe might be false; in other words, false belief is possible. However, when I know something, what I know cannot be false; in other words, false knowledge is impossible. For example, if I believe that you have a headache and you don't, I have a false belief. It makes no sense to claim, by way of contrast, that I know that blue is soft or that 5 is smaller than 4. Since blue is a color (and not a tactile sensation) and 4 is smaller than 5, it's simply impossible to know that blue is soft or that 5 is smaller than 4. So, false believings are possible, but false knowings aren't.

Believings and knowings are ways of apprehending. What is apprehended is different from apprehending it. This is why there should be a systematic coherence between how we understanding apprehending (which is the subject of the discipline of epistemology) and how we understand what-is (which is the subject of the discipline of ontology [metaphysics]). In the <u>Republic</u>, Plato sets up the following correspondence:

1. Being   Knowing
2. Becoming   Believing (Opining)
3. Nothing (Nonbeing)   Ignorance

1. Strictly speaking, we are only able to know Being, that which is fully real. Again, one cannot know what is not. For

Plato, the objects of knowledge are in the category of Being, which means that they are timeless (eternal, immutable, permanent). For example, it's possible to know that 5 is greater than 4 or that crimson is darker than pink. Why? Numbers and colors are Forms, unchanging abstractions. Judgments about Forms, which are objects in the domain of Being, are always necessarily true or necessarily false; such judgments cannot be otherwise.

2. When we have an opinion (belief), it may be true or false. For Plato, the objects of opinions (believings) are in the category of Becoming, which means that they are temporal (unstable, impermanent, mutable). For example, it's possible to believe that my shirt is red. However, it's also possible that my belief is mistaken because, for some reason, I may be misperceiving its color. Furthermore, even if my belief that it is red happens to be true at this moment, it may not be true tomorrow (because, say, the shirt could be dyed a different color or even cease to exist). Unlike the objects of knowledge, the objects of opinions are temporal. Judgments about objects in the domain of Becoming are always contingently true or contingently false; they could be otherwise.

3. Of course, if there's no apprehension at all, we are simply ignorant. Obviously, since it's the absence of apprehension, ignorance has no objects.

At least initially, this is a coherent system that makes sense. One mark of a great philosopher is that, even if he is wrong, he's wrong in an interesting way. Plato is a great philosopher.

Plato's view is also interesting. I recall initially learning it from a Spanish friend when I was a junior in high school. I found the Platonic thesis that there is a permanent realm of

Forms behind the incessantly changing perceivable objects of daily experience strange but fascinating.

What's most peculiar about Plato's view is that he thinks that reality comes in degrees and that, because they are unchangeable and knowable, abstract qualities are more real than changing individuals. For example, the color of the shirt is more real than the shirt. It's possible, for Plato, to know that red is a color but it's not possible to know that the shirt is red. Aristotle, Plato's greatest student, thinks his mentor's view here is exactly backwards. Aristotle thinks that individuals are more real than their attributes.

This is a major issue in philosophy. Should one distinguish an individual from its qualities? Should one distinguish the concrete from the abstract? If so, how? What, exactly, is an individual?

Furthermore, if there is an ultimate distinction, which is more real? Which is more important?

If you are attracted to such questions, you have a disposition to philosophical theory. However, rest assured, if such questions only serve to give you a headache, answering them is only important for those determined to conceptualize well. Again, fortunately, it is not necessary to conceptualize well to achieve mastery or to live well. It is, though, necessary to conceptualize at least decently in order to understand mastery (excellence), which is the subject of this book.

There's another important reason why permitting yourself to think hard about these questions is important: doing so weakens the tendency to fanaticism. These questions are difficult to answer. As we've just seen, great philosophers disagree with each other. Obviously, then, greatness is not the same as correctness.

Who is correct? That is a question you should *answer for yourself*. It is only thinking clearly through the important and fundamental issues for yourself that yields some degree of confidence in whatever answers you accept, however tentative your acceptance. It's good to have confidence in those answers, but it's also good always to be willing to re-examine them in the light of further experience. This is why *it's best to develop a philosopher's tentative, skeptical, probing attitude. It's best to keep a beginner's mind.*

If this is your first time doing any serious fundamental thinking, congratulations! It's not comfortable. I warned you: when you initially loosen your attachments, you may seem to be in free fall. You may feel like an eaglet who has been abruptly pushed out of the nest. However, I assure you, you have what it takes to soar. Therefore, it's only a matter of persistence.

Just work your way through this book at your own pace. Initially, you may find it helpful to lean on the ideas presented here. Think of them as tools (or lily pads): they are useful, but it doesn't follow that better tools aren't available. Don't attach to them, but it's fine to use them initially to help you.

I've deliberately chunked the chapters down into what I hope are digestible sections. If you need a break after any section, please take one. Whatever section follows won't disappear.

Please be kind to yourself. I happen to believe that it's fine to underachieve a little every day. It is not necessary to challenge oneself to the maximum on a daily basis; in fact, in my experience, it's counterproductive. Just push the envelope a little bit every day and, soon, you'll be amazed at your progress.

3.2. Abstract Goods

If I've been clear, you have already done enough good thinking to identify the central problem that mastery cures, namely, **we are stuck using inadequate self-concepts.** Specifically, your self-concept is a literate one that separates you from the more-than-human world. This central problem spawns a multitude of secondary ones.

Ask yourself honestly: "Do I go through life with an underlying feeling of separateness? Does everything else seem rather alien? Am I fully at home in my own life?" If such thoughts trouble you, you now understand why. You think yourself apart from the more-than-human world.

Furthermore, in our culture, this is *normal.* The other humans who surround us usually feel the same way. We tend to take it to be a natural part of the human condition.

It's not. Those who master life no longer feel that way.

Fortunately, though most are quickly disappearing, there are still opportunities for actually learning how to live a different way. People like David Abram and Jared Diamond have made it a point to experience living in significantly different human cultures. Fortunately, they haven't just thought about their experiences; they've written about them, which help the rest of us to understand what's causing our ailments.

[*Sidebar quotation* from Jared Diamond: "My own impression, from having divided my life between United States cities and New Guinea villages, is that the so-called blessings of civilization are mixed."]

Nevertheless, few people correctly identify the central problem or its source; even fewer solve it. Identifying a problem and explaining why it's a problem are not the same as solving it.

Let's contrast **two different models of excellence**, two different ways of being excellent, namely, the success model and the mastery model. Each model purports to solve the central problem. My thesis is that *only the mastery model works for living well*. The success model does not solve the central problem, but the mastering model does. I am not claiming that it's bad to be a success. Of course there's nothing wrong with being a success. I am claiming, however, that even being a success doesn't work for mastering life.

In order to understand why this is so, it's critical to continue examining qualities and individuals.

Here's the structure: The rest of this section is about qualities, and the next section is about individuals. The rest of this chapter relates those two subjects by considering the nature of desire and then specifies the difference between the success model and the mastery model.

Abstract goods are valuable qualities considered in abstraction from all individuals.[30] A value is a preferred (wanted, desired) quality. A power lifter trains to become physically stronger, so physical strength is a value. A monk or nun trains to become spiritually enlightened, so spiritual enlightenment is a value. A physicist investigates to understand the truth about matter in motion, so understanding is a value.

Different people have different values. In fact, disagreements about values seem ubiquitous. There is no agreed-upon list of abstract goods. Furthermore, there is no agreed-upon ranking of abstract goods in order of importance.

Here is a partial list of values (in no particular order): life, friendship, spiritual enlightenment, consciousness, activity, health, fitness, physical strength, pleasure, satisfaction, happiness, erotic love, contentment, truth, knowledge, wisdom, beauty, aesthetic experience, virtue, harmony, peace, justice, power, creativity, freedom, security, adventure, and honor.

Notice that all of these values are concepts, which means that they have opposites. Abstract evils are the opposites of abstract goods. A natural language like English may not have neatly corresponding terms in all cases, but abstract evils can easily be named: death, enmity towards friendship, being spiritually asleep, unconsciousness, and so on.

Understanding the success model depends upon understanding abstract goods and evils.

Qualities aren't successful or unsuccessful: individuals are. What is a successful individual?

Let's assume that you are unsuccessful and think through how you might become successful. Success is something to be gained (achieved, accomplished, won). You'll become successful by making important abstract goods concrete in your life and by minimizing the impact of important abstract evils.

What are your values? By itself, merely having a list of values isn't very helpful. Still, it's the place to start. If you don't have a written list of values, it would be helpful if you'd take a few minutes and write one out. Just sit quietly and jot down, in no particular order, a list of your values. What really matters to you? Go ahead. Use the list above for assistance; some of them are much more important to you than others.

[*Sidebar quotation* from Lee Iococca: "The discipline of writing something down is the first step toward making it happen."]

It would be extremely unusual if you had only one value. It's nearly certain that you have several. One way to expose them is simply to examine your life from different perspectives. What would it be like for you to flourish physically? What would it be like for you to flourish intellectually or artistically? What would it be like for you to flourish morally? What would it be like for you to flourish spiritually? What would it be like for you to flourish emotionally? What would it be like for you to flourish financially?

Once you have the list, it's important to prioritize it. What are your most important values? Rank them in order of importance. Please actually do it. Don't worry: nobody else has to see or evaluate it!³¹

In order for this list to work well to help you make your life more successful, the values must be congruent with each other as well as prioritized. Do all your values harmonize or are any of them in conflict? For example, people from different spiritual traditions often believe that spiritual enlightenment doesn't go with erotic love, which is why many who are serious about awakening take vows of chastity. If it were true that spiritual enlightenment and erotic love are in conflict and both appeared on your list, then your values would be incongruent. The point is to examine your list and ensure that all your important values are in harmony.

In terms of the success model of living well, an individual whose life had as many important abstract goods as possible and lacked as many important abstract evils as possible would be living an optimific life. This is the ideal of a successful life. An optimizing life, which is much more realistic, would be a life that has more important abstract goods and lacks more important abstract evils than any alternative. In short, in a well-lived life, goods or successes outweigh failures; there's a higher ratio of goods or successes to failures.

Admittedly, if you think of yourself as having a lifespan of, say, fifty or a hundred years, it's difficult even to think of a successful life because of the temporal duration involved.

Nevertheless, this should be sufficient to communicate the idea. Once you have conceived what your life would be like if it were successful, the next step is to create such a life for yourself. Since success never happens by luck or accident, this requires planning properly for success and then executing the plan. Your life cannot become more successful until you begin to make consistently better decisions, and that cannot happen until your thinking improves. So becoming more successful involves taking better care of your thoughts.

The abstract goods that you particularly cherish are your dreams (wishes). They will remain only dreams until you make them real. Planning to become more successful is figuring out how to make those abstract goods concrete in your life.

How?

Notice that, for whatever abstract good you select to begin with, there have been many people who have been successful. The general method is simple: *first*, identify a group of people who have been successful in the way that you want to be successful.

Second, get close enough to them to figure out how they think and what they do. If you are unsuccessful in the relevant way, what you'll discover is that there are important differences between how they think and how you think and that there are, naturally (since our acts come from our thoughts), important differences between what they do and what you do. Though you probably never noticed them before, those differences are critical.

Third, once you have identified those differences, change how you think and what you do to emulate those who are successful. Copy them. Adopt them as your role models. Begin always to think and act as they do.

Finally, if a new way of thinking or acting begins to work for you after you have practiced it sufficiently, keep doing it. If not, change it and try a different way—and persist until you are successful. In other words, adjust what you are doing on the basis of the feedback you receive. If you have the talent, there will be a method of thinking and acting that will work for you to be successful with respect to that abstract good.

This makes sense. It's rational. In general, this is the way to become more successful. It's the method of self-improvement. You may use this method again and again to install the various abstract goods that you value most in your life.

It's not a secret method. There are plenty of self-help authorities who offer help. There's an ample supply of books, audio and video programs, courses and seminars on many important abstract goods.

Furthermore, once you become successful in one or two areas, you may well find that your self-esteem rises. If you increase your success rate, why shouldn't you feel better about your life? It can become an upward spiral: the more excellence you create in your life, the better you feel, and, the better you feel, the more excellence you create.

Imagine that you have become successful in whatever ways you desire. Throw yourself forward in your imagination ten or twenty years. In as much sensory detail as possible, imagine going through an ideal day as a successful person. Exactly how would your life be different? In exactly what ways would that day be different from today? Please do it now: exercise your imagination for a few minutes.

Once you have, you are ready for the critical question: would that be living well? Could you experience such a day and still be dissatisfied or unhappy? Could you still feel empty, as if something critical were missing?

3.3. The Time of Our Lives

[*Sidebar quotations:*

From Master Eisai: "We are giants dipped in time."

From F. J. Shark: "Success in anything comes from being very fussy about what you spend your time on, and who you spend your time with."]

Questions like those immediately invite others. Let's focus on time. How long must life last to count as living well? Must we wait until an individual is dead before making a judgment concerning whether or not that life was well lived, or is it possible that, say, just one day of living well is sufficient?

This is an important issue about which philosophers disagree.

Aristotle's position is clear: Because "life includes many reversals of fortune, good and bad," we should wait until the life span is complete before judging it: "For one swallow does not make a spring, nor does one day; nor, similarly, does one day or a short time make us blessed and happy."[32]

The Buddha's position is clear: "Better to live in freedom and wisdom for one day than to lead a conditioned life of bondage for a hundred years."[33] He recommends that we let go of the idea that we have a life span: "Do not pursue the past. / Do not lose yourself in the future. / The past no longer is. / The future has not yet come. / Looking deeply at life as it is / in the very here and now, / the practitioner dwells / in stability and freedom."[34] Similarly, he warns us not to attach to the ideas of a self or of a life span.[35]

Who is correct?

Since your conception of your self is a literate one, it is nearly certain that you will think that Aristotle is correct. In other words, again, you find it natural to think of yourself as having a life span of (usually) five or ten decades. This predisposes you to think of living well as success rather than as mastery.

My fundamental task in this book is to encourage you to let go of thinking that living well is a matter of being successful in favor of thinking that living well is mastering life. In other words, on this issue I agree with the Buddha: one day of mastering life is sufficient for living well.

Again, there's nothing wrong with success. It's just that success is insufficient for living well.

Perhaps you have realized this from your own experience with success. Have you ever been successful at accomplishing something very important to you and then had a brief episode of elation followed by a curious kind of emptiness? You wonder, "Is this all there is?" You wonder why you worked so hard only to experience a letdown. How could the fruits of years of working hard spoil so quickly? You want the elation that success brings to last, but instead it soon evaporates. You may have quickly begun taking it for granted and become interested in something else. Next.

Whether or not you have experienced this yourself, surely you are aware of many others who have been successful only to discover the painful truth that **being successful is not the same as being happy.** People who are thought of as divas, people who seem to have everything, are frequently exposed as being dissatisfied and suffering just like the rest of us.

It's normal to value success. Why? It's normal to think of ourselves as having a life span. Again, though, this is a conception of ourselves that comes from literacy. Our preliterate ancestors didn't have it.

What is normal is not necessarily what is natural. What is normal is certainly not necessarily what is best. If, upon examination, that turns out to be the case in this instance, it would be best to let go of or, minimally, loosen your attachment to the thought that you are a separate self with a life span. Doing so will automatically loosen your attachment to the thought that you need to be successful to live well.

What other way of thinking about ourselves in relation to time is there? Excellent question! That's the spirit.

To learn about something new is to relate it to what we already understand by noting the relevant similarities and differences.[36] Let's first ask: How is it normal for us to think about time? Then let's ask: What alternative is there?

We normally think of time as being linear as well as abstract. Our idea is that time is directional. Time points from the past through the present to the future. In other words, time is like an arrow moving forward. Time is irreversible.

It's important to understand that alphabetic writing is a critical part of the explanation for the emergence of time's arrow. It's difficult to get our heads around the thought that time's arrow hasn't always been with human beings. Of course, the lives of preliterate humans were temporal. Being temporal is a quality of every concrete entity. However, nonliterate humans don't think in terms of time's arrow, of irreversibility, which we literate humans take to be the essential feature of temporality.

This is why the introduction of the idea of time's arrow initially aroused fear and even terror. Irreversibility is threatening. It implies instability and change. Instead of pointing towards rebirth and renewal, it points toward the end of the world. "It was the Judeo-Christian tradition which had established 'linear' (irreversible) time once and for all in Western culture."[37]

Hope is the other side of fear. Time's arrow spawned fear, but it also opened more hopeful possibilities. Specifically, with irreversibility comes the potential for lasting progress. After Steno laid the framework for modern geology, western thinkers began to grasp the idea of "deep" time, the disorienting discovery that human history is merely a recent and brief episode in the multi-billion-year-old history of our planet. Once Hume had undermined attachment to the Causal Principle, the door was open to Darwin's great theory of descent with cumulative genetic modification. In brief, the emergence of time's arrow underpins the whole imposing edifice of modern science.

Is time's arrow an inherent part of the ceaseless flux? Is time intrinsic and fundamental to the universe? Aristotle thinks so, but Archimedes does not. Again, great thinkers disagree.

What is important here is that time's arrow is not necessarily the last word about time. Once again, it's good to be skeptical, questioning, probing. Once again, it's good not to be fanatically attached to a particular view. It's possible we are mistaken in thinking of time as having a beginning and an end. Perhaps we are even mistaken in thinking of our lives as having life spans, as having beginnings and ends.

The alternative is to think of time as eternally present, which really is the idea that time is circular or endlessly cycling like the seasons. This is how oral people think of time. We know this because anthropologists have discovered that, for example, the languages of some indigenous, oral American Indians lack terms for the past and the future. Why? It's because they think of everything as being present.

The reason this seems strange to us is that we live apart from the more-than-human. Cut off from the rest of the world by alphabetic writing, *we live in our heads*. In other words, **we live abstractly**. As David Abram writes, "The senses of an oral people are still attuned to the land around them, still conversant with the expressive speech of the winds and the forest birds, still participant with the sensuous cosmos. Time, in such a world, is not separable from the circular life of the sun and the moon, from the cycling of the seasons, the death and rebirth of the animals—from the eternal return of the greening earth."[38]

What's the cure for living abstractly? It's to teach ourselves to live more and more concretely.[39] To anticipate: living concretely is living masterfully.

Furthermore, anyone can do it: success is not a requirement for living well.

To live in the world of an oral people is to live in a world without time's arrow. Notice that, without time's arrow, there can be no progress. Nothing permanently can be improved; *no gains can last*. It does not follow that human lives are meaningless; rather, their meaning comes from their location within the more-than-human. "The multiple ritual enactments, the initiatory ceremonies, the annual songs and dances of the hunt and the harvest—all are ways whereby indigenous people-of-place actively engage the rhythms of the more-than-human cosmos, and thus embed their own rhythms within those of the vaster round."[40]

[*Sidebar quotation* from Stephen Batchelor: "Life is neither meaningful nor meaningless."]

Do you have the sense that, if you fail to become successful or to accomplish or gain something important, your life will not have meaning? Are you attached to the idea that you have to do something valuable in order for your life to be meaningful? Do you think you need to be successful to live well? If so, that idea depends upon your attachment to time's arrow.

Once you become aware of that attachment, it becomes possible to hold it out and examine it. Is success the same as living well? Will becoming successful enable you to master life itself (and not just some part of it)? How could gaining something yield living well indefinitely?

[*Sidebar quotation* from Joseph Campbell: "When people say they're looking for the meaning of life, what they're really looking for is a deep experience of it."]

The issue here is how time is part of the human condition. There's no question that our lives are temporal. The question concerns how we should understand that temporality.

[*Sidebar quotation* from Roshi Bodhin Kjolhede: "In Zen we are learning to live *in* the moment but not *for* the moment. Living for the moment is living irresponsibly. Living in the moment is the opposite, for it is a state of responsiveness."]

As philosophers, what we must not do is simply assume that our normal answer (namely, that time's arrow is part of being human) is correct. We should examine it and follow the argument wherever it leads.[41]

Before clarifying the distinction between success and mastery, let's examine an aspect of our human condition that nobody disputes, namely, that we have desires. Desires connect temporal individuals with abstract goods.

3.4 Desire

[*Sidebar quotation* from George Bernard Shaw: "There are two tragedies in life. One is not getting what you desire. The other is to gain it."]

If you pay attention and it happens that it's been several hours since you've eaten, you'll notice that you are hungry. If you are like me, hunger recurs several times daily. If I don't eat when I'm hungry, the hunger gets worse. When I am hungry, my life seems incomplete. The hungrier I am, the more incomplete my life seems. Though it's possible (by fasting) to break the conditioning, I'm conditioned to eat when I'm hungry.

If I've just eaten a good meal, I do not experience hunger. Hunger is the desire for food; to be hungry is to want to eat. Food is the object of hunger. Without hunger, it's still possible to eat and it's still possible to enjoy the taste or smell or texture of food. However, without hunger it's natural not to want to eat.

Hunger, then, is noticing the gap between me (the hungry I) and food. When I am hungry, I notice that I'm over here and the good stuff, food, is over there—and I want the gap closed. Unless I am hungry, there's no gap.

To be hungry is to be in pain. Pain itself is intrinsically evil, something bad.

Being in pain can have good consequences. If I am hungry and satisfy my hunger by eating food that nourishes my body, the consequences can benefit my physical health. Please do not, however, confuse the pain itself with its consequences. There's nothing intrinsically good about being in pain. (This is even true for masochists. Pain hurts masochists just like it hurts everyone else. The difference is that masochists enjoy being hurt. That enjoyment is a second-order enjoyment. Pleasure and pain are interesting subjects, and there's much more to be said here. Nevertheless, perhaps this is enough to satisfy you that pleasures are goods whereas pains are evils.) The more we are in pain, the more intense is our desire to reduce or eliminate it.

Here's the critical question: what is the good with respect to hunger? In general, what is the good with respect to any desire?

Long before the Axial Age, some philosophers had answered this correctly. The longest and one of the oldest of the Upanishads is <u>The Forest of Wisdom: The Brihadaranyaka Upanishad</u>. Its author invites us to notice that someone without desires is "in that unitive state" in which "all desires find their perfect fulfillment."[42] In a state of completeness or unity there is no gap I want closed between whatever I desire and me. No gap, no desire. To be fulfilled is to be without desire. **The good with respect to any desire is the end of the desire.** The good with respect to hunger is the end of the hunger.

[*Sidebar quotation* from Master Thich Nhat Hanh: "Desire disappears when you see that the true nature of the object you desire is impermanent, has no separate self, and cannot be grasped. If you are not satisfied with what is available in the present moment, you will never be satisfied by attaining what you think will bring you happiness in the future."]

To have a desire is to be greedy (grasping, wanting [in other words, hungry, thirsty, lustful, and so on]). Without a gap, there's nothing to desire. If I am not hungry, I cannot desire to eliminate the hunger. It's impossible to desire what one already has.

This seems an almost trivial insight. It's not. Its importance is difficult to overestimate.

This chapter ends the first section of this book, which is entitled "The Way of the World." What exactly is the way of the world?

With one exception[43], all desires are egocentric (egoistic, selfish). Desires are either attachments when they are positive or aversions when they are negative. Hunger is an attachment; to be hungry is to want to gain something, namely, the food that one lacks. The desire to be rid of pain is an aversion; to want to eliminate pain is to want to get rid of something, namely, the pain, that one has.

It's normal to be conditioned to desire pleasures and to avoid pains. There are many different kinds of goods that we desire and many different kinds of evils that we want to avoid. (Please reconsider your written list from section two from this perspective.) This is *the way of the world: ordinary life is a ceaseless quest to gain what we like and to avoid what we don't like.*

The way of the world is what grounds the success model of living well. According to this model, to live well is to be relatively successful in gaining what is valued and avoiding what isn't. To be successful is to get what you want and avoid what you don't want (with little or no effort); the higher the ratio between what you want and what you get, the greater the success. To be successful is to get ahead.

[*Sidebar quotations*:

From Meister Eckhardt: "There is no stopping place in this life, --no, nor was there ever for any man no matter how far along his way he'd gone."

From Sir Winston Churchill: "Success is never final."]

Isn't that how everyone lives? Anyway, what's the alternative? If there is one, why might it be better than the way of the world?

[*Sidebar quotation* from Richard Bandler: "one of the most important steps in the evolution of your consciousness: *be suspicious of success.*"]

3.5 The Success Model and the Mastery Model

To live well is to act in a certain way. So both the success model of living well and the mastery model are about our acts (actions, doings, behaviors).

The purpose of ethics is to provide guidance for living. *What should I do?* Ethics exists to answer this question.[44]

Actions are temporal. Actions are preceded by causes and followed by consequences. Let us agree that the **what** of an action is the content that a full description of it would have, and let us agree that the **how** of an action is what remains when we abstract it from its causal precedents and its later consequences. In other words, its *how* is its intrinsic character. So, at least with respect to human actions, the *how* includes the actor's state of mind.

The difference between the success model and the mastery model concerns the *how* of actions and does not concern the *what* of actions. So if person S is using the success model and person P is using the mastery model, S and P may both commit acts that are identical with respect to their *whats*; however, at least if both S and P were following their respective models perfectly, the two acts would have different *hows*.

We should therefore be very cautious about judging the acts of other persons. Why? It's impossible to know *how* another is when performing an act.

With respect to *what* is done, those who advocate the success model and those who advocate the mastery model may advocate identical *whats*. Conceived externally, there is no difference.

With respect to *how* acts are done, those who advocate the success model and those who advocate the mastery model advocate radically different *hows*. Conceived internally, there couldn't be more difference between the two.[45]

If there may be no external difference between the acts, what's the big deal about the different *hows*? Excellent question.

Though some philosophers treat it as if it did, ethics doesn't exist in isolation. Considered in abstraction from the rest of what we understand, ethical questions are insoluble. No progress in ethics is possible unless the answers that are given to ethical questions are grounded in "first" philosophy, which is ontology (the study of being) and epistemology (the study of apprehending).

It turns out upon examination that, with respect to what we should do, it is impossible to know the difference between right and wrong acts. The reason for this is that the rightness or wrongness of an act is a function of its consequences and, since it is impossible to know all the relevant consequences of any act, it is impossible to know the difference between a right and wrong act.[46] You probably already understand this from your own experience with respect to important medical or economic decisions.

[*Sidebar quotation* from Brad Blanton: "It is a milestone in growing up to get this: there is no way to be right. There is no right way to behave. There is no way to know you have done the right thing."]

This leaves us with a very serious problem, namely, given that we cannot know the difference between what would be right to do and what would be wrong to do and that we want to live well, what should we do?

Fortunately, it also turns out upon examination that, with respect to *how* we should do what we do, it is possible to know the difference between right and wrong acts. In Part II, I attempt to explain clearly what this difference is. To anticipate: this difference is grounded in the concept of self, which is intimately connected to time. How we think of ourselves with respect to time turns out to be critical.

Even if we act with the right *how*, it does not automatically follow that *what* we do will be right. This serious limitation is built into our human condition. However, getting the *how* right is doing the best that it is possible to do.

I'm not sure about you, but, whenever I do my best, I'm satisfied. It makes no sense not to be satisfied with one's best.

The mastery model, then, is not about improving *what* we do; instead, it's all about improving *how* we do whatever we do.

If, as I hope, doing your best is very important to you, I encourage you to devour Part II with rapt attention. Once you clearly understand the mastery model, then critically examine it for yourself. If it survives examination, then install it in your own life. Doing so will give you the best chance of increasing excellence in your life and actually living well.

Even if upon reflection you stay with the standard success model, the practical suggestions in Parts II and III concerning what to do would still be relevant. It would only be the ideas related to the *hows* of our acts that would be irrelevant.

[*Sidebar quotation* from Richard Bandler and John Grinder: "most people are very chaotically organized on the inside."]

Living wisely is the purpose of philosophy. Whether you do your best or not is wholly up to you. If the mastery model is superior to the success model and you abandon the way of the world, then, since getting your *hows* right is solely up to you, living as successfully as possible is solely up to you. There is no more exciting possibility than that.

If you are going to work hard to get *what* you do correct, why not take the extra critical step and get *how* you do what you do correct as well?

Doing that involves loosening or releasing attachment to your self-concept. It's a simple idea, but it's difficult to execute. Practicing that by focusing on the present moment will, however, enable you to live better by letting go of many problems that are obstructing you from living well.

There are a number of ways to do that; all are ways of meditating.

[*Sidebar quotations:*

From Master Charlotte Joko Beck: "The truth is most of us . . . love our problems. We want to stay imprisoned in our constructions, to spin and twist and be the victim, to feel sorry for ourselves. Eventually we may come to see that such a life does not work very well."

From Eknath Easwaran: "Someone once asked the Buddha skeptically, 'What have you gained through meditation?' The Buddha replied, 'Nothing at all.' 'Then, Blessed One, what good is it?' 'Let me tell you what I lost through meditation: sickness, anger, depression, insecurity, the burden of old age, the fear of death. That is the good of meditation. . ."]

Part II:
The 7 Steps to Mastery

Chapter 4: What-Is

Part II presents a theory of mastery. It may be helpful to imagine a circular stone monument of seven layers. Like the layers of a wedding cake, each layer of the mastery monument is smaller than the one that supports it. Unlike the layers of a wedding cake, each layer is sufficiently high that it cannot be skipped.

The master's journey is to climb layer by layer from the bottom to the top. Anyone who understands how to climb layer by layer from the bottom to the top understands how to become a master. Anyone who climbs to the top becomes a master.

The purpose of understanding mastering is to help achieve it.

The foundational ideas presented in the first three chapters of this section may be more fundamental than you find initially comfortable. If so, please proceed slowly—or quickly! The territory will become more familiar at the higher levels. It's important, however, to understand at least the gist of them because the higher levels are based on them.

4.1. Transition

If you are like me, you prefer being secure to being vulnerable. Being vulnerable is risky. We feel naked, exposed, confused, and weak. Being vulnerable is no fun.

At least with a modicum of success at living, as we mature we think of ourselves as enjoying increasing security. Being secure is being in control. The more we feel that our lives depend upon our own decisions and the less we feel they depend upon alien powers, the better we feel. The more we think we have taken control of our lives and have minimized the control that others have over us, the happier we are. We trust ourselves to take better care of ourselves than having to leave our fates to others or happenstance.

The reality is that there is no security. It's impossible to protect ourselves from disasters. It makes no difference how firmly we are attached to our wealth or our health or our families or our homes or our views or anything else: **to be alive is to be insecure.** There is nothing to prevent ill fortune from occurring at any moment. Happiness based on a feeling of security is a delusion.

We adults may realize that such happiness is a delusion, but we cling to it anyway. Death may be imminent, but isn't this strawberry delicious?[47]

If we are ever to grow, we must muster the courage to let go of this delusive happiness. As long as we are content to settle for a good life, we'll never experience a great one. Good is the enemy of great. In other words, living better requires letting ourselves become vulnerable. As long as we remain stuck to life as it has been, we'll never enjoy life as it could be.

We all have different security blankets. What are yours? Are you willing to let them go?

[*Sidebar quotation* from Master Hakuin: "Students who wish to reach the realm of authentic peace and happiness . . . I urge you not to wait until you've grown old and tears are streaming down your cheeks."]

If you keep waiting, nothing will help you. You can become a student of mastery for years. You can read book after book, listen to audio program after audio program, watch DVD training program after DVD training program, and take seminar after seminar. You'll probably pick up a lot of new ideas, but none of them will make any real difference in your life. Mastering theory is not mastering life.

Learning is of little use until we let go and become vulnerable.

It is scary. It always has been. Hesitation is normal; if you hesitate, there's nothing wrong with you. To learn to swim, we need to get naked and let go of whatever is supporting us—and we only do that if we really want to learn to swim.

[*Sidebar quotation* from Soren Kierkegaard: "In order to swim, one takes off all one's clothes—in order to aspire to the truth one must undress in a far more inward sense, divest oneself of all one's inward clothes, of thoughts, conceptions, selfishness, etc., before one is sufficiently naked."]

However, once we commit ourselves to doing whatever it takes and let go, everything can begin to improve rapidly. When we are open, fresh ideas can take root and improve our decisions quickly.

Why not the best?

Becoming vulnerable is risky. It requires courage. It means resolving not to let fear, doubt, or laziness stop us any more.

[*Sidebar quotations*:

From Samuel Johnson: "Nothing will ever be attempted if all possible objections must first be overcome."

From Napoleon Hill: "Do not wait; the time will never be 'just right.' Start where you stand, and work with whatever tools you may have at your command, and better tools will be found as you go along."

From Herbert V. Brocknow: "The fellow who never makes a mistake takes his orders from one who does."

From Bob Burg: "Realize the following fact of life: The longer you wait to do what you know you should do now, the greater the odds are that you'll never actually get around to doing it. I call this the Law of Diminishing Intent."]

What is your approach to the theory of mastery? Are you looking to pick up some new ideas to chat about while having cocktails, or are you serious about mastering life?

If you are not now a mastery of anything, admit it. Confront the truth. Nothing bad will happen. In fact, it can be liberating. If you are not yet a master, that does not entail that you are a failure. All it means is that you haven't yet learned what works. It's just that you have learned a lot about what doesn't work. All that stands between you and mastery is your attachments. If you will resolve to loosen and let go of them, you will immediately find yourself transitioning from a poor, average, or good life to a great one.

You are preventing yourself from living well to the extent that you are a fanatic.[48]

The central problem we all have is loosening and letting go of our attachments. It's simple, but it's also far from easy. It requires deliberately letting ourselves become uncomfortable, confused, and insecure. There's no greater courage than the courage to challenge ourselves to let go.[49]

The less confidence we have, the more difficult it is to let go. Perhaps, though, you are not giving yourself enough credit. Perhaps you are not being fair to yourself. Let's see.

4.2 Confidence

Humor me and try this experiment: I assume that you don't happen to be in front of a mirror. Touch your right index finger to the top of your right ear. Actually do it.

Easy? Unless you happen to be severely physically disabled, yes, it's easy. It's easy *now*.

Think about what is required for you to be able to do that. You weren't born knowing how to do that. Think of the skill involved in learning how to maneuver your arm, hand, and fingers. Think of the many hours your parents spent with you encouraging you to learn how to control your movements. How would you teach a baby to do what you just did? Think how extraordinarily difficult or impossible it would be even just to use words to describe precisely what you just did. You touched your fingertip to an unseen location and sensed that location with both your ear and your finger: amazing. How long do you suppose it took you to learn how to do that?

You just did some excellent work. You think little of it; you take it for granted. However, imagine what it would be like to do it excellently when you are, say, very drunk or have suffered a stroke. If you let yourself really think about your feat, you'll realize that it is nothing short of miraculous.

You take a lot of excellence for granted. We all do. It's quite likely that you undervalue what you are already able to do. Perhaps you haven't made a million dollars or raised some wonderful children or written a great poem or done much to ease hunger in Somalia, but you have enjoyed a lot of excellent accomplishments in your life.

You may not be a classic success in the eyes of the world, but you have enjoyed some genuine successes.

Aren't you an excellent walker? Don't you usually walk so well that you don't even think about walking?

Aren't you an excellent talker? Don't you use language easily and automatically?

Aren't you an excellent driver? Don't you usually drive so easily that you take it for granted? Beginning drivers must pay attention to driving, but you don't. You pay attention to your thoughts or the radio or a conversation with a passenger.

The point is that you do all kinds of activities so excellently that you hardly pay attention to them. I don't mean, of course, that you are mindless when doing them. I mean that you don't have to think about them as you are doing them. In that sense, you've mastered them. If I knew you personally, I could give you example after example of activities that you routinely perform excellently.

If so, then shouldn't you have the confidence to learn how to do additional activities excellently? Why shouldn't you have the confidence to let go of where you are in favor of where you'd like to be? You've done it before, and there's no reason why you cannot do it again.

Yes, doing so requires being able to endure the transition. So? There's no living well without paying the price. Living well is interesting in part because it is a challenge; if something comes easily for us, we don't value it.

Like the rest of us, you are naturally lazy. So? Why not let go of being attached to laziness? Why not resolve to do whatever it takes to live well?

It's not as if you are doing anything more important, because **nothing is more important than living well.**

Furthermore, it's not exactly stepping alone into the void. Fortunately for us, lots of humans have preceded us. They have charted the course. Again, the mastery monument presented here in Part II has been around for at least the better part of three thousand years (and it's probably been around much longer than that, except that we lack the written records to know it).

Nobody can let go of your attachments for you. On the other hand, there are many, many people who have lived well and who are available to encourage and guide you.

The way to overcome irrational doubts and fears is to confront them. You'll conquer them yourself. However, if you let others who have gone before help you, you need not conquer them feeling alone.

[*Sidebar quotation* from James Bryant Conant: "Behold the turtle: He only makes progress when he sticks his neck out."]

Please make the decision to let go of whatever secret excuses are holding you back. Just resolve to do whatever it takes.

[*Sidebar quotations*:

From Andrew Matthews: "It's more about effort than luck . . . When you say, 'I'll do this thing. I don't care how hard it is.' Life then starts to support you."

From Malcolm Forbes: "Failure is success if we learn from it."]

How should you start? You already have. If you don't have a better plan, here's a suggestion. It has five parts:

(1) Reading at least fifteen minutes daily, read this book from beginning to end. If you are comfortable reading more than that and want to progress more quickly, read thirty or sixty minutes daily. Do it each day without fail. That's not too much for excellence.

(2) Then reread the whole book again, but read no more than one section per day as you really let the ideas sink in. Each day critically think through for yourself and evaluate the ideas from that section. Absorb them, or reject and revise them.

(3) Use Chapter 11 to select an activity that suits you well and begin investigating that activity seriously. If it doesn't seem that it's a good match for your abilities after reading seriously and thinking about it for a while, select a different one.

(4) Commit to doing whatever is required to perform that activity excellently. Write your ultimate goal(s) clearly. Decide exactly how you will tell whether or not you are doing successfully or masterfully. Then write out a daily activity plan to use for the next ninety days.

Decide what you going to sacrifice for one hour daily and let that other activity go for the next three months in favor of working your plan. Begin immediately to work your plan.

(5) Twice a month, take an honest look at the results you are achieving. Tweak your daily activities accordingly. After ninety days, recommit yourself to success or mastery. Write out a daily activity plan to use for the second ninety days. Continue working each day without exception (except for serious illness or accident) until success or mastery. Persist. As a refresher, skim a chapter or two from this book occasionally.

When you have mastered that activity, you may want to repeat steps 3, 4, and 5 for an additional activity.

Steps 1 through 3 may go smoothly. All that is initially required is giving up something that you are doing now for at least 15 minutes daily in favor of reading and thinking. Part 4, however, won't go smoothly. There will be sticking points and obstacles, and the purpose of step 5 is to use them as opportunities for growth.

Whenever I get stuck, I always find that I'm unintentionally creating my own sticking points. Without realizing it, I've trapped myself. I am able to free myself by thinking better about my situation. My guess is that your experience in this respect is like mine. If so, here are two web pages that I wrote that will help you free yourself:

http://www.lasting-weight-loss.com/trap.html
http://www.lasting-weight-loss.com/obstacles.html [50]

The more you practice excellently, the more confidence you'll enjoy. The fact is that you should already have enough confidence to begin at least reading about doing what will give you more confidence. It may be difficult to get yourself unstuck. The trick is just to start. Don't wait until you feel sufficiently confident, just start. It's positive action that generates confidence and dissolves doubts.

In fact, you have already started! You are already reading this. Excellent! If you'll just continue every day to read in this book (or a similar one) for at least fifteen minutes, you'll continue to progress. Why? It's impossible to come to understand potentially powerful ideas without eventually having to test them for yourself!

[*Sidebar quotation* from John Fuhrman: "If you are unwilling to change, you have already reached your maximum potential."]

4.3 Coming To Our Senses

We have been speculating about what-is (reality, ultimate reality, the world, being itself) for thousands of years. However marvelous all that wondering may be, it's not my intention to add to it. *Speculation is endless.*

This book is about mastery. There's nothing speculative about mastery. As any successful person or master will confirm, excellence is concrete. It's as real as right here, right now.

Living is primary; speculation is secondary. Without immediately lived experience there would be nothing to speculate about.

Speculation begets speculation. It's possible to get so carried away with discursive thinking that we forget our direct experience of living. We can get so absorbed in our theorizing that we forget our lives.

It's incongruous and laughable when this happens to great thinkers like Thales or Newton. We expect them to do better. It can be a serious affliction, however, when it happens to us. Like absent-minded professors absorbed in their theories, we may stumble though life—and miss a lot of living as a result. Whenever that happens, it's sad. Getting lost in our ideas is unnecessary and never leads to living well.

Please don't misunderstand: I'm not against thinking well. There are times when it is important to think. During those times, we should think as well as we are able to think. What I'm against is wasting life uselessly speculating. Getting attached to speculating is as counterproductive as getting egocentrically attached to anything else.

Where should we begin? With our direct experience of living. It's not only the natural starting point, it's the only one that doesn't quickly degenerate into mere speculation. We are already living. Our concern is to see if we can live more masterfully.

[*Sidebar quotation* from David M. Buss: "Every living human is an evolutionary success story."]

We are animals living among other animals. Our experience of what-is is grounded in the intersubjective world of life, which Husserl called the Lebenswelt, which means "life-world." The life-worlds of humans from different cultures are different, and the life-worlds of other animals are different from human life-worlds. What do they all share? Husserl thought that the most fundamental, primordial feature of all life-worlds was the spatiality of the earth itself.[51]

The subject who experiences the life-world, thought Merleau-Ponty, is the body itself. *I am this living breathing body.* The same for you and others. This is important because it must be the starting point for thinking about what-is. Why? There's no other option that is more fundamental that our immediate sensory experience. Such grounding promptly deflates most speculative balloons.

Husserl's slogan was "Back to the things themselves!" I suggest that we follow Husserl in his determination to take seriously the facts as we find them, to pay serious attention to how the world reveals itself to us. To do otherwise, to begin with scientific, religious, or philosophical theories, merely inflates speculative balloons. That way is also the way to fanaticism.

To think about our immediate sensory experience is to think about **perception.**

The reason to think carefully about perception is because it's quite likely that you were taught a theory about it that is inadequate. Because you were taught it years ago, it's a theory that probably seems quite natural. Because everyone else was also taught it, it is quite popular. If you proceed carefully through what follows, you'll be rewarded by freeing yourself from some insidious thinking.

Perceiving is an occurrence, an activity by which animate organisms orient themselves to their surroundings. David Abram correctly calls it a "dynamic blend of receptivity and creativity . . . [an] ongoing interchange between my body and the entities that surround it . . . a sort of silent conversation."[52]

Let's consider an example.[53] To keep it as simple as possible, let's limit it to vision and tactual feeling. Suppose that you are reading this book in a physical format, that you take a break from reading, and that you put it down on the wooden table beside you.

Please look at that table. You see its top. You see how the light hits it rather unevenly: some parts of its surface, where the light reflects off it, are much lighter in color than other parts. The steaks of grain are darker than the rest of its area. What color is its underside? If it happens to be an oak end table, you expect its underside to be similar to its top even if it isn't a finished surface. However, you cannot see it.

Please get down below it and look upwards at the bottom of the tabletop. Either the color and the striations of the grain of the bottom of the tabletop are similar to its top or they aren't.

However, as long as you are underneath it looking up, you cannot now see its top. It's still there, of course. Reach up and feel it. Does it have the same colors it had before?

What color is the inside of that table top? Presumably, it's not hollow. You can tell by the heft of the table that its top is made of solid oak. How, though, could you ever see the color of its insides? Even if you sawed the top in two and looked, you'd only have exposed additional surface area. Are its insides colorless? Does it even really have insides?

Here's the point: the table is more than you perceive. However you see or touch it, you cannot exhaust its presence. It has dimensions that are wholly inaccessible to your senses. *The reality of an entity is its inexhaustibility.*

So an object is anything we are able to notice, and a real object is an object that we are able to notice multiply.

[*Sidebar quotation* from Maurice Merleau-Ponti: "the house itself is . . . the house seen from everywhere. The completed object is translucent, being shot through from all sides by an infinite number of present scrutinies which intersect in its depths leaving nothing hidden."]

Furthermore, that real table beside you is a temporal entity in flux. As time goes by, sunlight, dust, grease, stains, wear, decay, and even polish or insects or abuse will take their toll on it. If we believe the scientists, your solid oak table is mostly air! The molecules that constitute it are in incessant motion. The micro-table is quite different from the macro-table. Even if it weren't, the table itself would still be slowly evolving over time.

Similar considerations apply to other bodies. Do they suddenly seem more interesting?

Of course, the word 'table' itself isn't in flux. If we get attached to our concept of a table, we may think ourselves fortunate in having attached to something stable in our instable world. What we would have actually done, however, is to substitute one object for another. *We attach to our concepts because they are comfortingly static; however, the world we inhabit is dynamic.*

[*Sidebar quotation* from D. T. Suzuki: "The main trouble with the human mind is that while it is capable of creating concepts in order to interpret reality it hypostatizes them and treats them as if they were the real thing."]

If you will still the usually incessant chatter of words and attend to your actual perceivings, you will find these interesting occurrences to be like wordless dances. (Notice the analogy!) **The more we conceptualize, the more we miss the lived world.** It's impossible to conceptualize without separating (and, to anticipate, separation is the root of all suffering).

In other words, to the thinking mind, the ordinary objects about us seem utterly passive, inert, dead. For that reason, we quickly lose interest in them. After all, when was the last time you paid any attention to your end table? However, to our sensing bodies, objects are never utterly passive, inert, or dead. *What we perceive is animated.* Perception is a participation that is a reciprocity between our awarenesses and incessantly mutable objects around us. Noticing is an interchanging activity.[54]

Also, it's important to notice the absence of anything about causation in the description of perceiving the table. Presumably, certain causal conditions must be satisfied or there wouldn't be any perception at all. However, the idea of causation is irrelevant in this context.

If you deny this, it's probably only because you were taught the philosophical causal theory of perception ['CTP'] in school. You probably haven't thought about it since junior high school. It's time to question it. Let's examine it briefly to enable you to detach from it.

Remember, if you would practice philosophy well, it's important to begin with our experience and not with whatever theories we happen to have picked up. Let the theories you accept be grounded upon experience (instead of just upon someone else's theory).

According to the CTP, when you see the table, something like this chain of events happens. Light is reflected off the surface of the table into your eyes. That pattern of light hits your retinas, which are composed of rods and cones that convert the energy from the light into electrical energy. Your optic nerves transmit this pattern of impulses back to the visual projection areas of your brain and you "see" the table. Or, rather, you see the "table-message" that supposedly comes to you via this causal sequence of intermediaries from the table.

Do you notice something odd about this view? If not, you are too close to it. Step back and consider it from a distance.

Here's what's odd: it is supposed to explain how you see the table but this is exactly what it can never explain!

How could anyone know that the CTP is correct? *There could be no evidence for it.* Suppose it's advocated by Joe Psychologist. According to Joe's own theory, he never sees tables. He only sees table-messages. The same for all the other senses. Therefore, there's no perceptual connection between Joe's awareness and the (putative) bodies that surround him; there's only his awareness of objects that he supposes are messages that he postulates (speculates, hopes) come from surrounding bodies' (There may not even be any such bodies at all; Joe's world may be nothing but a series of messages.) He never perceives bodies. How could there be a worse theory of perception than that?

I mention this for four reasons.

(1) It's practice in examining your own theoretical attachments. Just because you happen to have accepted some theory doesn't entail that it's an adequate theory. Theories need to stand up to critical examination.

(2) Notice that nothing bad happens if you let go of the CTP. It's perfectly all right simply to admit that you don't know how perception works. It is strange. It's uncomfortable to admit that we really don't understand something that we thought we understood, but, far from being a fatal admission of error, letting go of theoretical attachments can actually make the world much more interesting.

(3) Thinking this through may boost your confidence in your ability to think for yourself. There are plenty of well-known thinkers who have attached to the CTP. You may have just surpassed them all. Doesn't that show that you are able to play the game of theorizing also? There's no need for you ever to be intimidated. Just resolve to proceed slowly whenever it is necessary.

(4) It's important to realize why the CTP fails so miserably. It's because it is an indirect theory of perception. According to it, there are intermediaries between awareness and perceptual objects. Not.[55] Even many of the major thinkers of modern western philosophy have been misled into thinking that there is a screen of "ideas" between us and the objects that make up the world. The right kind of theory of perception is a direct theory of perception.

Perception is direct. To claim that perception is direct is to claim that in every episode of perception there is the perceiving awareness and the perceived object, whether that object is real or unreal. (This is unpacked in the next two sections.) It's false that perception is indirect, that there are intermediaries between the perceiver and the object perceived. All indirect theories of perception crash just like the CTP.

Whether what is perceived is real or unreal, or taken to be real or unreal, perception is direct. This is supported by the ways in which we usually think and talk—often even when we are discussing dreams and hallucinations.

The chief reason to think that perception is direct, though, is based on a careful examination of the lived-world. It merely acknowledges what Butchvarov calls "the most intimately known fact about ourselves."[56] It's important to clarify this. After all, *claims about what-is that are not ultimately grounded in perceptual experience are vacuous.*

4.4 Awareness

Perception is direct awareness between ourselves and material objects and their qualities. When perception works well, when those objects and their qualities are real, it is "veridical"; when it doesn't, when those objects and their qualities are unreal, it's "nonveridical" (in other words, an illusion or delusion).

Is there an intrinsic difference between veridical and nonveridical perception? No. Of course there isn't. Otherwise, we'd always know the difference and couldn't ever be fooled by illusions or delusions.

When you perceive your table you are aware of it. A chief reason why people get confused about perception is because they have not sufficiently examined awareness (consciousness) itself.

Just as there are two kinds of theories about perception, namely, direct and indirect, so there are two kinds of theories about awareness, namely, direct and indirect. (The indirect kinds are often called the "mental contents" or sometimes the "three-term" theories.)

What is awareness?

It's peculiar in that it's neither an individual nor a quality' It's neither a monadic nor a relational quality. It's <u>sui generis</u>, which makes it an irresistible magnet for philosophers.

It does, however, have a nature: it is always directed toward something. In other words, it's always about some object or other. Following Brentano, this is called the thesis of the "intentionality" of awareness. (I use scare quotes to quarantine the world 'intentionality' to show that it is a technical term. Like all technical terms, it should be explained in nontechnical language, which I have just done.) You have the same familiarity with awareness as Brentano or anyone else. Ask yourself: "Am I ever aware without being aware of something?"

When you love, don't you always love something, some object such as another person? When you hate, don't you always hate something? When you perceive, don't you always perceive something? When you think, don't you always think something? When you dream, don't you always dream something? When you hallucinate, don't you always hallucinate something? And so on.

It's important here not to confuse being aware of nothing and being aware of an unreal (nonexistent) object. It's easy to imagine, for example, an unreal object; perhaps you did it while dreaming last night. It is impossible, on the other hand, to imagine nothing. When you imagine, don't you always imagine something or other?

It's simply a fact that awareness is always about some object or other. There is no such thing as an "empty" or "blank" awareness. (If there were, how could we notice it?)

It's also simply a fact that some objects we are aware of are unreal (do not exist). When this happens in perception, it's a nonveridical perception. The reason we may get fooled at least occasionally is that there may be no intrinsic difference between veridical and nonveridical perception.

Sartre is the one who clarified this. He thought that all awarenesses necessarily have objects and that, considered in abstraction from what they are about, awarenesses are nothing at all. In other words, there is nothing "in" awareness; instead, usually, material objects are *before* awareness.

In other words, Sartre's point is that awareness is perfectly transparent. There's nothing in it; it has no inhabitants. It exhausts itself in its objects. Awareness itself is nothing but the genuine revelation of an object.

This is the fact that Butchvarov had in mind when he claimed that it is "the most intimately known fact about ourselves." *There is no way to separate awareness from its objects.* Awareness is because objects are; objects are because awareness is. Like everything real, they are interdependent, in other words, their arising is conditioned by other entities.

Awareness has no varieties or species or levels. For example, the only difference between so-called auditory awarenesses and visual awarenesses is that the former are about auditory objects while the latter are about visual objects. Please don't be misled by talk that the mind has different "faculties": all it means is that there may be awareness of different kinds of objects. All episodes of awareness are the same: all they are are the presentations of various objects. Awareness of an object is no thing (nothing) distinct from the object itself; "they" are inseparable.

In the case of perception, there is no way to separate our perceptions from their objects. Those objects may be unreal. Therefore, this provides us a good motive for always being willing to be skeptical about perception. In particular, to perceive something is not to know that it is real. In general, to be aware of something is not to know that it is real.

Descartes's dream argument is the best way to show this. You may read it for yourself in his First Meditation.[57]

What matters here is only the possibility of dreaming—not its actuality. Even if you have never had a dream, you could. Similarly, even if you never have, you could perceive unreal objects.

Remember: let go of the idea that awareness in dreams is not the same as awareness when awake. There are no different kinds of awareness. So a dream is just awareness of dream objects. (Of course, some dream objects may be real, in other words, it's possible to dream about real objects.)

Here's the best way to make this argument vivid: are you certain that you are not dreaming right now? Do you know that you are reading this book? Isn't it possible that you are only dreaming that you are reading this book?

Could you imagine waking up five minutes from now? Why not? Couldn't you wake up and then realize that a short while ago you'd only been dreaming that you'd been reading? True, it would have to be an amazingly vivid, realistic dream, but it's still possible, isn't it?

In that case, did you really awaken from a dream? Could you have only dreamed to have woken up? How could you rule out that possibility?

Have we have clarified the nature of awareness only to have created a worse problem about perceiving what-is?

Let's not jump to premature conclusions. What we have actually done, I hope, is to have worked you very close to a big "Aha!" (So don't worry if thinking hard about this gives you a headache. The headache will soon pass, but the insight will remain.)

4.5 The Obstructed Obvious

So, after all this thinking, what is reality? What is ultimate reality? Let's begin with reality and then turn to ultimate reality.

Reality is inexhaustibility. In other words, it's a concept: whatever is inexhaustible is real and whatever isn't is unreal.

Imagine being on your first camping trip as a youngster. It's some time after midnight and you and your friend are lying in your tent too afraid to sleep. You think you hear a twig snap as it would if a large mammal stepped on it. You whisper to your friend in a trembling voice, "Did you hear that?" If your friend replies affirmatively, you think that that sound was real and not a figment of your imagination. In other words, if you and your friend heard the same sound, you'd naturally think it was a real sound. If your friend didn't, you'd either begin to have doubts or suspect that, perhaps, your friend had momentarily drifted into sleep.

Similarly, if you and I notice the same shooting star, we'd naturally think it was a real shooting star and not, say, our old eyes having simultaneous peripheral light flashes. If we were both looking in the same direction in the night sky and you didn't see it, I'd probably wonder if my eyes were tricking me.

Similarly, if I see the same cashier at the bank today and remember seeing her last week, of course I think she's real. I might, though, be mistaken. Perhaps I'm misremembering or the cashier last week has a twin sister who happens to be working there today.[58]

There's no point multiplying examples beyond necessity.

To be real is to be inexhaustible.[59] Anything that is multiply noticeable. Anything that can be noticed multiply is real.[60] By way of contrast, anything that can only be noticed once is unreal.

Reality is a concept, a way of sorting objects into two groups. Again, an object is anything noticeable. Not every object is real; only those objects that are multiply noticeable are real.

'Multiply' may mean one person at one time (for example, I'm seeing the table while I'm touching it) or one person at different times (the table I'm seeing now is the table I saw yesterday).

Mistakes about judging reality are possible. Of course they are! We are not infallible. If I'm having a nightmare in which a polar bear is attacking me, I may think it's real during the dream but, after awakening, I'd conclude that, fortunately, I was mistaken.

Let us, then, resolve always to be humble when making existential judgments, which are judgments about the reality or unreality of something. Attaching to such judgments is the fundamental mistake of fanatics. This is why it is foolish to be a fanatic. It's always possible to be mistaken about the reality of individuals.

[*Sidebar quotation* from Saki Santorelli: "We are all seeking solid ground. Yet if we look closely we see there is really no such place to stand."]

In short, reality is a concept for sorting objects. Inexhaustible objects are real, whereas exhaustible objects (in other words, objects that can only be noticed once) are unreal.[61]

Ultimate reality is obvious.

This, of course, stands in direct opposition to the view that ultimate reality is hidden. It is not at all hidden: it is right here, right now. Whence the popular idea that it is hidden and beyond the grasp of most humans?

Ultimate reality is also obstructed. **Ultimate reality is the obstructed obvious.**

How can it be both obstructed and obvious?

It's because *we obstruct it by conceptualizing*. All it takes to apprehend ultimate reality is to let go of incessant conceptualizing. That's not easy to do[62], but it's simple. The important point is that doing so reveals how obvious ultimate reality is.

[*Sidebar quotation* from Keith Johnstone: "I belatedly thought of *attending* to the reality around me . . . I [previously] saw what *ought* to be there, which of course is much inferior to what *is* there."]

How should we understand ultimate reality? What is it like?

These, of course, are foolish questions. If to apprehend ultimate reality is to apprehend it without conceptualizing it, it is impossible to describe it conceptually. So please drop that requirement. If you want to apprehend it, train yourself to let go of conceptualizing. If you were to let go of conceptualizing even for a moment, you'd enjoy direct access to ultimate reality. It really is obvious.

[*Sidebar quotations*:

From The Buddha: "They abide in peace who do not abide anywhere."

From Sharon Salzberg: "It is only due to our concepts that we feel separate from the world."

From John Wheeler: "There is no *out there* out there."]

Either you will or you won't. If you think it a project worth undertaking, there's no reason why you cannot undertake it successfully. If you don't, you won't do what is required. There's nothing more to be said about that. You will undertake that noble quest or you won't.

So, **reality is conceptualized ultimate reality.** Our conceptualizations distort reality by separating unity.

For example, is the world red or not red? Either answer is misleading. Some individuals are red and some individuals aren't. Reality itself is both red and not-red, or beyond both red and not-red. The point is that reality is always more than we conceptualize it to be.[63]

It is not that reality and ultimate reality are somehow different in kind: it's the ineffable difference between conceptualized and unconceptualized apprehension of the same subject matter.

The most obvious and important fact about reality is that, except for abstractions, **every real individual is impermanent and conditioned by other objects.** Every event is connected to every other event. Nothing exists independently. Nothing exists immutably. Nothing exists permanently. What-is is flux. What-is is process.

[*Sidebar quotation* from Steve Hagan: "If all is truly flux, where do we find beginnings or endings? . . . Both the beginning and the end are inconceivable."]

This is not merely theory: it is experienced by each of us all the time. Every real object is a dependent process. There are no exceptions. Just try to think of a single one. Think of a sunset or a table or a galaxy or a lake or a cloud or an animal or a love affair or a pain: none of those are permanent and nothing at all like them is permanent.

Not everyone agrees. Let's briefly mention the two extreme views.

One extreme view ("metaphysical absolutism") is that there is a transcendent ultimate reality that is immutable. Isn't this *obviously* either unintelligible or wrong? Unless the phrase "a transcendent ultimate reality" denotes unconceptualized reality, I find it unintelligible; I been a philosopher for about fifty years and have no other idea what metaphysical absolutism might mean. If so, it's eliminable.

The other extreme view ("metaphysical nihilism") is that nothing is real. However, this is absurd. Many objects are noticeable in multiple ways. Of course everyday entities are real; it's just that they are processes dependent upon other entities. If so, this is also eliminable.

In a word, then, what is the nature of reality? **Impermanence**.

Therefore, the bottom level of the mastery monument is nothing but impermanence (flux, instability)!

The implications of this concerning what we should do are impossible to overemphasize. In particular, with respect to mastery, its goal cannot be a state. Even masters never are: they are in a process of becoming. Mastery is real, but, like everything else that is real, it isn't permanent; mastery is a process. The Buddha would say that, like everything else that's real, it's "dependently arisen."

In general, with respect to satisfaction, it makes no sense to aim at permanence. Why? There is no permanence!

Haven't you experienced this yourself? Haven't you noticed that, whenever you tried to grasp something that would yield permanent happiness, you were disappointed? Haven't you noticed that whenever you thought "If only I could have X, then I'd be happy" and then successfully grasped X, you nevertheless failed to achieve lasting happiness?

We have all made that mistake. The only interesting question is whether or not we mature enough before dying to learn the lesson that **grasping never works.** Many, or so it seems to me, die without ever learning the lesson. Attachments are poisons. This explains why all fanaticism is foolish.

The goal of the mastery journey is a process. If you undertake the journey, understand that you'll never arrive at the destination. There's no permanent, or even stable, destination. However great your accomplishments with respect to mastery, there will always be more to do, more to master.[64]

It's important to understand this at the beginning. Please release the idea that, even if you undertake to discipline yourself in the appropriate ways for the kind of mastery you have selected and even if you work hard and enjoy significant successes, you'll eventually achieve a plateau beyond which it is impossible to go. There will always be more.

Mastering is open-ended. The ideal that it is not is as unreal as the horizon.

This may initially disappoint you, but, if you think hard about it, you'll realize that this is the way it should be. Do you really want the challenge to end? Even if you do, be assured that it won't.

That's just the way it is. That's the nature of reality.

Chapter 5: Creating Your Reality

Unless you are a fully enlightened sage, your "surreality" is not exactly the same as reality. Your surreality is your world, the reality you inhabit.

Sometimes, we notice the difference. Once when I was seventeen, my friend Humpty and I were driving nonstop from Del Rio, Texas, to where we lived in Toledo, Ohio. We were in my mother's station wagon. It was the middle of a dark night and, after having already covered many hundreds of miles, we were tired. I went to lie down in the back, while my friend drove for a while. We were cruising (probably doing about 75 mph) along Route 66 somewhere in Missouri.

Suddenly, the car swerved abruptly; I instantly feared for my life as I was rolled up against the inside back of the car. I stabilized myself and looked up: there seemed no reason for Humpty to have swerved. The traffic was very light. Fortunately for us, he didn't lose control of the car. He said he saw a large truck coming right at us on our side of the highway. But there was no truck!

What he actually saw were the headlights of our automobile reflecting off the girders of a bridge. As tired as I was, I started driving again (and we eventually made it home safely). The point is that his world, his surreality, was not the same as the world, as reality.

That time nothing untoward happened. Sometimes, though, the gap between reality and surreality can get you killed. Illusions and delusions can be dangerous.

[*Sidebar quotations*:

From Marcus Borg: "Both Jesus and the Buddha offered a similar diagnosis of the typical human condition: blindness, anxiety, grasping, self-preoccupation."

From Dan Cavicchio: "There's only one way out of a bad situation, and that's to stop believing in it. Don't make it real and it disappears."]

5.1 Worldmaking

We do not create reality; we discover it. However, **we create our surrealities.** We don't make *the* world, but we make the world we inhabit.

We make our worlds, our surrealities, by making existential judgments. All judgments are decisions. If I decide or judge that the student I'm seeing in my office now is the student I saw in class yesterday, I am judging that student to be real. If it's the same student, I'm right; if it isn't, I'm wrong.

Most of our decisions are habitual, automatic.[65] We make them without paying attention to them.

[*Sidebar quotation* from John Kenneth Galbraith: "The conventional view serves to protect us from the painful job of thinking."]

What, for example, were you thinking about the last time that you got into your car, started it, and drove off? Are you able to remember?

It's highly unlikely that you were thinking about getting into it, starting it, and driving off; you have done that so frequently that the whole sequence of decisions that completing that task involves was habitual or automatic.

You may have been thinking about your destination or what would happen when you arrived. You may have been worried about whether or not you needed to stop for gas soon, or you might even have been meditating. In other words, you weren't thinking about what you were doing because you no longer have to.

It's as if you have so programmed your brain to do what is required that you are able to do it without thinking about it. In fact, the only time you likely think about it is when the sequence doesn't go well for some reason, for example, when the car fails to start.

It would have been different if, for example, you were only a beginner or you were seriously ill or injured.

[*Sidebar quotation* from Tor Norretranders: "It is everything we *cannot* figure out that we think about. After all, we have no reason to puzzle over what we are really good at. We just do it. Without consciousness."]

It's similar with respect to our existential judgments. As experienced adults, we almost always make them habitually, automatically, without thinking about them. It's only infrequently we pay attention to them. We are likely to do that only when something has gone wrong or we suspect that something may have gone wrong or might go wrong, for example, when we've been drinking or dreaming.

As explained in Chapter 4, we have no guarantee that our existential judgments are correct. Sometimes we are blind to what is real, and sometimes we hallucinate and mistakenly think that something is real when it isn't.

[*Sidebar quotations:*

From Robert Dilts: "Since you don't really know what is real, you have to form a belief—a matter of faith. . . beliefs are largely unconscious patterned thinking processes . . ."

From Andrew Matthews: "So long as you *believe* that everything is going wrong, it will keep going wrong . . . Things will improve the minute you say, 'There are no accidents in my life. I am where I am meant to be' . . . It is possible to accept the world as it is and still accept a share of responsibility to improve things."]

A mistake about something's qualities is an "illusion." A mistake about something's reality is a "delusion." There is no way to ensure that, in a given case, we are not being blind or hallucinating. There is no way to avoid illusions and delusions.

Of course, the problem isn't just in mistaken existential judgments themselves—it's in the actions we base on them. In other words, *the decisions that we make to create our surrealities affect how we behave.* This is one reason why we all make behavioral mistakes. Sometimes those mistakes can have very important, very real, negative consequences (as well as unanticipated positive outcomes).

This is why, from the standpoint of an individual, it is so dangerous to be a fanatic. If you happen to be attached to incorrect existential judgments, your actions can be counter-productive for yourself as well as for others.

Essentially there are two kinds of mistakes:

(1) Sometimes we take two (or more) different objects to be the same. Have you ever had someone you recognized walking towards you from some distance and hailed that person—only to be chagrinned moments later when that person turned out not who you thought it was but a stranger?

(2) Sometimes we take the same object to be two (or more) different objects. Did you ever go to a class reunion and find yourself chatting with a stranger—only to realize belatedly that you actually knew that person?

Such mistakes can be amusing. On the other hand, they can also be very dangerous. The next truck that you swerve to miss might not be real and yet you might wind up dead.

This is what forces *the distinction between reality and surreality, between what is real and what we think is real.* For every object, either it is real or it isn't. However, for any individual, it's impossible to be certain whether it is real or not.

[*Sidebar quotations*:

From William James: "Each world, *whilst it is attended to*, is real after its own fashion . . .

From William Cullen Bryant: "Weep not that the world changes. Did it keep a stable, changeless state, it were cause indeed to weep."]

This doesn't go for all objects. The exceptions are **abstract objects**, for example, numbers. Whether you are awake or asleep, 2 + 3 = 5. If you were ignorant of arithmetic, you wouldn't know that. However, given that you understand arithmetic, you cannot be mistaken about it.

Notice that you are so attached to your arithmetical understanding that you wouldn't let any perceptual experience override it. Suppose that you were in a bar late some night and someone challenged you to add 2 shot glasses to 3 shot glasses. You counted them and got 6. What would you do? Would you think, "Aha! I now know that it's false that 2 + 3 = 5." Of course not. You would, I hope, realize that you are so drunk that you counted one twice. Drunk or sober, 2 + 3 = 5. Similarly, you know that crimson is a red and that triangularity is a shape.

Abstract objects are always qualities or combinations of qualities; they are never individuals. All individuals are concrete. Qualities, again, are commonalities, what two or more individuals may share or have in common (or what may be true of two or more individuals). Since two shirts can be blue, blueness is a quality. Qualities are concepts. (Recall that concepts are principles of classification.) They may be considered in abstraction from the individuals that instantiate them; in other words, we can think of them in isolation.

By way of contrast, individuals are always concrete, always temporal and usually spatial. They are unified clusters of qualities. It's impossible to think of them in isolation from their qualities.

The reason why we may ignore abstract objects qua abstract objects in this book is that, because they are eternal (non-temporal, timeless, outside time), they are immutable.[66]

Nothing concrete inhabits the domain of being. Everything temporal (in time, whether momentary or enduring) inhabits the domain of *becoming*. Everything temporal is unstable. Like our very lives, mastery is a process. There's nothing fixed or stable about it. Everything in the domain of becoming is unstable. Concrete objects are dynamic, lively processes. Their relations are always contingently one way rather than another (for example, you used to be shorter than your mother but now you are taller than your mother). Everyone understands that concrete objects can be fascinating, alluring, and even beautiful. Since there's no necessity about mastery, since mastery is always a contingency, let's restrict ourselves to the domain of becoming.

So, for any given concrete object, for any individual, it's impossible to be certain whether it's real or not. Since making a mistake can have terrible consequences, we have a problem.

What's the solution? How should we guarantee that we don't make mistakes when we make judgments about concrete objects? In the domain of becoming that we inhabit, how can we avoid making decisions about what to do or what not to do that will have bad consequences?

[*Sidebar quotation* from Roshi Philip Kapleau: "what works for one person may not work for another. If what is said applies to you, use it; if it does not, discard it. There is no one way, no should's or ought's . . . you must find your own way."]

There is no solution. There's always the possibility of a gap between reality and surreality. **Our acts are inevitably shots into the dark.** Again, mistakes go with our human condition. There's no way to avoid them. We are not perfect.

[*Sidebar quotation* from Kalu Rinpoche: "You live in illusion and the appearance of things. There is a reality, but you do not know this. When you understand this, you will see that you are nothing, and being nothing you are everything. That is all."]

So, let's stop attaching to the idea of perfection. That idea is a trap; it prevents mastery.[67] It's as if the ego pushes the idea of perfection forward so that we'll get discouraged and stop practicing. **Mastery requires ego reduction**, which is the chief goal of practicing. So, from the ego's point of view, trying to prevent practicing is a life-or-death concern. If it can get you to quit practicing, it will continue to live; otherwise, it won't.

[*Sidebar quotations*:

From Marshall Stamper: "The most important words you'll ever hear are the ones you tell yourself."

From Robert Dilts: "Since you don't really know what is real, you have to form a belief—a matter of faith. . . beliefs are largely unconscious patterned thinking processes. . . they are hard to identify. . . If you're going to change your identity or a limiting belief you hold: (1) You've got to *know how to do it*. (2) You have to *be congruent about wanting your outcome*. (3) You also have to have the belief that it's *possible* for you to make the change."]

What's this chapter on surreality doing in a book on mastery? It's not just that paying sufficient attention to surreality prevents us from having the wrong goal with respect to mastery, namely, that the wrong goal is a state rather than a process, but it's also that failing to appreciate our fallibility permits us to attach to the idea of perfection, which prevents mastery.

If you are like me, even though they don't withstand critical examination, the two ideas that a state of mastery and perfection are possible have a strong psychological attractiveness. Fully absorbing the ideas about surreality presented here will undermine that attractiveness.

5.2 Interbeing

Until we become fully enlightened sages (and, again, that may only be an ideal), the best we can do is to minimize the gap between reality and surreality, which automatically minimizes mistakes. How should we minimize the gap?

[*Sidebar quotation* from Master Dogen: "To carry yourself forward and experience myriad things is delusion. The myriad things come forth and experience themselves is awakening. Those who have great realization of delusion are buddhas; those who are greatly deluded about realization are sentient beings. . . "]

The only way to minimize it is to keep challenging ourselves, to keep questioning and examining.[68] Again, doing that is doing what philosophers do. So, if you don't already, please practice philosophy and never stop. Please practice philosophy even when you are reading this book. In fact, I hope this book is an effective introduction to practicing philosophy well.

[*Sidebar quotation* from T. S. Eliot: "And the end of all our searching will be to return to the place where we began, and to recognize it for the first time."]

In fact, it's difficult to imagine that, at least to some extent, you don't do this already. Suppose that, late some afternoon, you drop by my cottage and we enjoy a cup of tea together. You leave to meet someone for dinner and drive directly and quickly to a nearby restaurant. As you enter the restaurant, you see me already sitting there midway through a meal. You wouldn't believe your eyes, would you?

In this case, in effect your understanding would be questioning your noticing. Perhaps, there is some bizarre explanation for how I had beaten you to the restaurant, but, more likely, you take a second look and realize that you weren't really seeing me but someone who closely resembled me.

Our understanding is the combined totality of our judgments. How we understand affects how we notice, and how we notice affects how we understand.

Since becoming is flow (flux, process), whenever our understanding of it is not in flow but stuck, rest assured that the gap between reality and your surreality is increasing.

Obviously, for example, someone who is blind and always has been has no understanding of colors. Also obviously, we all have different experiences and use different analogies and conceptual systems, which explains why different witnesses typically perceive the same accident somewhat differently.

Our understandings depend on our noticings, and our noticings depend on our understandings. There is an ongoing interaction between them. As a matter of fact, this interaction is so close that, except in theory, it's impossible for ordinary humans to separate them.

This is the idea of interbeing.[69] The Buddha said it repeatedly: "This is, because that is. This is not, because that is not. This comes to be, because that comes to be. This ceases to be, because that ceases to be."[70]

In other words, cause and effect are because of each other. Everything concrete is the result of multiple causes or conditions. This is called the doctrine of "dependent arising" (or "interdependent co-arising").

In the last chapter, I claimed that nothing real is independent. In other words, everything real is dependent on multiple causes or conditions. I hope that you asked yourself, "Is that true?" I hope that you thought about it and didn't just accept it because I seemed to know what I was talking about.

If the doctrine of dependent arising is correct, then we can rely on it. Whenever our noticings don't fit it, we should question them. This doctrine could be a useful tool. For this reason, let's look at it more closely and see if it stands up to examination. If it does, then we may have provisional confidence in it and begin to use it.

Let's see. Let's continue with the example of your oak end table. It's real. You are able to see it and touch it. Doesn't it exist independently from everything else—or does it exist dependently?

Considered solely as a visual object, notice in the first place that it is part of a whole visual field. In particular, it's not floating by itself; it is dependent for support on the carpet, which is in turn supported by the floor, which is in turn supported by the foundation of the building, which is supported by the earth. (Recall from Chapter 4, section 3, how Husserl thought that the common feature of all life-worlds was the spatiality of the earth itself.)

Don't you also take it that the table has an unseen backside as well as solid insides?

Do you "see" the sun and rain and minerals from the soil in the table? No? Look more deeply. This table is primarily made of oak, which comes from oak trees. No sunlight, no oak trees. No rain, no oak trees. No minerals from the soil, no oak trees.

Do you "see" other animals in it? What about the squirrel who buried the acorn that grew into the tree? What about the deer who ate the plants around it that enabled that oak to soak up sunlight? What about the earthworms who aerated the soil?

Do you "see" all the people in the table as well? What people? Do you see the logger who used a machine to harvest the oak tree? Do you see his parents and grandparents? Do you see all his ancestors stretching back tens of thousands of years?

That oak would not have become a table if it were still a tree. What about the craftsmen at the furniture factory? What about those good folks in marketing and sales? What about the executives who ran the company and the investors who financed it? What about the truckers who shipped it? What about those who manufactured the truck and built the highways? There are lots of people in your table if you will look deeply enough.

Do you "see" the wheat in the table? What wheat? The wheat that the logger ate as the bread on his sandwich that fueled his body enabling him to run the machine that harvested the oak tree.

Do you "see" yourself in the table? You should. The table is part of your perception; it's what you have in mind. You aren't seeing nothing; your mind isn't blank or empty. You are seeing something, namely, your table. It's part of your life. There's no separating awareness from the objects of awareness. Furthermore, you purchased it and gave it its present location.

Do you "see" our society in there as well? After all, that table is your property. Perhaps property is like a game that we play. According to the rules of our property game, nobody else may use or take your table without your permission.

Unlike some bodies (such as other humans or oceans or clouds), this one is a body that you are able to own. Ownership drags with it our laws and the whole criminal justice system we have for enforcing them.

The idea of ownership is one that philosophers have seriously considered and debated, and philosophy encompasses the whole history of ideas. Your labor produced the money you used to purchase it. Your moneymaking occurred in our economic system. No economic system, no table in your home.

Do you "see" time in your table? You should. Obviously, it's a temporal object.

In fact, what if you were time itself? Are you separate from time? Maybe the reason that you are "seeing" the table as a temporal object is because you are bringing time into the perception. (This idea comes from Kant.) Perhaps to live well is to be time. If so, this would explain that, although sages look to be bound by time like the rest of us, they really live, as William Blake puts it, "in eternity's sunrise."

[*Sidebar quotation* from Joan Stambaugh: "Instead of a supposedly permanent ego anxiously watching time fly past or slip away, I *am* time. As long as I am time, it does not slip away. Any activity involving intense concentration and absorption bears witness to this. A musician performing a concert, a writer engaged in writing, an athlete playing on the sports field—none of those, if they are really doing what they are doing, is aware of the flying away of time. If asked, they would answer that they are not aware of time at all, and this answer shows that they *are* time."]

In fact, is there anything in the domain of becoming that is not in your table? There's space and time in it, the light of sunshine and the dark of night, rain and clouds, minerals and earth itself, people living and dead, animals, plants, ourselves, our society, and our ideas. Goodness!

This table is a miracle. Far from being independent, it co-exists along with everything else. Its reality depends on the reality of everything else.

These are wonderful ideas, aren't they?

[*Sidebar quotations*:

From Sir Winston Churchill: "Men stumble over the truth from time to time, but most pick themselves up and hurry off as if nothing happened."

From Thomas Edison: "Make it a habit to keep on the lookout for novel and interesting ideas that others have used successfully."]

5.3 Identity

[*Sidebar quotation* from Tor Norrentranders: "Whether we want it that way or not . . . individual continuity . . .has no material foundation."]

What, essentially, is this table? What makes it up? This table is composed of non-table parts.

In fact, **every individual is composed of non-individual parts**. A non-individual part is a quality. Therefore, individuals are composed of qualities, commonalities. Since an individual is precisely that which is not a commonality, since an individual is something unique, this is astounding.

Of course, the table is itself. Every object is itself and different from every other object. That is the law of identity, which is necessarily true. Let's label this table "A." So, A is A. That's true. Of course A is A.

However, we have just seen how this A, this individual, is a cluster of commonalities. So, in that sense, A is not A. How could a unique individual be a cluster of commonalities? (I return to this in the next chapter.)

The correct view, though, is that the A that is not A really is A.[71] The reason for this is that being an individual, like being a quality, is a concept. We are able to separate objects into individuals and non-individuals, just as we are able to separate objects into qualities and non-qualities. The real (true) table is beyond our concepts and classifications.

In other words, the problem is that *the reality of the table lies beyond our conceptual horizon.* We never fully grasp the table with our concepts. Our concepts never exhaust it. Because, as we have seen, our noticings never exhaust the reality of this table, this begins to make some sense, doesn't it? The river water passes through our nets.

This doesn't mean that there's anything hidden about the table. It only means that the real table is the obstructed obvious.

The A that is not A really is A. The individual table that is not an individual (because it is a set of qualities) really is itself.

The reality of the table is beyond our conceptualizations of it. In that sense, the table is only real when it is not grasped conceptually. In general, again, ultimate reality is beyond our conceptualizations of it.

If so, the truth about the world cannot be conceptualized. This is why we should locate what is true in the world rather than in our conceptualizations. At best, our conceptualizations are weak approximations that are sometimes useful.

Isn't your table suddenly much more interesting? Looking deeply enhances our lives.

This is yet another reason to avoid fanaticism. Fanatics think that they know the truth about reality. Not! They think the world is static and boring when it is dynamic and interesting. The judgments of fanatics don't penetrate reality any further than the judgments of anyone else.

The reason is that judgments are conceptualizations and conceptualizations cannot penetrate reality. Reality is always beyond our thinking that it is this or that. Where 'F' denotes some concept or other, reality is always beyond F or not-F. Reality encompasses both F and not-F, or, put differently, it is neither F nor not-F.

Do you know the lines from e.e.cummings's wonderful poem "If Everything Happens That Can't Be Done": "and birds sing sweeter / than books / tell how." Perhaps what he is telling us is that reality is better than we think it is.

Conceptualized reality isn't reality. Reality is – thus!

5.4 Mastering and Conceptualizing

What's the relevance of all this to mastery?

The chief lesson is this: for the most part, mastery should not be confused with conceptualizing.

The qualification 'for the most part' is necessary because it is possible to master bodies of knowledge, masses of related concepts. This is what graduate school is all about. We are able to master book-learnings of various kinds.

Still, and everyone understands this, there's a big difference between someone who has mastered a theory and someone who has mastered a practice. If you needed an operation, would you want a surgeon to operate on you who was fresh out of the classroom and doing his first surgery or a master surgeon who had twenty years of practice to complement his medical and surgical schooling?

Mastering is practicing.

To claim that mastery should not be confused with conceptualizing doesn't mean that conceptualizing isn't a part of mastery. It is. There's no mastery without conceptualizing. However, the heart of mastering is practicing—not conceptualizing.

Think of mastering a new dance step. At first, you'd think about what you were doing. You'd be self-conscious. You'd begin by deliberately practicing moving in certain ways, probably imitating someone who had already mastered the step. It would seem awkward initially, but soon it would begin to feel a bit less strange and more comfortable.

The more you practiced the step correctly, the more and more comfortable you'd feel. Eventually, you may be able to dance without thinking about dancing. You might, for example, be thinking about how to make your partner look good instead of thinking about what you were doing with your feet. In fact, at the level of mastery, if you started thinking about your feet, you might stumble!

I've actually seen that happen. Permit me a true story.

Years ago I played hockey, and my friend John was a teammate. Like the rest of us, John had been playing hockey since he was a boy, and he was a master skater. In fact, he was either the fastest or the second-fastest skater I ever played with in my long hockey career. I was never a fast skater, but I could skate well—especially backwards. (I played defense.) Yet I once beat John in a race on skates.

Here's what happened. The college where I teach has a varsity hockey team. John had played on that team and was friends with its coach, who also managed the rink. That enabled John to get us some extra ice-time, which is how it happened that day that we had the ice surface to ourselves. Tired of just skating around passing and shooting pucks, I challenged John to a short race backwards. I proposed racing from a blue line just to the red line at center ice. John accepted the challenge.

Of course, he knew that he was a much faster skater than I was and, so, should win even such a short race easily. He figured that I must have some trick up my sleeve, some special technique that would enable me to get off to a faster start than he could. I didn't have any such trick up my sleeve; I was bored doing what we had been doing and had merely proposed an alternative.

We stood on a blue line with our backs to center ice. "One, two, three—go!" We each took off backwards. Instead of just taking off and beating me as he surely would have, John thought about what he was doing: he watched my feet and tried to emulate exactly how I started so that he, too, could begin by using this trick I supposedly had. What happened?

He fell down. It was hilarious! We both laugh about it to this day. (And, of course, knowing what would happen next time [namely, John would have just skated], I never raced him again.)

Lesson: masters who start thinking fail.

Of course, mastering begins with conceptualizing. We need some idea of what we want to do before we begin training. Eventually, though, as one persistently practices well, it's as if our brains more and more take over and the conceptualizing drops away. Practicing well requires us to let go of thinking.

Mastering is not thinking about doing. **Mastering is doing.** To master is to perform some task excellently without thinking.

Furthermore, it's a selfless doing. **All excellent doings are selfless.**

Understanding that requires understanding the self, which is the subject of the next chapter.

Chapter 6: Understanding Yourself

What am I? What kind of thing am I? What am I not? Am I the same through time? How did I begin? How will I end? Is my self real or only surreal?

[*Sidebar quotations*:

From Jack Parr: "Looking back, my life seems like one long obstacle race, with me as its chief obstacle."

From Thomas Merton: "What can we gain by sailing to the moon if we are not able to cross the abyss that separates us from ourselves? This is the most important of all voyages of discovery, and without it, all the rest are not only useless, but disastrous."]

It is not easy to understand the concept of self. There are at least three reasons for this.

First, it is a concept. Like all concepts, we weren't born with it. We learned it. We learned how to identify with some objects and to separate from others. So, we may have learned it well or poorly; you and I have picked up at least slightly different self-concepts. Thinkers, as we shall see, have even proposed very different concepts about what selves are.

Since it's always possible to unlearn what has been learned, it's possible to revise our self-concepts. In fact, it's common to do so, for example, in adolescence. This is what identity crises are. (If there were no serious question about what selves are, how could there be identity crises?) So, second, any particular self-concept is a moving or evolving target.

Third, if we are selves, then we are trying as selves to understand ourselves. How could this be easy? It's never easy to be clear, impartial, and disinterested in our own cases.

Valuable conceptual work is always one of three kinds: creating valuable new ways of understanding, preserving fruitful ways of understanding, or eroding poor ways of understanding.

Most of us have a tendency to place too much emphasis on the first. In the case of mastery, however, since it has been around for several thousand years, we need not even try to be creative. There's nothing new about it to invent. We would be wise to concentrate heavily on eroding poor ways of understanding and preserving valuable ways of understanding. This emphasis is never more important than with the concept of self.

Is a self what we most intimately identify with? This is a promising beginning. However, as soon as we begin to get specific, we begin to see the difficulty: what are the similarities and differences between myself and everything else?

The young protagonist of James Joyce's <u>A Portrait Of The Artist As A Young Man</u> tries, like the rest of us, to relate himself to everything else:

Stephen Dedalus
Class of Elements
Clongowes Wood College
Sallins
County Kildare
Ireland
Europe
The World
The Universe[72]

Perhaps figuring out what our selves are is figuring out how we fit into reality. How could we come to understand ourselves if we are unable to relate ourselves to everything else?

6.1 Nothing, Everything, or In Between?

Accounts of the nature of the self come in three varieties:
 (1) the self is nothing,
 (2) the self is everything, or
 (3) the self is something in between nothing and everything.

There's no fourth alternative. Let's consider these in turn.

(1) Could it be that the self is **nothing**? This view is so bizarre that I'm not sure that any philosophers have ever held it—and that's saying something.

The serious possibility here is that such annihilationism amounts to the doctrine that it's false that the self is a continuant. A "continuant" is just an individual that is real at two or more consecutive times. If your table remains itself through time, it is a continuant. Let's interpret the claim that the self is nothing to mean that it's false that the self is a continuant.

"Ontology" is the name of the study of reality. A standard issue is ontology is: "Are any continuants real?" This question is about concrete individuals; it is not about abstract objects (because, since abstract objects are not temporal objects in the first place, they obviously could not endure as temporal objects).

There are two major problems with the claim that selves are continuants, which provide two reasons for being tempted by the view that it is false that selves are continuants.

First, the initial problem about claiming that selves are continuants is apprehending the reality of any continuant. If selves were continuants, how could we tell that they are? More generally, if some individuals were continuants, how could we tell that they are?

For example, is your oak table a continuant? Suppose, as is natural, you think it is. Why do you think that? You think it because its qualities are unchanged from this moment to the next moment. Notice that, even if that is the case, it may not follow that there is something underneath the qualities—an independent (separate) individual—that is enduring through time.

This is not merely an issue about selves. It's an issue that encompasses all individuals. Are independent individuals real? If so, are any of them continuants (as opposed to their all being momentary)? By "independent individuals" I am referring to "substrata," which are, supposedly, substances or whatever is underneath an individual's qualities that holds those qualities together.

Second, what are continuants? Could continuants be substrata?

Let's examine this notion of substrata. If we were to abstract an independent individual from its qualities, what would it be? Try it with your oak table. Imagine abstracting (taking away, isolating) all its monadic qualities: its shape, its colors, its hardness, its texture, its weight, its mass, and so on. After all, these are commonalities, in other words, they are not unique to this table; two tables could share exactly the same shape and color and so on. What would be left?

Well, *have you ever noticed an object that had no qualities?* Of course not. How could you notice (think, single out, pick out, identify) an individual that lacked all qualities whatsoever? It is unintelligible to claim that something would be left after such a process of abstracting. So, it must be that nothing would be left. In other words, there are no independent individuals, no substrata. So continuants could not be substrata. The claim that independent individuals are real is unintelligible. Since a claim must be intelligible to be either true or false and, since it's false that the claim that independent individuals are real is intelligible, it cannot be true.

Since this applies to selves and all other individuals as well as to tables, this is an important ontological point. **No individuals are independent of their qualities.** There are no real independent individuals, no substrata. All individuals are nothing but clusters of qualities. In this context, the claim that a self is nothing would mean that no self is independent.

If so, **a self is a cluster (aggregate, congeries, togetherness, unity) of qualities;** it is not a (continuant or even momentary) substratum underneath its qualities. Similarly, all individuals are nothing but clusters of qualities.

[*Sidebar quotation* from John Daido Loori: "We cannot see things as they really are until we let go of the idea of a separate self."]

Does it follow that individuals cannot be continuants if they are not substrata? Does it follow that I (my self, my ego) am not a continuant if I am not a substratum?

It's important to see that *individuals may be continuants even if they are not substrata*. In particular, I may be a continuant even if I'm not a substratum—and the same for you and all other individuals.

Imagine two individuals, two clusters of qualities, and ask: are they one or two? Is it one cluster noticed twice or two different clusters that may only resemble each other? If the two clusters were separated temporally, how could we tell if they were one continuant?

This is a fascinating question. Arguing for an answer to it would take us far beyond the scope of this book.[73] Permit me to make three points about its answer, but I refrain here from arguing for them lest we get too far afield.[74]

First, based on an examination of the qualities of the two clusters, there's no way to tell whether they are really one or not. The qualities, for example, may or may not stand in a one-to-one correlation. So? If the qualities don't, the two apparently different individuals may still be the same; if they do, they may still not be the same.

Second, because there's no way to tell based on an examination of the qualities of the two clusters, we must simply *decide* either that they are the same or that they are not. (Again, decisions can be automatic, habitual.) In such decisions, we are creating our surrealities. In doing so, we may or may not be creating a gap between what we think is and what-is.

Third, it's normal to think that continuant individuals are real. After all, don't you think you are the same person you were an hour ago? Don't you think that your oak table is the same table it was a minute ago? If continuant individuals are real, then those continuant individuals are clusters of qualities that lack substrata. They remain, in other words, dependent individuals even though they are also continuants.

Our surrealities are full of dependent, continuant individuals. In fact, it would be nearly impossible for you to think of yourself as anything but such a self.

(2) Could the self be **everything**?

This is another fascinating idea. It is what mystics have always claimed. The problem is rendering it intelligible.

Could all identity judgments be true? Recall that an identity judgment is a two-in-one judgment. For example, the table that I'm seeing now is the table that I saw earlier (a is b). If true, there is one real table noticed at two different times; if false, there are two different objects. There's no difficulty about the fact that there are two noticings. The question in this case is whether there is one continuant or not. Is the present visual object the same as the remembered one? It's at least logically possible that it isn't, that someone substituted a second table for the first and that the two tables only exactly, or closely, resemble each other.

Notice that, since the affirmative answer to the question 'Could the self be everything?' requires concepts (such as judgment and truth) to be thought and concepts are principles of division, it's not clear that it's possible to think that all identity judgments are true. It's easy, of course, to say or write the words, but that's not the issue. In other words, what could it mean to claim that, in reality, there are no correct applications of concepts? Would not such a claim undermine itself?

Mystical pronouncements are ineffable.

The problem is not necessarily with the mystics. As some philosophers like Bradley have argued, it may be that conceptualization is falsification. This is another reason why fanaticism is foolish. It's good to be skeptical of all attachments that involve concepts.

Furthermore, it's difficult to achieve a unitive experience. Any lack of understanding them may come from us and not be due to a problem with the language of the mystics.

[*Sidebar quotation* from Mohandas Ghandi: "Identification with everything that lives is impossible without self-purification . . . But the path of self-purification is hard and steep. To attain to perfect unity one has to become absolutely passion-free in thought, speech and action; to rise above the opposing currents of love and hatred, attachment and repulsion."]

Minimally, then, the question 'Could the self be everything?' must be interpreted before it can be answered.

The best interpretation among many interpretations of the claim that the self is everything comes from The Upanishads. They teach that Reality is atman-Brahman, which is transcendent. In that sentence, 'Reality' is capitalized to indicate ultimate or absolute reality. The claim that the self is everything means that a permanent Self [atman-Brahman] different from our ordinary immanent mortal selves is real.

There is certainly such a phenomenon as a mystical experience of a unitive state. Plenty of mystics over the centuries have testified eloquently (though obscurely) to that.

[*Sidebar quotation* from C. D. Broad: "To me, the occurrence of mystical experience at all times and places, and the similarities between the statements of so many mystics all the world over, seems to be a really significant fact."]

The critical question concerns the correct interpretation of such experiences. What seems to happen is that people who have such experiences interpret them according to the conceptual systems that they already have. That's perfectly natural; we all do it all the time. So a Hindu would naturally think that the experience was one of union with atman-Brahman. A Christian would naturally think that the experience was one of union with the Biblical God. An atheist would naturally think that the experience had some naturalistic explanation and interpretation or other. And so on.

If so, this leads us back to questioning the adequacy of various possible conceptual systems. Is our interpretation of such experiences contaminated by the ways that we naturally understand them?

Here's the point: *there's no necessity about interpreting mystical experiences in any particular way.* For example, having a mystical experience does not prove that atman-Braham is real. Suppose that someone suspected that atman-Braham is real and then that person had a mystical experience. That person would naturally interpret that experience as union with atman-Braham. Is that the correct interpretation of that experience? Not necessarily. We have seen that there's an important difference between believing that something is correct and knowing that it is.[75] Since that interpretation would still be questionable, that person would still not know that <u>atman</u>-Braham is real.

In fact, as I have already admitted, I do not think there is anything hidden beyond ordinary reality. *Reality is the obstructed obvious.*

It does not follow that there are no mystical experiences. Of course there are. It's just that they do not have to be interpreted as contact with a reality that is usually hidden.

The way to convince yourself of this is temporarily to set aside the obstruction provided by all your conceptual attachments, in other words, to have a mystical experience. If you do, what you'll find if I'm correct is nothing that isn't obvious. It will be a radically different kind of experience (because it will be direct rather than indirect), but it won't be of something radically different. What you won't find is <u>atman</u>-Brahman, the Biblical God, or any other transcendent reality. Instead, you'll have the profound sense that what's revealed has been there all along.

Could I be blind? Yes. If you disagree with me, could you be hallucinating? Yes. Fortunately, there is a way to settle the issue, namely, by removing all conceptual obstructions. Furthermore, although it isn't easy, anyone can do it.[76]

So let's let go of the idea that a self is the Self.

(3) If there are three options and two don't work, that leaves us with the third. Since a self is neither nothing nor everything, it must be **something in between** nothing and everything. This is, in fact, the usual concept of a self.

What kind of thing is a self? It's an individual. Like all individuals, it's made of qualities, non-individual parts, and it is dependent on other individuals. Individuals are nothing except their qualities; they do not have substrata.[77]

[*Sidebar quotation* from Shunryu Suzuki: "There is no you to say 'I.' What we call 'I' is just a swinging door which moves when we inhale and when we exhale. . ."]

Again, the usual conception we have is that selves are continuant individuals. Unfortunately, most people seem to think of themselves as continuant substrata rather than as continuant dependent individuals. However, once we let go of the idea that we are independent individuals and accept that we are like all other individuals in that we are dependent, we have made important intellectual progress and are ready for the logically next question:

What kinds of qualities do we have?

6.2 Our Sort

We have seen[78] that we are lazy, greedy, ambitious, impatient, selfish, vain, and ignorant. What kind of thing is lazy, greedy, ambitious, impatient, selfish, vain, and ignorant? It's a dependent continuant cluster of some more fundamental (general) kinds of qualities.

Naturally, different thinkers have proposed different accounts. Let me propose a list for your consideration. There's nothing original about this list. The order of the five qualities listed makes no difference. Perhaps this list will work well for you, and perhaps it won't. What's important is that you think it through for yourself. In each case, please ask, "Is this really me?"

(1) In part, I am a body, physical processes, but I am not only a body. If I weren't a physical being, how could I be alive or lazy or hungry or lustful? Human beings are animals, and all animals are, minimally, bodies. There's more to me than my body, but I am at least a body. I am a spatial being; I occupy space. I share that quality with rocks! I am also alive,

which is a quality I share with, say, trees. I have a human form, internally and externally.

(2) In part, I am aware, and awareness is a conscious process, but I am not only aware. If I lacked mind (awareness), how could I be ambitious, impatient, selfish, vain, or ignorant? A human body without a mind would not be a human being. I am able to make universal as well as singular judgments, which would be impossible without awareness.[79]

(3) In part, I perceive, and perceiving is a noticing process, but I am not only a perceiver. If I weren't able to perceive, how could I think or understand anything? What would awareness be about? I am a sentient being, and sentience is a quality I share with, say, horses and dolphins. Like other animals, I have desires; when, for example, I am hungry and perceive food, I want it.

(4) In part, I have feelings; I experience emotional processes, but I am not only emotional. If I lacked feelings, how could I ever be anxious, embarrassed, guilty, proud, afraid, or resentful? I don't know if, say, elephants also feel grief, but my interpretation of their behavior is that they do. I believe that I share feelings at least some with other kinds of mammals.[80]

(5) In part, I am disposed to act, and acting is an active process, but I am not only inclined to act. If I weren't disposed to act, how could I ever want to make a friend or eat or go for a walk? My decisions to act may not always work; if I am paralyzed and decide to get up and go for a walk, I won't be able to do it. However, whether they are causally efficacious or not, I am naturally disposed to take action.

If so, and if other human selves are like my self, then a self is a cluster composed of the physical qualities of a human form, consciousness, perceptions, feelings, and dispositions to act.

This is not an original account. The Buddha articulated it 2500 years ago[81], and it may not have been original with him. What is most significant about his view of the self is that it is exactly the right kind of view. He thinks the self is neither nothing nor everything. He is justly renowned for arguing against the view that selves are substrata and against the view that a self is the Self. He thinks of the self as a continuant, dependent cluster of these five qualities.

[*Sidebar quotations:*

From Roshi Shunryu Suzuki: "Our body and mind are not two and not one. If you think your body and mind are two, that is wrong; if you think that they are one, that is also wrong. Our body and mind are both two *and* one . . . in actual experience, our life is not only plural, but also singular . . ."

From Grey Owl [Archie Belaney]: "Remember, you belong to Nature, not it to you."]

6.3 Mind

There is a lot more to be said about each of these five qualities, but, with one exception, it's not necessary to go into them in more detail here. Consciousness (awareness) is the exception.

The reason for this is that, at least after Descartes here in the west, it may seem more natural for us to identify more with consciousness than with any of the others.

[*Sidebar quotation* from Napoleon Hill: "You have absolute control over but one thing, and that is your thoughts. This is the most significant and inspiring of all facts known to man!"]

To be conscious of an object is to have it in mind, to be aware of it, to notice it.

There's a difference between *paying attention to* an object and just *being conscious of* it. For example, right now you are, I hope, paying attention to what you are reading, but you are also aware of the position of your body, the warmth or coolness where you are, occasional extraneous sounds, and so on. Normally, we are aware of lots of objects, but we select only one or a few of them for devotion by our attention.

If I were to ask you if you had a **mind**, you might well reply, "Of course I have a mind!" You know how to use the noun 'mind' correctly. The problem is that we tend to reify experiences. Which object, really, is your mind?

That noun came from the verb '(to) mind.' Of course, you understand the correct use of that verb, too. 'Did you mind that no one asked you to the dance?' 'Mind that you don't bump your head when you go down the cellar stairs.' 'Did you mind the baby as you were asked to?' What these and all similar uses have in common is the notion of paying attention. If you were not conscious that no one asked you to the dance, you didn't mind not being asked.

Instead of assuming that the mind is a more-or-less static individual, let's take ordinary episodes ("acts") of paying attention as being examples of mind. They are acts of consciousness, dynamic mental episodes that are similar[82] to silent conversations. The reason that this is important is that, otherwise, we have a tendency to think that our minds are stuck over here whereas their objects are things that are over there. In this way we set up a misleading bifurcation.

This is how we come to think of our selves as minds. After all, if my mind is over here and everything else is over there, on which side of the bifurcation is my self? Well, I think, I must be my mind. If so, then my mind must be connected (presumably by consciousness, which then must be a relational quality) to all those other things. So I'm separate from everything else. This puts me in a very lonely position.

It's also unnecessary to think this way. In fact, it's the wrong picture. As noted earlier, the only difference between an episode of awareness and the object that that awareness is about is theoretical. There is no separation except conceptually; since they cannot be separated, they are like two sides of a single piece of paper. It's impossible to have one without the other. This is why there's no need to reconnect with all the world's objects: except in words and concepts, there never was any separation.

This is an excellent example of how our conceptualizing obstructs reality. The notion that there is a problem of breaking out of my mind to encounter the "external" world is a pseudo-problem.

The idea that minds are individuals puts a spell on us. What's the best way to break that spell?

There are, of course, individual episodes of awareness, in other words, there are many different individual objects. That's different from thinking that minds are individuals.

Here's a simple question: do you think that other people in addition to you are conscious? In other words, is awareness (consciousness) a quality? (Recall that a quality is what two or more individuals may share, that qualities are commonalities.) Don't you think that other people are also conscious? I do.

Consciousness is <u>sui generis</u>. Suppose, though, that we had to classify it as either an individual, a monadic quality, or a relational quality. Where would it go? Various thinkers have put it into all three categories, which indicates how peculiar it is. What we normally think, however, is that other humans and many animals are conscious.

This isn't just theory: if you have ever unexpectedly locked eyes with, say, a bear or a moose or a walrus in the wild, you had no doubt whatsoever at that moment that other beings are consciousness. Consciousness, therefore, is more like monadic qualities than it is like individuals or relational qualities. It's somewhat like a monadic quality of all objects.

So what?

Do you take yourself to have been born? Do you take yourself to be mortal? I do, and I assume that you do as well. The natural cycle is for animals to be born, grow, and die.

In other words, you correctly take yourself to be a temporal being. (It doesn't matter here whether or not you take yourself to be a continuant.)

This is why you are not consciousness. Consciousness is not a temporal being.

At least it's not if it's a quality. No qualities are temporal beings. Hence, it's false that consciousness is a temporal being.

Qualities don't go in and out of existence. If they did, there'd be such a thing as an unreal quality. However, there are no unreal qualities. Qualities, considered apart from the individuals that instantiate them, are abstract objects. All abstract objects are real. Of course, since they are abstract, all abstract objects are nontemporal denizens of the domain of being. They may not be very interesting, but they are always available for us to be interested in.

You yourself are a temporal object. Consciousness is not. So, you are not consciousness.

You should decide for yourself whether or not this argument is sound. Is it true that no qualities are unreal? That part of the argument is sound. Just try to think of one. **Suppose that you are able to think of a color that no real** individual has ever seen. Is that color real? Well, could you think of it in an hour? Could someone else think of it? Why not? There's nothing to prevent it. If so, then it could be noticed more than once, which would make it the subject of a true identity judgment. Any subject of a true identity judgment is real.

This argument does not work for individuals, but it does work for all qualities. Of course qualities are commonalities. It is impossible to have a commonality that couldn't be noticed multiply.

Still, this argument depends upon taking consciousness as a quality, which, as I have admitted, is misleading. Is there an alternative?

A better way to break the spell that you are a mind is simply to examine (introspect) any episode of awareness carefully. Suppose that you look at your end table. Now, isolate (abstract, pay attention to) the awareness itself; attend only to it and not to the table. Can you do it? How could you notice *that* awareness without guiding off the table? How could you pick out (specify, identify) *that* episode of consciousness without referring to the table? Because, as we have seen, the only quality of consciousness is "intentionality," whenever we try to notice an episode of awareness we always fall through to the object of that awareness.

What this means is that your mind is not over here at all: **the mind is all objects**. We foolishly talk as if we have objects in mind; the reality is that mind is in objects.[83] Sages have been saying this for centuries. For example, Master Dogen, arguably the greatest thinker in the history of Japan, wrote: "You think that your mind is thoughts and concepts, but it is really trees and grasses and pebbles and tiles."

Once this sinks in, you'll naturally detach from the pernicious idea that you are your mind. Consciousness is one of your essential qualities; without it, you would not be the individual, the cluster of qualities, you are. That's true. On the other hand, identifying with your consciousness fails. You are much more than merely awareness. You are very well endowed; your nature is very rich.

A similar kind of argument could be made for your other four essential qualities.

Again, you are a cluster of qualities. You are not to be identified with any one of them, and you would not be you if you lacked any one of them. You are a dependent cluster of qualities; you are not a substratum that exists beneath them. You may also be a continuant; at least you naturally take yourself to be a continuant. If so, you are a dependent cluster of qualities, or, rather, a continuing sequence of quality clusters. That's all a self is: *a continuing sequence of quality clusters.*

An individual's having a quality is due to a complex of causes and conditions. For example, the consciousness you enjoy is a result of a host of factors.

The particular cluster of qualities that is your self had a beginning, and it will have an end. Whether they are momentary or continuants, that's true for all individuals. Qualities don't go in and out of existence, but individuals do.

It's not that individuals come from nothing and will become nothing. Their births are due to a complex of causes and conditions, and their deaths are due to a complex of causes and conditions. We individuals came from something and will become something. How could nothing beget something or something become nothing?

Distinguish the doctrine of *reincarnation* from the doctrine of rebirth. The doctrine of reincarnation, when applied to you, means that you will have another life span after this one. (I remind you that the Buddha urged us to let go of the idea that we have a life span.) You may enjoy fifty years of life this time around, and next time around you may enjoy a hundred years, and the time after that you may enjoy eighty years, and so on. I have no clue what that means. It seems that it must refer to the reality of a continuant substratum, but that idea is incoherent.

On the other hand, the doctrine of *rebirth*, when applied to you, means that there is an ongoing process from moment to moment that you identify as your continuant self. You have a kind of ontological momentum. This is the natural view. As long as it doesn't rely on the reality of a continuant substratum, it may well be the right view. We could think of our selves as a sequence of momentary clusters of qualities, perhaps something like space-time worms that are segmented at every moment. Again, individuals are made of non-individual parts (qualities). These parts do not go in and out of existence, but individuals do.

[*Sidebar quotation* from Ajahn Amaro: "more often than not the Buddha talks about the rebirth process in moment-to-moment terms."]

If you think Elvis is still alive, you are deluded.

On the other hand, if you think his qualities are still around, you are correct; furthermore, they always will be and they always were. It's not that they exist at all times; it's that they exist timelessly.

6.4 Selflessness

This is the section of this chapter most directly relevant to mastery.

Much of our concern with the concept of self has to do with dissolving conceptual obstructions regarding selves. If you were attached to the idea that you are a continuant substratum in which qualities inhere (something like the way in which pins inhere in a pin cushion), you might think of mastery as a simple matter of adding another quality (sticking another pin into the pin cushion) that, once added, would simply remain there until death. It's important to realize that mastery is not like that.

Mastery is a process, an ongoing activity. Everyone agrees that Michael Jordan used to be a master basketball player. Is he now, many years after retiring from the game? It doesn't work that way, does it?

[*Sidebar quotation* from The Bible (Ecclesiastes 9: 10): "Whatever task lies to your hand, do it with all your might."]

Any activity can be performed selflessly. In that sense, mastery is always possible. This is why many thinkers have tried to get us, in effect, to let go of the idea that we have a life span and instead to focus on the present moment. **Life is now**.

[*Sidebar quotations*:

From William George Jordan: "The individual can attain self-control in great things only through self-control in little things . . . He must . . . live each day as if his whole existence were telescoped down to the single day before him. With no useless regret for the past, no useless worry for the future, he should live that day as if it were his only day, the only day left for him to assert all that is best in him, the only day left for him to conquer all that is worst in him . . . Each day is a new existence."

From Wallace Wattles: ". . . guard your thoughts . . . Put your whole mind into present action."

From Yasutani-Roshi: "You can never come to enlightenment through inference, cognition, or conceptualization. Cease clinging to all thought-forms! I stress this, because it is the central point of Zen practice. And particularly do not make the mistake of thinking enlightenment must be this or that."

From Roshi Philip Kapleau: "In Zen everything one does becomes a vehicle for self-realization; every act, every moment is done wholeheartedly, with nothing left over. In Zen parlance, everything we do this way is an 'expression of Buddha,' and the greater the single-mindedness and unself-consciousness of the doing, the closer we are to this realization. For what else is there but the pure act—the lifting of the hammer, the washing of the dish, the movement of the hands on the typewriter, the pulling of the weed? Everything else—thoughts of the past, fantasies about the future, judgments and evaluations concerning the work itself—what are these but shadows and ghosts flickering about in our minds, preventing us from entering fully into life itself? To enter into the awareness of Zen, to 'wake up,' means to cleanse the mind of the habitual disease of uncontrolled thought and to bring it back to its original state of purity and clarity."

From David Loy: "To wake up is to realize that I am not in the world, I am what the world is doing right here and now."

From Jack Kornfield: "Everything we do in life is a chance to awaken."]

Until paying full attention to the present moment becomes usual once again, it requires constant practice. Constant practice is not what we really want to do, but, fortunately, it is something we are all able to do and, even, master.

[*Sidebar quotations*:

From Master Dogen: "Continuous exertion is not something ordinary people are fond of, but nevertheless it is the true refuge for everyone."

From William James: "The faculty of voluntarily bringing back a wandering attention over and over again is the very root of judgment, character and will."

From Thomas Edison: "Our greatest weakness lies in giving up. The most certain way to succeed is always to try just one more time."

From Andrew Matthews: "If there is an outstanding quality common to great [achievers] . . . it is not their talent—it is their *focus*."]

We'll consider selecting an activity to master.[84] The best activities provide room for endless improvement, continual mastering.

It's best to select an activity that is neither too big nor too small. The much more common error is to select one that is too small.

If you select an activity that is too small, you'll eventually run out of challenges and need to select something else. You'll become much less interested in it. This doesn't mean that it's wrong to master a small activity. Still, it's vitally important to tackle at least one that isn't too small for you.

[*Sidebar* quotation from Peter McWilliams: "If you're not playing a big enough game, you'll screw up the game you're playing just to give yourself something to do."]

Have you ever met people who were unhappy because they found themselves stuck in an activity that was too small?

When I was an undergraduate, through a family connection I met a business professor at my university. When we met for the first time, we talked. He asked me what I was majoring in. When I told him that I was a philosopher, he said that he wished that he had gone into a field like that. Whether correctly or incorrectly, he thought the field he had chosen was too small for him. However, he had a tenured job teaching it at a good university that enabled him to own his own home and support his wife and children. He had come to hate being stuck, but he didn't see any way out.

That made an impression on me.

This happens more frequently outside the academy. I have not infrequently observed people who have become quite successful at a job or even a business of their own who became stuck. The work had become too small to sustain their full interest, and, unfortunately, they had become economically dependent upon it and fearful of moving on.

Isn't it better to aim too high than too low? What if you aim too low and make it? Then you'd either have to quit trying or start anew.

If you make it your business to do anything less than master life itself, you are in danger of aiming too low. [85]

[*Sidebar quotation* from Michelangelo: "The greater danger for most of us is not that our aim is too high and we miss it, but that it is too low and we reach it."]

If you think of mastery as an ongoing process instead of as just another achievement (just another pin to be stuck into the pin cushion), you may be more likely to avoid the mistake of aiming too low.

Whatever activity it is about, mastery requires **selflessness.** Unfortunately, 'selflessness' is a misleading term. Why? What should we replace it with?

Archery is an activity that can be mastered. Suppose that you are a master archer. I picked this example because there's a classic, short book about it, namely, Herrigel's <u>Zen in the Art of Archery</u>. It's an account of how he set about mastering archery. "Steep is the way to mastery."[86] How steep? Before one even releases an arrow for the first time, one must draw the bow. It took him *a year of diligent practicing* before he could draw the bow correctly!

The problem was that he would constantly think about what he was doing. He came to believe that he "would never hear anything but the monotonous answer: 'Don't ask, practice!'"[87] His Master warned him not to "practice anything except self-detaching immersion."[88] Herrigel's fault is our fault: he was *too full of thinking and of ego*. He kept holding back from throwing himself completely into his practice.

What was the goal of the persistent practicing? Purposelessness and egolessness and self-abandonment.[89] Hits on the target were merely the outward signs of hits on this inner target. Finally, after years of relentless practicing, the bowstring finally cuts through him: "Bow, arrow, goal and ego, all melt into one another, so that I can no longer separate them. And even the need to separate has gone . . ."[90]

This is a description of the realization of selflessness, the perfection of the "artless art." This is the true target, which Herrigel's Master said he could name the Buddha.[91] It's transforming. His Master told him, "You have become a different person in the course of these [five] years."[92] It's liberating. Living becomes characterized by "purposeless detachment."[93] **Sages lead lives of purposeless detachment.**

How does one become a sage, a master of living well? By "long and eventful years of untiring practice."[94]

Please select an activity to master that is sufficiently big to be worthy of your years of relentless practicing.

Of course, Herrigel was still shooting the bow even after crossing the mastery threshold. In that sense, his shooting was still a product of himself, in other words, not selfless.

So, words can here trip us up.

The process is one of ever-increasing focus on practicing. Mastery involves thinking about doing something in order to learn how to do it and then practicing doing it persistently until one is able to do it excellently without thinking. This process is one of ever-increasing "mindfulness."

To be mindful is to pay attention. If you are washing the dishes while thinking about what you are going to do after you finish washing the dishes, you are washing the dishes mindlessly, which is the opposite of washing them mindfully. To wash them mindfully is to devote your full attention to washing them without a single extraneous thought, to wash each dish as if it were as valuable as an infant.

To live mindfully is to live fully in the present moment without a single extraneous thought. The present moment is the only time we have to live.

Living mindfully is automatically living selflessly.

We are all capable of this. I hope that you have occasionally experienced it, lost yourself in some activity. Perhaps when you were a child you became totally engrossed in creating a finger-painting. You forgot yourself and just became what you were doing. Perhaps then your teacher came along and, meaning to encourage you, said, "That's really good. Keep it up." What happened? It broke the spell. You became self-conscious. You got caught up in evaluating rather than in doing. You transitioned back from selfless to selfish.

[*Sidebar quotation* from John Stuart Mill: "Ask yourself whether you are happy and you cease to be so."]

Mastery is living selflessly. The only way to mastery is to practice living more and more mindfully.

At every moment we are either mindful of what we are doing or not. Moment after moment, life offers us another opportunity to live masterfully.

A simple way to tell the difference between living poorly and living well is if you are noticing time. To be aware of the passing of time is to live poorly. Think, for example, of any experience in which time drags: you are an employee watching the clock waiting for the work day to be over so you can be released or you are a parent waiting for the surgeon to tell you how your child's operation went. To be oblivious to the passing of time is to live well, to be fully engaged in life with no separation between mind and body. Think, for example, whenever as an athlete during a competition you were "in the zone" or when you were giving a music recital when "it" (not you) seemed to be playing the instrument. Such flow experiences are optimific experiences.

When has time stopped for you? What kinds of activities were you engaged in? What might life be trying to tell you?

Think about them. Notice in particular that those activities were all ones that you had become good at because you had rehearsed or practiced well for a long time. That's how practicing relates to living well. **There's no living well without practicing well.**

The right attitude fosters practicing well. In fact, it's impossible to practice well with a bad attitude. What exactly is the right attitude for living well?

Chapter 7: Adjusting Your Attitude

You may have the sense in parts of this chapter and the next that the territory is becoming more familiar. The higher we go on the mastery monument, the more comfortable you may feel. If you do, at least part of the explanation is that making the effort to clarify more fundamental material first automatically helps to clarify what is less fundamental.

Furthermore, presumably because more fundamental ideas are more difficult to understand, less fundamental ideas are more popular to discuss. Examining both kinds is important.

Even though we all know what attitudes are, they seem slippery, difficult to stabilize or notice. This isn't just because attitudes may evolve and change; it's also because attitudes are *dispositional qualities.*

Consider the china mug from which you are sipping tea. You are able to perceive in a moment its color, shape, size, hardness, smoothness, location, and all its other phenomenal (monadic and relational) qualities, but you are not able at this moment to see its brittleness. If you were to drop it on the slate floor of your kitchen, you'd find out that it is brittle as well as, say, white. Brittleness is a dispositional quality; whiteness is a phenomenal quality. Dispositional qualities are more difficult to apprehend than phenomenal qualities.

Attitudes are dispositional qualities to think in certain ways. They are automatic reactions waiting to be triggered by living. Since our thoughts spawn our behaviors, they have enormous impact on the quality of our lives. The advertiser's slogan "Attitude is Everything" isn't just hype.

[*Sidebar quotations*:

From Thomas Jefferson: "Nothing can stop the man with the right mental attitude from achieving his goal; nothing on earth can help the man with the wrong mental attitude."

From William James: "It is our attitude at the beginning of a difficult task which, more than anything else, will affect its successful outcome. . . Human beings can alter their lives by altering their attitudes of mind."

From Karl Menninger: "Attitudes are more important than facts."

From Earl Nightingale: "The most important single factor that guarantees good results[:] attitude!"]

Another reason why they are sometimes difficult to identify is that we, like Samuel Gulliver in Gulliver's Travels, lie to ourselves about our own attitudes: we shade events to favor ourselves. Instead of examining our own attitudes, we *assume* that they are serving us well and create our surrealities around that assumption. We foolishly believe that it's not in our interest to examine them.

Ignorance isn't curable when we are attached to it. Even though we are being close-minded and negative, we assume that we are merely being realistic. You've probably noticed this in others. If someone were not open to looking at something that you know would be of benefit, since **no argument will open a closed mind**, any attempt you make at persuasion would be useless. Without vigilance, it's easy to slip into a negative attitude ourselves.

If you watch for instances of this, they can be quite amusing. I know a man who has a seven-figure annual income from his network marketing business. Recently, he showed the business plan to a prospect who was interested in earning additional income. When the prospect had seen the plan, he said simply, "That'll never work." The man I know said that he was so astounded he was momentarily speechless!

[*Sidebar quotation* from W. Clement Stone: "There's very little difference in people. But that little difference makes a big difference. The little difference is attitude. The big difference is whether it's positive or negative."

From Chuck Coonradt: "Negativism is like a cancer of the mind."

From Price Pritchett: "Life always gives us a choice. We can focus on what's wrong or what's right. Whichever one we feed our attention to will grow. The one we tend to ignore will wither, weaken, and sometimes die."]

Is your attitude serving you well? Is it enabling you to enjoy life more and more, or is it preventing you from growing wiser? It's important to examine your attitude as honestly as possible. It may not be serving you as well as you think it is. There's no need to tell anyone the results of your examination.

Consider enlisting the help of a close friend or two; after all, they may be more objective in their analysis. If you ask for and receive such an appraisal, please genuinely thank your friend for the assistance and avoid becoming defensive. Even if you hear something you'd prefer not to hear, even if you think your friend is wrong about something, resist the temptation to defend yourself or to argue about any part of the evaluation; instead, just listen carefully and be grateful that someone loves you enough to speak honestly to you about you. After cool consideration, if you think that your friend has spotted a weakness, take appropriate action to strengthen your attitude; otherwise, let it go.

The purposing of examining your attitude is to improve it. You have the power to improve it. Once you admit that your attitude needs improvement in a certain way, it's possible deliberately to nurture growth in that way. How?

The instant you become aware of a less than helpful thought kicking in, replace it with a more helpful one. As simple as that tactic is, it will work for you *if* you persist in using it. It may take a few months, but it may only take a few weeks. The long-term benefits of sticking with it may astound you.

[*Sidebar quotation* from Cynthia Stamper Graff: "Whatever obstacles you face . . . you always have a *choice* as to how to react. You can choose to feel bad and give up, or you can use your experience as an opportunity to learn and grow. Your attitude—the mindset with which you approach problems—has a direct impact on your ability to transform obstacles into opportunities."]

I'm not a sage, and I don't know what an ideal attitude is. On the other hand, I have some ideas that may help you to improve your own attitude. Please think of the following eight criteria as suggestions on how to evaluate your own attitude. *The purpose of this chapter is to enable you to use this checklist to identify weaknesses where your attitude could be strengthened.* Unless you happen to be a fully enlightened sage, it is possible to improve your attitude.

There are other criteria that could be used, but they are all secondary to these eight. If you are strong with respect to these, there's nothing else you need to worry about in terms of attitude adjustment. As indicated in each section, each of the eight is grounded in something already discussed. All eight are important, but I have not attempted to rank them in order of importance.

(Since character virtues are also dispositional qualities, others sometimes discuss some of these eight as virtues.)

An excellent attitude is one of detachment, gratitude, accepting responsibility, humility, philosophical courage, compassion, abundance, and cheerfulness.

7.1 Detachment

Though it is relatively unknown and unpopular in our culture, detachment may be the most important aspect of an excellent attitude. The great medieval Christian mystic Master Eckhart thought so: "No one is happier than a person who has attained the greatest detachment . . . I praise detachment above all love . . . above all humility . . . above all mercifulness."[95] His point is not that love, humility, and mercifulness are not excellent; his point is that they come from pure detachment. When we detach, we are at our most divine. What does this mean?

[*Sidebar quotations:*

From The Buddha: "when a bodhisattva gives rise to the unequalled mind of awakening, he has to give up all ideas . . . that mind is not caught in anything."

From Master Muso Kokushi: "There is ultimately no means of safeguarding anything in this world; anything you can gain can be lost, destroyed, or taken away. For this reason, if you make the acquisition and retention of goods or status your aim in life, this is a way to anxiety and sorrow."

From Pope John XXIII: "Every day is a good day to be born, and every day is a good day to die."]

What is detachment?

As we have seen in Chapter 4, ultimate reality is the obstructed obvious. It's obstructed in the sense that it is impossible to conceptualize it. Is ultimate reality temporal or timeless? It is beyond both time and eternity. Is ultimate reality dynamic or static? It is beyond both becoming and being. And so on. Many mystics make this point by claiming that *ultimate reality is emptiness,* nothingness.

For example, Eckhart asks, "What is the object of pure detachment?" He answers his own question: "My answer is that neither this nor that is the object of pure detachment. It reposes in naked nothingness. . . ."[96] Therefore, "a heart in detachment asks for nothing." If nothing is desired, satisfaction is inexhaustible. That's genuine happiness.

So detachment is grounded in the nature of ultimate reality; it is rooted in emptiness.

There is no mastery without detachment.

This is the critical difference between the success model and the mastery model.[97] Recall that success is grounded in the way of the world, which is the ceaseless quest to gain what we like and to avoid what we don't like. We are able to become relatively successful by getting what we want and avoiding what we don't want. In other words, *being successful is still being a slave to one's preferences.* Since new desires constantly arise, success can only be fleeting and relative.

Anyone attached to the success model is attached to certain achievements, to gaining, to grasping certain *whats*. If we attach to becoming successful, we may actually succeed. However, being successful should not be confused with being happy. Being a champion athlete or a famous movie star or a powerful politician or a wealthy CEO doesn't produce lasting happiness.

By way of contrast, anyone attached to the mastery model is attached to doing everything in a certain way; it's attachment to certain *hows,* not to doing certain *whats*. What does this mean? It means doing whatever is done with detachment, without trying to achieve some valued outcome. Mindfully getting the *how* right, which is acting with detachment (especially from one's self-concept), is only possible within the present moment.

Freedom is the difference between mastery and success.

Attachment to mastery is the one nonpoisonous attachment. *The only valuable attachment is to detachment!*

To be detached is *not* to be attached to gaining whatever one desires and avoiding whatever one desires to avoid. In other words, the way of mastery is the opposite of the way of the world. Becoming successful and becoming masterful are radically different.

It is not that masters don't have desires or preferences. Everyone has desires and preferences. The difference between ordinary people and masters is that masters have let go of their attachments to their desires. **Masters desire nothing.** They live freely, which is the opposite of living in slavery to preferences. This is why they are so peaceful: in their heart of hearts there is tranquility, pure detachment. Unlike the rest of us, they are not attached to their own egocentricity. This is why sages (saints, buddhas) are selfless. They have successfully detached from their own self-concepts.

It is because they have done so that such masters of life are so loving. As I've explained elsewhere[98], to love is to overcome separation by identifying with the beloved and acting accordingly. In other words, it's understanding what is best for the beloved and promoting it. It's giving selflessly with no expectation of a reward. It's impossible to love while being attached to oneself. The more selfish we are, the less we are able to love. The more we practice detaching from our self-concepts, the less selfish we become and the more loving we become.

Many thinkers have appreciated and articulated these ideas.[99]

[*Sidebar quotation* from <u>The Bhagavad Gita</u>: "Seek refuge in the attitude of detachment."

From Lao-Tzu: "No desire is serenity."

From Rumi: "detach yourself . . . separate yourself from the house of desire."

From Pascal: "I have discovered that all of man's unhappiness derives from only one source—not being able to sit quietly in a room."

From Master Sheng-yen: "Desire indicates aspiration for future gain. Attached love indicates holding on to something possessed . . . Attached love and desire are causes and consequences of each other. Together, they give rise to craving, attachment, and all sorts of vexation . . . they are the root of all afflictions . . . Genuine love is selfless giving . . . give without expecting something in return . . . Only when one is completely unselfish does genuine love arise. This genuine love is Buddhist compassion."

From Will Durant: "One of the lessons of history is that nothing is often a good thing to do, and always a clever thing to say."

From John Daido Loori: "The presence of self, the subtlest hint of self-centeredness, creates the difference between a 'do-gooder' and the manifestation of true compassion. . . It is very easy to understand not attaching to things that are evil . . . But the same problem exists when we attach to good . . ."

From Andrew Matthews: "Even enjoying life takes practice . . . **The challenge of life is to appreciate everything and attach yourself to nothing** . . . When you chase things, they run away . . . Nature seeks balance . . . "

From Joseph Campbell: "centering is the whole thing."]

It is because masters are detached that they are so calm. Of course they are emotionally untroubled. As I explain elsewhere, all emotions are egocentric. The heart of every positive emotion is the judgment "this is good *for me*"; the heart of every negative emotion is the judgment "this is bad *for me*." The more we practice loosening our attachments to our self-concepts, the less emotional we become. The less emotional we become, the closer we become to mastering life and living in abiding joy. It is impossible to be selfless and emotional.

It is detachment that spawns the virtues of patience and forbearance.

If you do not live in abiding joy and want to, what should you do? Practice detachment.[100] This is what is required to master life itself. I believe that it is very *important for everyone to master, or at least become successful at, some specific activity* or other. Why? It's very difficult to like yourself very much or to enjoy life very much without some regular excellence. How could you be happy without liking yourself?

There is, though, a big gap between an excellent activity and an excellent life. Mastering, say, archery is not the same as mastering life—but mastering a specific activity does provide more than a mere taste of mastering life. It makes the ideal of becoming a sage seem attainable.

We get one shot at life: why not master it? Why not practice detachment daily?[101]

7.2 Gratitude

Life sometimes hurts a lot.

Our bodies suffer when, for example, we are ill or hungry or too cold or too hot or in pain.

Our minds suffer when, for example, we are discouraged, ignorant, anxious, or confused.

Our perceptions suffer when, for example, we perceive the world with pessimism or darkness or bigotry.

Our feelings suffer whenever, for example, we experience negative emotions like anger, jealousy, hatred, guilt, or fear.

Our dispositions to act suffer whenever, for example, we are motivated by ignorance or propaganda or despair.[102]

Such dissatisfactions are normal. Though such dissatisfactions can be dissolved, there's nothing abnormal about you if you suffer in these five ways.

On the other hand, what if it's true that abiding joy is possible? What if training ourselves in detachment really is able to free us from suffering? What if we, too, are able to train ourselves to become sages? What if living well really is possible?

What could be a greater reason to be grateful than that?

[*Sidebar quotations:*

From Zig Ziglar: "Show me one happy, ungrateful person!"

From Earl Wilson: "Success is simply a matter of luck. Ask any failure."

From Dennis Allen: "Help! I'm being held prisoner by my heredity and environment!"]

As frequently happens when we try to use ordinary language and concepts to express what is extraordinary, we need to stretch beyond the ordinary here. In using the word 'gratitude', I'm *not* referring to the feeling of gratitude. When we feel gratitude, it's because we think we have gained something and we are grateful to the person who is responsible for that gain; in other words, we think of ourselves as enjoying, as one philosopher puts it, "the dignified position of passively receiving."[103] The feeling of gratitude is a positive emotion that, like all emotions, is an attempt to boost our self-esteem.

I'm referring to the attitude of gratitude. Right now, in this very moment, I am able to be happy. If I am happy, it's because I have opened myself to what is available in the present moment by sufficiently mastering the art of detachment. Nobody gave me anything. Nor, since happiness is my birthright, have I gained something I've lacked; I've managed to realize what I've had all along. The practice of opening has nothing to do with gaining something; it has to do with letting go of conceptual obstructions. Once that gateless gate has been broken open, it's capable of endless enlargement.

[*Sidebar quotations:*

From Wes Borden: "[T]he purpose of Zen training is not to acquire enlightenment but to shave away ego-centered thoughts until one is able to see that fundamentally one lacks nothing."

From Pema Chodron: "the disease of ignorance and self-absorption affects us all. . . The journey to enlightenment involves shedding, not collecting. . ."

From Roshi Philip Kapleau: "Enlightenment is not a static condition; it is capable of endless enlargement."]

It's quite appropriate to feel gratitude to the sages who have shown me the way—and I do. I never would have figured it out on my own; at least in my own case, trial and error never would have worked. Still, to detach from the self is to release all emotions, positive and negative.

The best test of whether or not you have successfully cultivated an attitude of gratitude is if you are even genuinely grateful for obstacles. For example, do certain other people make your life a hell? Do they churn up spite and hatred?

Suppose a physician gives you a painful medicine that cures a serious ailment: wouldn't you be grateful to the physician? Why not think of your enemies like you think of such medicine? Why not treat all obstacles that way?

In other words, look at the final outcome. The medicine, though painful, was beneficial. It is the same with enemies and obstacles: because they can stimulate patience and compassion, encountering enemies should turn out to be beneficial. Remember, they cannot harm you without your consent. The final outcome is really up to you.

[*Sidebar quotations:*

From Pema Chodron: "In any encounter, we have a choice: we can strengthen our resentment *or* our understanding and empathy."

From Shantideva: "If there is a remedy when trouble strikes, / What reason is there for despondency? / And if there is no help for it, / What use is there in being sad?"]

The attitude of gratitude comes from realization of nonseparation, from directly experiencing the fact that there's no gap between what-is and me. The experience of the unitive state is, at least when developed, profoundly transforming and liberating. That is what grounds an attitude of gratitude. It's a lasting release from dissatisfaction. Anyone who has enjoyed and deepened the breakthrough experience has a profound attitude of being blessed or being lucky.

[*Sidebar quotation* from Pema Chodron: "Trungpa Rinpoche once said that enlightenment is like smelling tobacco or hearing a bugle for the very first time. We don't usually experience life this freshly."]

After Plato and Aristotle, Plotinus was the third greatest philosopher of the ancient West. He calls the mystical experience "awareness of The One": "The chief difficulty is this: awareness of The One comes to us . . . by a presence transcending knowledge . . . because knowledge implies discursive reason and discursive reason implies multiplicity."[104] He says that that is why Plato said we can neither speak nor write about The One, and that "[i]f nevertheless we speak of it and write about it, we do so only to give direction, to urge towards that vision beyond discourse." It cannot be conceived, but it can be directly experienced. "Anyone who has had this experience will know what I am talking about."[105]

The experience yields a lasting transformation. "The person who obtains the vision becomes, as it were, another being. He ceases to be himself . . . Absorbed in the beyond he is one with it."[106] That person has let go of attachment to the self-concept. That person has an attitude of gratitude. That person continually feels blessed, perpetually lucky.

Will you be one of those beings? Will you remain inside a conceptual box or become absorbed in what is beyond conceptualization?

7.3 Responsibility

It's wholly up to you.

Did you have perfect parents? Is your genetic endowment perfect in all respects? Has your health always been excellent? Was your formal education the best? Did you grow up in a perfect society? Have you glided through life without a single important mistake?

I'm not suggesting that there isn't an enormous difference in the advantages that some of us have had. Life is quite unfair with respect to that distribution. What I am suggesting is that we all have access to excuses if we want them.

Stop making excuses for yourself. Accept full responsibility.

[*Sidebar quotations*:

From St. Bernard: "Nothing can work me damage except myself. The harm that I sustain I carry about with me, and am never a real sufferer but by my own fault."

From William George Jordan: "Most people sympathize too much with themselves."

From Price Pritchett: "Where's the logic in not trying because you might not succeed, when in not trying you guarantee failure?"]

I have repeatedly observed gifted undergraduates who seemed stuck being in their own way because they really had never admitted to themselves that they were responsible for the quality of their own lives. They'd blame their parents or siblings or friends or teachers or coaches—anyone except themselves. It's easier to blame others than to examine oneself. Some grow past that attitude, and some never do. Some forfeit their lives on meaningless distractions. Some commit suicide.

We all have found ourselves in systems: the school system or the criminal justice system or the corporate system or the social system or the bureaucratic government system and so on. My experience has been that no system suits me perfectly. After all, I'm unique and the system wasn't specifically designed for me. The same is true for you and everyone else. This presents us with two choices.

We can rebel against it or work to improve it. I've tried both. The latter works better.

For example, suppose that you have a job in a corporation and that you encounter a problem with a client or a supplier. You can try various ways to avoid it, or you can accept responsibility for solving it and tackle it. Which is the immature way and which is the mature way? If you want to become a much more valued employee, when you are on the job deliberately look to assume more responsibility for the quality of goods or services produced.

The system doesn't determine the quality of your life. You do.

What is accepting full responsibility?

Life is a sequence of moments. Moment after moment life, offers us the opportunity to respond to it. **Accepting full responsibility is responding with ability moment after moment.** To respond with disability is to live without accepting responsibility.[107]

For example, if you are upset and yell at me, what will happen? Nothing will automatically happen. I would be a fool to give control of my life over to you or anyone else. What happens is my choice. If I decide to join you in being angry, I will yell back at you. On the other hand, if I decide not to join you in being angry, I may invite you to tell me what's bothering you or, simply, withdraw—anything except becoming angry myself. If I were to let you or anyone or anything else push my buttons, I would not be accepting full responsibility; I'd be abdicating responsibility.

[*Sidebar quotation* from Napoleon Hill: "Without doubt, the most common weakness of all human beings is the habit of leaving their minds open to the negative influence of other people."]

Deliberately accepting full responsibility for the quality of one's own life has always been a mark of the wise. For example, the Stoic philosopher Epictetus wrote: "The position and character of a non-philosopher: he never looks for benefit or harm to come from himself but from things outside. The position and character of a philosopher: he looks for all benefit and harm to come from himself."[108]

The key to accepting full responsibility is the realization that *nobody else can benefit or harm you*. How can that be? After all, someone could give you a million dollars or someone could kill you. Wouldn't that be benefiting or harming you?

Actually, perhaps not. Each would be an attempt to benefit or harm. In the big picture, would either attempt work? What would all the consequences of either act be? Nobody has any idea. Perhaps you'd unintentionally use the money to ruin your life and the lives of loved ones; perhaps a quick death would actually prove better for you than the alternative. Who can say what the future will be like? Again, it's part of our human condition that we are unable to know the future.

We don't always control what happens to us; however, we *always* have the ability to control how we react to what happens to us. We *always* have the option of responding well.

Epictetus says that the key to adopting this attitude is always to be on guard against yourself as if you were an enemy lying in wait. He recommends challenging yourself to make progress. Censure yourself, but don't praise or blame anyone else. Never talk about yourself as if you were an important or wise person. If something blocks you from obtaining what you want, blame yourself for the obstruction. If someone criticizes you, don't respond and let it go; if someone praises you, accept it graciously and let it go (he even recommends laughing inwardly to yourself). Most importantly, ignore what isn't up to you and only pay attention to what is up to you.

Personally, I've always found Stoic ethics attractive. The idea of dissolving my attachment to the way of the world, to getting what I want and avoiding what I don't want, has always resonated with me.

"Some things are up to us, and some are not up to us. Our opinions are up to us, and our impulses, desires, aversions—in short, whatever is our own doing. Our bodies are not up to us, nor are our possessions, our reputations, or our public offices, or, that is, whatever is not our own doing. The things that are up to us are by nature free, unhindered, and unimpeded; the things that are not up to us are weak, enslaved, hindered, not our own . . . if you think that only what is yours is yours . . . you will not be harmed at all."[109]

Perhaps living well is not only possible but also simple. If we will take full responsibility for what is up to us and let go of what is not up to us, we will be on the right track. We should be concerned only with our opinions, our impulses, and our desires, in other words, our thoughts, and the way to wisdom is to control them rather than have them control us.

Though not easy, living well is simple. The key is to take charge of what is up to us, take full responsibility for it, and then master it until we achieve the detached wisdom of a Stoic sage. The way to find out what is up to us is to examine the world, to put life to the test; sometimes we have much more, and sometimes much less, influence than we anticipate.

If we do that, we could live the rest of our lives in solitary confinement or an iron lung and still live well.

[*Sidebar quotation* from Art Buchwald: "Whether it's the best of times or the worst of times, it's the only time we got."]

In fact, multiple blessings can distract us. For those of us who have obviously been lucky (finding ourselves, for example, healthy and loved and living in free societies), we can forget to take full responsibility for what is up to us. Bad move.

7.4 Humility

In theory, it's easy to be humble. After all, once we accept the ideas that (1) the future consequences of our decisions are very important to us and (2) we have no idea what those consequences will be, unless we happen to get lucky because in the relevant respect the future happens to resemble the past, then we accept the important idea that we don't know how to bring about the consequences we most value.

Remember your first boyfriend or girlfriend? Remember your first kisses? Whenever you kissed that person, he or she always kissed you back, right? Now, suppose you encountered that person right now and pushed your puckered lips out: what would happen? Might you not be rejected or even slapped? The point is that, just because two kinds of events have always been conjoined in the past, it does not follow that they will always continue to be conjoined in the future.[110]

In practice, it's not so easy to be humble. One reason is that often the future does, in fact, frequently turn out to resemble the past in some respect. I drive home drunk, and, yet again, I get home safely without getting in an accident. I cheat on an exam, and, yet again, I don't get caught. I'm late for work, and, once more, nobody notices. I have a second dessert, and, still, I don't get fat. Pile up enough of those experiences and I start thinking I'm smarter than everyone else. I can break the rules and get away it. Why be humble?

Experience usually takes care of it. Sooner or later I'll get into a traffic accident, get caught cheating, get fired for tardiness, and wind up fat.

In the long run, we'll all be dead; also, in the long run, we all become more humble. We realize more and more that we know less and less. The objects of knowledge more frequently seem to be in the domain of being rather than in the domain of becoming where we'd like them. We find that we can't do what we used to do without piling up a lot of dissatisfaction; also, we may discover that we weren't really getting away with what we thought we were getting away with.

Whenever the thought "I know the right course of action in this situation" occurs, delete it. Even when actions have beneficial consequences, force yourself to remember that they were shots into the dark. If you keep reminding yourself of that truth, your humility will grow.

[*Sidebar quotations*:

From Charlotte Joko Beck: "No matter what the discipline—art, music, physics, philosophy—we can pervert it and use it to avoid practice . . . The important thing is who we are at any given moment and how we handle what life brings to us. As body and mind become more integrated, the work becomes paradoxically far easier. Our job is to be integrated with the whole world. . . real practice . . . moment by moment, just facing the moment."

From Eknath Easwaran: "[S]incere questioning . . . is the beginning of wisdom."

From Eric Hoffer: "In a time of drastic change it is the learners who inherit the future. The learned usually find themselves equipped to live in a world that no longer exists."]

7.5 Philosophical Courage

In using 'philosophical courage' I'm neither referring to physical courage or to having the courage of one's convictions. It's different.

Physical courage is exhibited whenever one takes calculated risks with one's body. It's exhibited in battle, for example, or on the gridiron or on the ice of a hockey rink or in everyday emergencies like saving a drowning child. As Aristotle points out[111], too little physical courage is being cowardly and too much physical courage is being foolhardy. Physical courage can be stimulated through proper training, which is why soldiers and football players are required to practice.

Have you ever heard a politician praised for having the courage of his convictions? That courage is overrated. Every fanatic has the courage of his or her convictions; every fanatic is tightly attached to his or her most cherished beliefs. The courage of a fanatic is the courage of a stubborn jackass. It's worthless because it's based, ultimately, on delusion and fear. *Nothing abides.* If your views aren't evolving, rest assured that you are delusional. You are attached to them probably because you are afraid of what you'll find if you examine them.

[*Sidebar quotations*:

From Bishop Fulton Sheen: "Most of us do not like to look inside ourselves for the same reason we don't like to open a letter that has bad news."

From Price Pritchett: "Life tests us—sometimes with problems, on other occasions with opportunities. The first question on life's many exams, though, is always the same: 'How will you explain the situation to yourself—with a positive or negative point of view?'

From Price Pritchett: "Usually success is a direct byproduct of screw-ups."]

Fanatics keep thinking as they have always thought. Fanatics keep doing as they have always done. Fanatics keep living as poorly as they have always lived. They condemn themselves to living poorly because of the ever-increasing gap between their static surrealities and the dynamic flux of what-is.

[*Sidebar quotation* from Olga Korbut: "Don't be afraid if things seem difficult in the beginning. That's only the initial impression. The important thing is not to retreat; you have to master yourself."]

The most admirable courage is philosophical courage, the courage of philosophers. This is **the courage to challenge our convictions.** It requires genuine courage to challenge our most important and fundamental beliefs.

This courage is rooted in the nature of becoming. We live in the domain of becoming—not in the domain of being.

Here's a simple everyday example based on the fact that we are in the midst of the Internet revolution. How we access information and how we do business are rapidly evolving. For youngsters who have lived their whole lives in the computer age, there's no courage required for them to be computer literate. However, for oldsters, it does require courage to let go of old ways and adopt new ones. You probably have yourself known elderly people who won't go near computers. It's sad, isn't it? You also probably know elderly people who have embraced the Internet revolution and greatly enriched their lives by doing so.

Here's a key test: do you welcome or resist change? Do you prefer motion or being stuck? What-is is becoming.

If you resist accepting that, you resist change. You don't like new experiences. You avoid getting out of your familiar ruts. You aren't open to meeting new people or new ideas. You won't try new foods or ways to exercise. You don't like traveling to new places. You resist life.

On the other hand, if you embrace life, you welcome change. You find it exciting and liberating. You like to travel physically, intellectually, or spiritually. New cuisines and new people are opportunities—not dangers.

If we are lucky, we, too, will become elderly. Our judgments are, in fact, constantly being challenged because they are constantly becoming obsolete as the world turns.

Sometimes, we should let go of judgments and adopt new ones. When? There's no easy way to tell the difference. All we can do is to practice, constantly, re-examining what we believe. Again, the only alternative to the examined life is much worse.

(Does it surprise you that a philosopher recommends living as philosophers live?)

[*Sidebar quotation* from Zig Ziglar: "Don't be distracted by criticism. Remember the only taste of success some people have is when they take a bite out of you."]

7.6 Compassion

[*Sidebar quotation* from Albert Einstein: "Our task must be to free ourselves . . . by widening our circle of compassion to embrace all living creatures and the whole of nature and its beauty."]

Masters are inherently compassionate. Provided that the interest of others is genuine, their impulse is always to be generous with their wisdom. Being willing to share what is best in one's life with others marks someone who is compassionate.

To be effective, compassion must be guided by understanding. Blind compassion is as likely to be harmful as beneficial. It's very difficult to acquire the skill to be compassionate. This explains why sometimes a compassionate act might not look compassionate. A parent who disciplines a child or a Zen master who strikes or yells at a disciple might not appear to be acting compassionately when they are.

There are two kinds of compassion: attached and detached.

[*Sidebar quotation* from Michael Novak: "The quantity of sheer impenetrable selfishness in the human breast (in *my* breast) is a never-failing source of wonderment."]

The paradigm of attached compassion is erotic love. When we are in love, we want not only what is best for the beloved but we also want the beloved. Wanting the beloved is selfish. It's a desire to take rather than a desire to give, a desire to use rather than a desire to be used. In other words, the desiring element in erotic love is as surely present as the loving element. Everyone knows that great love affairs entail immense benefits. Everyone values them.

However, the wise also know the truth I've expressed as Bradford's Law of Conditioned Life. Where 'G' stands for the satisfaction that comes from gaining whatever is desired and 'L' stands for the dissatisfaction that comes from its loss, the law is: $G + L = 0$.[112]

The paradigm of detached love is the love of a saint for a sinner. The saint desires only what is best for the sinner, and the love isn't even slightly tinged with selfishness. A saint will understand what is best for the sinner and skillfully promote it. The impulse is one of selfless giving. As Saint Francis of Assisi put it in his great prayer, he wants to seek less "To be consoled as to console, / To be understood as to understand, / To be loved, as to love." The key to detached love is, as he puts it, "is dying to self."

It is only in dying to self, in detaching from our self concepts, that we become able to do what the Buddha said we should do, namely, "cultivate boundless love to offer to all living beings in the entire cosmos."[113] He doesn't tell us to love only those beings who have something to offer us in return. Love tainted in any degree by selfish attachment is not love.

When a master is being masterful, there is no selfish attachment. How does anyone become masterful? It's by devotedly practicing in a right way. There are multiple ways to practice simply because there are multiple activities that may be mastered; furthermore, it's often the case that there are multiple ways to master a single activity. Some involve physical activity, and some don't. What all those ways have in common is persistent mindful practicing.

As we have seen[114], all episodes of consciousness are characterized by "intentionality." Obviously, to practice mindfully is to be focused only on one's practice. "Mindfulness is always mindfulness of something."[115] One way or another, successful masters always communicate this to their students. It doesn't matter whether one is practicing meditation or prayer or a martial art or a craft or any other activity: *mindfulness is the essence of practicing.*

Therefore, **loving is the essence of practicing**. To love is to act in an informed way to benefit the beloved. To practice to become a master is to practice loving.

At first this may seem odd. However, it's really not. Suppose your neighbors send their son to karate class. Why would they do that? It's not so that their son will be able to use karate to beat up his classmates. It's to help develop their son's character through the discipline required to master karate. In other words, it's an effort to help their son overcome his selfishness, to grow, to mature.

How is someone working to master, say, archery loving? Well, do you think that the target is on that bale of straw over there? Not. The target is the overcoming of separation (the unitive experience, realizing our Buddha-nature). If not union, what is love?

This is obviously true with respect to practicing a spiritual practice. As Master Thich Nhat Hanh notes, "The heart of Buddhist meditation is mindfulness . . . [and] . . .The practice of mindfulness is the practice of love."[116]

This is why an attitude of compassion is the opposite of a violent, aggressive, or harming attitude. The Dalai Lama defines compassion as "a mental attitude based on the wish for others to be free of their suffering and is associated with a sense of commitment, responsibility, and respect towards the other."[117]

An important caveat is that it is critical to have compassion towards oneself in order to have compassion towards others. Self-love precedes other love. We are unable to love others more than we love ourselves. We are able to love ourselves by overcoming selfishness. To overcome selfishness is to detach from our self-concepts. To detach from our self-concepts is to focus on others. Thich Nhat Hanh says, "when you are able to love yourself, you can love anyone."[118] *To love is to identify with the beloved.*

There's nothing new about any of this. The Buddha challenges us to "Go beyond your [selfish] likes and dislikes" until they disappear.[119] Someone who is living well "never asks what life can give, only what he can give to life."[120] He is "egoless" and naturally lives a life of "selfless service" with "friendship toward all."[121]

This is why a sage, a master of living well, plays big rather than small. Someone who stays at home plays small. He identifies only with himself. A sage has no special home. He is "homeless" because he is "ever at home."[122] The world is his home.

This doesn't mean that a sage may not live alone. A sage is free from being attached either to living alone or living with others. Similarly, a sage loves others without being attached to loving others.

Suppose that you have mastered something. Might your understanding benefit others? If so, there'd still be no point in arrogance, in going about telling others how to live. Arrogance is counterproductive. On the other hand, why hide what can be helpful?

Here's an example from my own life. Probably because my father was an internist, I've always had an interest in health. I've also a tendency to eat too much and to exercise too little, which results in my having too high a percentage of body fat for excellent health. I've learned a lot about lasting weight loss, and I've permanently lost a significant amount of weight. I've made my understanding available to others, at no charge, at a website. Some have expressed gratitude to me for my helping them to help themselves.

Have you considered doing something similar? Why not? What understanding do you have that might help others help themselves?[123] Even if you live alone, thanks to the world wide web, you can be ever at home online. If you were more open to others, might not that help them to live better?

In other words, are you challenging yourself enough? Could you become more compassionate?

[*Sidebar quotation* from Mike Rayburn: "It is impossible to give more than you receive."]

The Buddha said, "If a man who enjoys a lesser happiness beholds a greater one, let him leave aside the lesser to gain the greater."[124] Have you enjoyed success in some field or other? If so, terrific. However, have you mastered that field? *Please don't settle for success if you are able to become a master.*

As you master, help others to master.

7.7 Abundance

Is your surreality one of abundance or scarcity?

As a practical matter, self-help authors always advise acting from an attitude of abundance. Suppose, for example, that you are a young man who wants to master dating. Would it be better for you to adopt the attitude that the supply of suitable lovers is abundant or scarce? There's no question that you'd be better off adopting the attitude that the supply of potential mates is unlimited.

If you are poor and want to start a business and make money, would it be better for you to adopt the attitude that the supply of money is abundant or scarce? There's no question that you'd be better off adopting the attitude that the supply of money is unlimited. In fact, this attitude is behind the huge economic expansion created by capitalism in the last several centuries. It's not that there's a fixed quantity of wealth that has to be shared, it's that wealth can be created, indefinitely expanded.

As a theoretical matter, should we adopt attitudes of abundance or scarcity?

Modern western ethics has taken these questions as characteristic: "Should I promote my good or the good of others? To what extent should I promote my good or the good of others?" Unfortunately, the more fundamental questions, "What is a good?" and "What is the self/other distinction?" have received woefully insufficient attention.

Who am I? What is my self? Who are the others?[125]

The chief point to be made with respect to the question, "Should we adopt attitudes of abundance or scarcity?", is that any coherent answer depends upon some self/other distinction and upon the good in question.

If you and I are enemies and shipwrecked on a small island with a very limited supply of fresh water, then water that I use will not be available to you and vice-versa. On the other hand, if we were friends, then I would value what is best for you and you would value what is best for me and, undoubtedly, we'd share the water peacefully.

It's extremely important to notice that adopting an attitude of abundance is appropriate with many (or, perhaps, most or even all) *important abstract goods*. For example, there may be a fixed quantity of fresh water on a desert island, but *there is an unlimited quantity of friendship or understanding or forbearance or health.*[126]

If so, at least with respect to many important abstract goods, there are both practical and theoretical reasons for adopting an attitude of abundance.

Hoarding is not saintly behavior.

7.8 Cheerfulness

[*Sidebar quotations*:
From Shantideva: "Put on an ever-smiling countenance."

From Michel de Montaigne: "The clearest sign of wisdom is continued cheerfulness."

From Martha Washington: "I am determined to be cheerful and happy in whatever situation I may find myself. For I have learned that the greater part of our misery or unhappiness is determined not by our circumstances but by our disposition."

From Hugh Downs: "A happy person is not a person in a certain set of circumstances, but rather a person with a certain set of attitudes."]

Sages are cheerful. Always.

Sages are masters and being a master always provides one with a reason to be cheerful, to be upbeat, to be confident. Even just being successful at some important activity is a good reason to be cheerful.

It's sometimes notoriously true that being successful does not always go with being cheerful. Some successful people are curmudgeons. Some are famously pessimistic. Some are rude and unkind. Some speak hateful words. Some are criminals.

Their defenders will always write that criticism off to their heroes being concentrated on their work. There's truth in that defense: successful people are often so busy concentrating that they can be quite forgetful of everything else. Think of an absent-minded professor so entranced in his thoughts that he fails to return the greeting of one of his students simply because he doesn't notice it. That student shouldn't take it personally.

On the other hand, that whole mindset is askew. The fundamental problem is that it presupposes that the work of a successful person is what is of maximum value. Not.

A well-lived life is the most valuable creation.

I confess that I used to be of the other opinion. I would see someone being idle and I'd sneeringly ask myself, "What is that person accomplishing?" It's the attitude adopted by many artists and intellectuals: productive or creative work is what is most important.[127]

The greatest creation is a masterful life. The most valuable masterpiece is a well-lived life.

We've come back to the beginning of this chapter: a masterful, well-lived life is characterized by detachment. A sage is not preoccupied with his or her own interests; to be a sage is to be detached from the concept of self. Being detached is the opposite of living abstractly by being wholly absorbed in one's thoughts. Sages are always centered. They are never lost in thought. A sage, therefore, is always open to others. This is why sages lead lives of selfless service.

You may object that you have seen masters who appeared to be angry and quite lacking in cheerfulness. No doubt. The question is: "Was that anger genuine?" Sometimes, loving-kindness requires harsh discipline. It may seem incongruous if, for example, you see a Zen master yelling at his students or rushing around the meditation hall thwacking them with a stick. Two minutes later, though, he may be calmly sipping tea with you, which may leave you all the more puzzled. What he was doing was loving his students, encouraging them to push themselves harder because he understands that that is what is best for them.

Please challenge yourself to be more cheerful. If you are not naturally cheerful, it may be because you are preoccupied with your own problems, stuck within yourself. The cure is to master something, which will require you to let go of such self-attachment. Since sages have already done that, this explains why they are always full of good cheer.

[*Sidebar quotations*:

From Viktor Frankl: "The last of the human freedoms: to choose one's attitude in any given set of circumstances. . ."

From Bernard Baruch: "The greatest freedom you have is the freedom to discipline yourself."]

Chapter 8: Organizing Your Values

[*Sidebar quotations*:
From David M. Buss: "Humans don't seem well-designed for dispassionate intellectual discourse about domains that have profound personal relevance."

From Andrew Weil, M.D.: "If you simply condemn unwanted behavior without acknowledging what you are getting out of it, you may not be able to give it up no matter how much harm it is causing."]

Have you noticed how we teach other people to treat us? The next time you are waiting somewhere and people are around, please play investigating novelist. That man over there, you'll imagine, would be perfect for a minor role in your novel. Study him closely.

What does his body language say about his self-image and self-esteem? Is he confident and relaxed or uncertain and anxious? Any nervous ticks or mannerisms? What do his clothes, footwear, and grooming say about how he values himself? Judging from his facial expression, what is his mood? Is he waiting calmly or impatiently? What's his level of formal education? What's his occupation? Is he healthy? How will he die?

If he's talking with a companion, so much the better. See if you can listen in on their conversation. What can you tell about him from the way he talks, his tone of voice, his vocabulary, his volume and diction? Is he showing deference to his companion or is he assuming it? Does he have an air of superior social standing or does he realize that his place is far below the top? Is he conscious of how others around him see him or utterly indifferent to them? Would you be willing to trust him? Is his word his bond or not? Is he politically liberal, conservative, middle-of-the-road, or indifferent? Did he have a normal or very abnormal childhood? Are his eyes kind and open or wary and distrustful?

[*Sidebar quotation* from Allison Lurie: "Long before I am near enough to talk to you on the street, in a meeting or at a party, you announce your sex, age, and class to me through what you are wearing and very possibly give me important information (or misinformation) as to your occupation, origin, personality, opinions, tastes, and current mood. By the time we meet and converse, we have already spoken to each other in an older and more universal voice."]

If you want some feedback about how you did, invent some reason to engage him in conversation and get him talking about himself. It shouldn't be too difficult: I assure you that, if he is normal, he will be his own favorite topic of discussion.

What major insights have you learned from observing people interacting with each other? Recall, for example, arguments you have observed between couples, siblings, or friends, in other words, people who know each other. Are you able to explain the nature of those arguments with the hypothesis that the one person actually taught the other person how to treat him or her?

If you investigate this seriously for yourself, you'll discover that *we teach others how to treat us*. If you yourself are having difficulties with someone in your life, challenge yourself to figure out why those problems occur. How did you contribute to them? How did you teach someone to argue with you or give you problems?

I am a small time real estate investor. When I purchased my cottage nearly a quarter of a century ago, it came with two small apartment buildings behind it (one of which I sold a few years ago). I had no experience as a landlord, yet I've personally managed tenants here ever since. Even if you've never managed real estate yourself, you've probably heard horror stories about how difficult it is to be a landlord. Well, it is difficult for many people. Why?

They don't pay attention. They assume it's easier to be excellent at it than it is. They fail to notice that landlords teach tenants how to treat them. Instead of deliberately learning from the mistakes and successes of others, they rely on trial and error—thus condemning themselves to making costly mistakes that are easily avoided. I realized my own ignorance; my first move was to read a long book on how to manage real estate. The result? I've never once been to court with a tenant. I've never once had a single serious dispute with a tenant. In fact, my tenants enjoy living here so much that they stay for years. (The current record is twenty-two years.) That's not because I have good people skills; it's because I took responsibility for learning how to set up mutually beneficial landlord/tenant relationships. Be fair, firm, and give good value.

Do you want to set up good relationships at work? Do you want mutually beneficial friendships and love affairs? If so, pay attention to them. Train yourself through books and programs and seminars how to establish such relationships, practice what you've learned, observe carefully what happens, and make adjustments to your behaviors on the basis of the results you actually obtain. Wouldn't it be very foolish, for example, to suffer through a couple of divorces before it occurs to you to pick up a book on how to create a terrific marriage?

Who knows you better than you? No one. Therefore, other people rely on cues from you about how to treat you. They've little else to rely on. (This explains why first impressions are so important. Others will form an impression of you in seconds, even before any words are exchanged.) If people don't treat you well, might that be because you have taught them how to treat you poorly?

[*Sidebar quotation* from Sonya Friedman: "The way you treat yourself sets the standard for others."]

How is this relevant to mastery?

Here's the key idea: once you begin seriously to examine how others treat you, *extend the examination to yourself.* How do you treat yourself? Mastery requires disciplining yourself, in other words, treating yourself in a certain way. Once you become self-conscious of how you actually treat yourself, you'll be able to identify ways that you can improve.

Do you treat yourself as if you were very important, extremely or infinitely valuable? (If not, why should anyone else?) For example, would a neutral observer quickly realize that you pamper yourself physically by fueling your body with excellent food; regularly training it with appropriate fitness, strength and flexibility exercise; and ensuring that it is well hydrated and well rested? Or, do you regularly abuse your body with drugs (including tobacco and alcohol), eat poorly, never exercise, drink too little water, and sleep whenever?

In other words, please focus your investigating novelist's eye on yourself. Pretend that you are observing yourself from outside yourself. Become self-conscious of everything you do and how you do it. *The way to mastering life is to pay attention.*[128] Pay attention to everything you do. This is precisely what sages have been teaching since the Axial Age.[129]

In particular, do you always act mindfully? What do your own observations demonstrate about how you value yourself? Do you have your life together or not?

If, as is likely, there's a gap between how you actually treat yourself and how you would like to treat yourself, then you have identified an important source of stress in your life. Once you recognize the gap, please admit that it doesn't have to be there. Often the most important step in solving a problem is identifying it.

In other words, unless you are a fully enlightened sage, you'll notice that at least in some ways you don't treat yourself as well as you should. That's normal. Let's work on straightening that out. *Discovering how to do that is the purpose of this chapter.*

Please avoid the excuse that you are too busy treating others well to worry about treating yourself well. *It's impossible to treat others well without treating yourself well.* You cannot give what you don't have. Without self-love, you cannot give love to others. Also, how you treat yourself automatically shows others how to treat you. Furthermore, if you happen to be a parent, if you treat yourself poorly you are teaching your children how to treat themselves poorly.

The first step is to help you identify your most important value. The second step is to examine it in comparison with your other important values.

All your core values are grounded in how you understand yourself and the world. To the degree that you are unclear about the nature of yourself and of your surreality, you'll be unclear about your values. If you are unclear about what really matters to you, how could you make those values concrete in your life? That's why clarifying your understanding of what-is[130], your surreality[131], and yourself[132] logically precedes clarifying your values.

[*Sidebar quotation* from Sidney Harris: "It's surprising how many persons go through life without ever recognizing that their feelings toward other people are largely determined by their feelings toward themselves, and if you're not comfortable within yourself, you can't be comfortable with others."]

Again, it's important that your values, the abstract goods that you consider most important, be congruent. In the next chapter, we'll consider how to make them concrete in your life. For now, let's come up with a list of values that may improve upon the list I asked you to make earlier.

(If you didn't make the earlier list, please go back to Chapter 3, section 2, and make it before you tackle the rest of this chapter. If you use the list of abstract goods that I provide there, it won't take long and it will maximize the value of what follows. It's fine not to want to bother, but just do it anyway. There's no mastery without discipline, and this is an exercise in self-discipline.)

Now, what you likely have is an unorganized list. Let's try to organize it. Doing so will help to ensure that it is complete, that you haven't overlooked something major. It will increase your confidence in it. Let's organize it on the basis of the five fundamental qualities that humans have.

First, though, let's dissolve the important potential objection that having such a list is useless, that it's impossible for you to improve your core value(s).

8.1 Personality

My father was a clinical internist. Though I don't recall how the subject arose, I was in my late teens when he told me about a patient he had recently seen. The patient was a young man who was troubled about being homosexual. My father had no idea how to help, so he called the best local psychiatrist he knew, Dr. Kenyon. Dr. Kenyon told him, in effect, "Well, Brad, send him over. There's nothing much anyone can do to change him, but I'll see what I can do for him."

I've thought a lot about that kind of thinking. We all have a tendency to fixate on some conception that we have of ourselves and assume that it is either impossible or nearly impossible to change it.

As we have seen, however, the idea that, for example, you are an underlying independent self is nonsense. There is no continuant substratum that is fixed one way rather than another. Like it or not, you are not your self-concept. You are free to create whatever self-identity you want.

It's helpful to distinguish "persona" from "personality." Your persona is the mask you wear for other people. It's like a role that you are comfortable at playing in interpersonal relations. Your persona is changeable. It may be uncomfortable to change it, but, with practice, it's not that difficult. Actors adopt different personas all the time.

For example, suppose that you are a normal, good-hearted young man. You are also short, fat, lonely, insecure, and terrible with women. You know that women say that they prefer tall, trim men who are confident. You have reluctantly come to the conclusion that you are stuck in friend zone for life. Not. That will be true only if you don't teach yourself how to break out of your conceptual box by adopting a different persona. Admit that you are ignorant and fix your problem. You are confusing what women say they want with what actually attracts them. If you will make appropriate changes, you'll soon discover for yourself that it's possible to be short, fat, and very attractive to women. There are plenty of good books, programs, and seminars available to teach you. Soon your confidence will grow and your loneliness will disappear—never to return. That will be your reward for learning how to become successful in attracting women.

Your personality, on the other hand, is a set of dispositional qualities that seem utterly natural to you. Some psychologists have thought that we are each born with a certain personality type, that we are hard-wired. What's clear is that it is extraordinarily difficult to change them; when we try, it's always a major effort that is so uncomfortable that we never feel very good at it. A good analogy is to handedness: think of naturally being right-handed and forcing yourself to become left-handed.

There are different systems for classifying the dispositional qualities that constitute a personality. The best one I've found is the Myers-Briggs Type Indicator (MBTI) that was developed from the ideas of Carl Jung, who was influenced on this topic by ancient Hindu thinking. According to it, there are four core dimensions that make up a personality. It's helpful to think of each dimension as like a scale: the stronger your tendency is in one direction, the more unbalanced the scale would be in that direction. In other words, each dimension comes in varying degrees.

According to the MBTI, the four core dimensions to your personality have equal weight. They are: *how you are energized, what you naturally notice, how you make decisions, and how you organize your surreality.* There are, then, sixteen possible personality types. Each dimension of each type has characteristic strengths and weaknesses. None is inherently better or worse than any other.

(1) If you are energized more by being with other people rather than being alone and if you like to direct your energy toward others rather than yourself, you are an "extrovert" rather than an "introvert."

(2) If you naturally focus on what is in the present moment (the trees) rather than focusing on the larger picture (the forest), you are a "sensor" rather than an "intuitive."

(3) If you make decisions logically, objectively, and analytically by weighing the pros and cons rather than relying

on how you feel the issue will affect you and others, you are a "thinker" rather than a "feeler."

(4) If you organize your surreality in a settled, closed way rather than leaving things in an unsettled, open way, you are a "judger" rather than a "perceiver."

Again, each of these dimensions comes in degrees. On some of them your balance may be tipped clearly in one way rather than the other, yet on others you may be nearer equilibrium.[133]

If you want to improve your people skills, I recommend learning this system. Once you have mastered it, you'll be able to meet a stranger, classify his or her personality, and then communicate with that person more effectively. *The <u>sine qua non</u> of good people skills is to forget yourself and focus on the other.* By using the other's natural language, you'll be able to establish rapport much more quickly and easily with fewer missteps.[134] However, that's not primarily why I'm mentioning this system.

Learning it can help you understand yourself. You'll fall into one of the sixteen possible classifications. It's not just important to realize that most (15/16ths) people have different personality types than you, it's important to realize that you have stable natural tendencies in certain directions. It can be quite helpful to take these tendencies into account when thinking about your values (and how different values may be more natural for others than for you) and when selecting an activity to master.[135]

There's a third reason (in addition to improving your relations with others and better understanding your own natural tendencies) to mention the BMTI: it's to set all such systems aside. In terms of mastery, it doesn't really matter what your personality type is. It's important to detach from the idea, if you happen to have it, that you are unsuited to mastery because you are stuck with a certain personality type that you think doesn't lend itself to mastery.

Why doesn't it matter? Because, again, mastery requires detachment. Whatever your natural tendencies, whatever your personality, if you are to master anything, you must set attachment to your self concept aside. It doesn't matter where you are coming from; all that matters is how you do what you do—and getting the *how* right requires absorption in the activity, in other words, letting go of attachment to your self concept.

[*Sidebar quotations*:

From Pema Chodron: "We can't overestimate the power of commitment."

From Dennis DeYoung: "Winners are losers who got up and gave it one more try."

From Denis Waitley: "It's not what you are that holds you back, it's what you think you are not."

From Vince Lombardi: "Winning is a habit; unfortunately, so is losing."]

This is **good news**: regardless of your personality type, you may become a master. We know that mastery isn't easy, so it's important to make it less difficult by not putting obstacles in our own way. The way to do this is to adopt values that make it easier to become a master.

Again, disciplined persistent practice of the right kind is critical for mastery. If you are fortunate enough to learn directly from a master, one way or another get used to hearing: **'Don't think—practice.'** Mastery requires focusing the mind. Focusing the mind requires focusing fully on some practice or other. Insofar as we are thinking, we are not practicing.

It's impossible to practice while thinking about and remaining attached to our personas and personalities. Mastery requires detachment from our self-concepts. So, whatever personas you adopt and whatever your personality type, since they will be left behind as you learn how to practice well, you are capable of mastery.

8.2 Eliciting Value

Values are preferences. We all have preferences.

The question here, then, is not about whether or not to have values. The only question is whether or not you should examine and, possibly, improve the values that you already have. Again, the first step must be to uncover what you already value. How?

Most of us are attached to our preferences. We choose the same ones so frequently that we bond with them emotionally. Assuming that you are normal in this respect, the fact that you are emotionally attached to your values permits you to uncover what you already value in an easy, two-step process.

[*Sidebar quotation* from George W. Crane: " . . . motions are the precursors of emotions."]

STEP ONE: Please imagine finding yourself in the following social situation: You have just begun talking with someone who interests you. You would like to decide quickly whether or not this person is worth much of your time and attention. You realize that it can be difficult not wasting time with banalities when getting to know someone. For example, we are not our jobs. Therefore, your asking the common question "What do you do?" would likely lead to talking only on a superficial level. Here's some sample dialogue to elicit that person's core value quickly.[136]

"Let's try an experiment. I'll ask you three questions that will let me know a little more about you. They're pretty easy.

Will you play along with me?" If you receive an affirmative answer, proceed.

[1] "If you had to choose one thing in your life that you had to have in order to feel that your life is worthwhile, what would it be?" Let's label the answer you receive 'X'; remember the exact word or phrase to use in the second question.

[2] "If you had X in your life, what kinds of things would that allow you to do?" (Alternatively, you may ask, "If you have X in your life, what kinds of things does that enable you to do?") Let's label the answer you receive 'Y'; remember the description to use in the third question.

[3] "Suppose that in the future you have Y. How would you feel? What emotion would you experience?" Let's label the answer you receive 'Z'; remember to repeat it as you continue.

"So, you are all about Z. It's your core value. As you thought about it, I noticed that you paused. You actually felt Z for a moment, didn't you?" When you receive an affirmative answer say, "So, we've fulfilled your life goal in three minutes. You can die now!"

A key to good people skills is this: *briefly be interesting and then interested.* This dialogue works because it demonstrates to the other person that you are an interesting person. You've kept it light in tone, but you are now ready, if you want, to follow it up with being genuinely interested in that person's life. If you want to build rapport, simply ask some good questions based on what you just learned and listen carefully to the answers you receive, watching for commonalities to point out.

As you'll confirm if you try it a few times, this procedure works. (You may discover that it works less well on a certain type of person. However, it is easily revisable to work on people who are less introspective and less self-aware. With people like that, it will work better if you elicit their core value by asking about behavior: "What do you most enjoy doing?" "What's your perfect scenario for doing it [repeat it]?" "So, [repeat the description of the perfect scenario] how would that make you feel inside?")

STEP TWO: How is this relevant to mastery? Please practice these questions on yourself.

You'll be able to uncover your core value if you ask yourself these questions and answer honestly. The procedure will work for you as well as it will work for getting to know a stranger.

Once you have clearly identified what you actually value, you are in a position to examine it critically. Is it really what you want your life to be about?

N.B.: the organization of values presented in the rest of this chapter depends upon the five-fold analysis of human nature given in Chapter 6. A set of values is confused unless it corresponds to an account of human being. It's an example of how to organize your values coherently.

What is your account of human being? How do your values correlate to it?

8.3 Physical

[*Sidebar quotation* from Ralph Waldo Emerson: "The first wealth is health."]

As we have seen[137], we are, in part, our bodies. What physical values (abstract goods) are important with respect to mastery?

Obviously, **life** itself. It's impossible to master life, or to master or be successful at some specific activity, without being alive.

It's best, also, to enjoy physical **wholeness**, in other words, to have a body that is intact and not missing any parts like limbs or important organs. It's possible to live well without, say, legs or while spending a lot of time hooked up to a kidney dialysis machine, but it would be better to be whole.

Descartes thought that **health** was the greatest good. Many people agree; if you have your health, you have all that you need, and, if you lose your health, you have almost nothing left. There no doubt that health is an intrinsic good. Is it really that important?

Some diseases (for example, leprosy) and some injuries (for example, quadriplegia) inhibit or eliminate our ability to feel our bodies. Please try to imagine for a moment how you would feel if you were unable to enjoy any physical **pleasure** such as the pleasures of touch or sex or taste or even just awareness of your limbs. Wouldn't you quickly miss them? Wouldn't the richness of life be diminished? More importantly in terms of mastery, being unhealthy inhibits practicing. No practicing, no mastery.

It's critical to distinguish having (or lacking) a quality from the consequences of having (or lacking) it. The consequences of being unhealthy can be good. For example, suppose that someone survives a life-threatening illness or injury. That person may forevermore live better because of having had that experience. However, it does not follow that it's false that health is a good. Of course it's a good.

Let's distinguish health from **wellness**. Being healthy is being free from disease, injury, and the symptoms of disease and injury. Enjoying wellness, however, is not merely being healthy: it's flourishing physically. It's being fit, strong, flexible, and energetic.

Given a choice, would you rather enjoy wellness or its opposite?

Health and wellness are very important goods. If you have any doubt at all about that, just ask someone who lacks either.

Are they, though, important to mastery?

[*Sidebar quotation* from James Joyce: "Mr. Duffy lived a short distance from his body."]

Yes they are. Remember that mastery results from a journey of practicing. Except for mastering a conceptual subject and meditation itself, all practicing involves bodily motions. A lack of either health or wellness puts a drag on bodily motions. It's difficult to practice anything if you don't feel well.

Therefore, if you enjoy health and wellness, I encourage you not to take them for granted. Work to preserve them. If you are unhealthy or unwell, please do whatever is possible to preserve whatever degree of health and wellness you enjoy and, if possible, to enhance it.

Beauty deserves mention. Physical beauty is a good, but having it is temporary and, furthermore, its consequences can be unfavorable. On the other hand, its consequences are often favorable. It seems, however, largely irrelevant to mastery. In fact, to the degree that beautiful people are distracted by the consequences of their being beautiful, they may be retarded in developing an appreciation of mastery. With respect to practicing, beauty makes no difference.

If so, these, then, are the important abstract goods that relate to us as bodies: life, wholeness, pleasure, health, and wellness.

8.4 Mental

We are, in part, our minds. What mental values are important with respect to mastery?

Consciousness itself is a good. If your friend is in a coma, don't you wish—even just for your friend's sake--for the coma to end? There's no issue about the value of consciousness.

Understanding is a good. It's true that the consequences of understanding can sometimes be unfortunate (as, for example, when a troubled person understands how to make a bomb and then blows up a building full of people), but it's better to understand than to be ignorant. Someone with a lot of understanding is someone with a lot of (theoretical or conceptual) **wisdom**.

The possession of any good can have bad consequences. We are here considering goods in abstraction from their causes and their consequences. Similarly, an abstract evil (such as ignorance or death or pain) that becomes concrete can have good consequences. Again, since we are unable to determine in advance all the consequences of our decisions to act in one way rather than another and since they are relevant to whether an act is right or wrong, we are unable to determine the rightness or wrongness of our acts. This is why it is foolish to attach to views about right and wrong. This is an important part of the Buddhist tradition.

[*Sidebar quotation* from Jianzhi Sengcan: "Both gain and loss, and right and wrong -- / once and for all get rid of them."]

Think back to episodes in your childhood when you didn't understand what was happening. How did that make you feel? Ignorance can be very troubling emotionally, can't it? *Of course* it's better to understand than to be ignorant. Ignorance hurts instantly, as soon as we realize it.

What if it were possible to have direct insight into the nature of ultimate reality? What if we could set aside all conceptual discriminations and enjoy an unobstructed vision of reality? What if there really is such a thing as **awakening** (spiritual enlightenment, satori)? The sages are unified in telling us that that is marvelous beyond all understanding.

Such an experience, at least if deepened and expanded by additional practicing, would be profoundly transforming. It's the moral transformation that really counts—not the awakening experience itself. If the sages are to be believed, awakening and enlightenment mean abiding joy and a permanent end to dissatisfaction. Therefore, any list of mental goods ought to include it. *Though being successful at or mastering a specific activity is possible without it, mastering life itself is impossible without it.*

Obviously, too, we should include **happiness**. There is no agreed-upon single conception of happiness. It must, though, have to do with having a good relation between one's self and the world. What relation?

I suggest **freedom** (liberation). There are different kinds of freedom: physical freedom, political freedom, financial freedom, and so on. Each kind makes us happy. (My own answer to the first question in the "Eliciting Value" section above is 'Freedom.')

All freedoms require discipline; there's no such thing as undisciplined freedom. We don't value what we don't have to work for, do we? If freedom or any other good were just handed to us, we would not appreciate it very much. We value only what we work for.

What is it to work for freedom? In terms of discipline, what is the price of freedom? The general answer is that it is freedom from the tyranny of incessant conceptualizing. To achieve that kind of freedom is to achieve the most important freedom, which also may be to achieve the greatest happiness. Mastering life is liberating.[138] If so, and if you want to be as happy as possible, why not liberate yourself?

Freedom enables us to work/play or practice at whatever we want. Appropriate activities result in excellence, either success or mastery. Happiness is the by-product of excellence.

[*Sidebar quotation* from David Deida: "Ego death, absolute surrender to the point of oneness, is ultimate freedom."]

The more we live in that way, the happier we are.

This is where **love** in its various varieties, including **friendship**, comes in. Many people think that the greatest good to enjoy is a great love affair. Many other people, including some famous philosophers like Cicero, think that the greatest good is friendship. Happiness generates an endless supply of love. By way of contrast, those who are unhappy have a diminished capacity to love.

The key point to notice is that all varieties of love are other-directed. Love is about giving to another; it's not about taking from another. *Being loving is the opposite of being selfish.* We are happy when we love, even happier than when we are loved.

Even though they have occasional bursts of generosity, children are naturally selfish. It takes a lot of work to overcome selfishness. Because it requires us to become less selfish, it takes sustained effort to love effectively. Sages break the back of selfishness, but, still, many of the rest of us overcome a lot of selfishness, which enables us to love. We may not love with the purity of a sage, but that doesn't mean that we do not love at all. It's not all or nothing.

[*Sidebar quotations*:

From the Buddha: "Little by little a person becomes good, as a water pot is filled by drops of water."

From Pema Chodron: "Taming the mind takes time. . . The fruits of the spiritual path are ineffable and usually not immediate."]

To love is to give diligently, generously, and inclusively with understanding.

What makes us happier than loving well? Imagine yourself on your deathbed. Will it comfort you to realize how much you have used other people in your life for your own selfish purposes? Hardly. It will, though, comfort you to realize how much love you have given to others. That's what really matters.

Freedom also involves **creativity**. Great artists, for example, break outside themselves and unleash wonderful new arrangements of colors, sounds, materials, and words. Notice that mastering any art requires discipline. Discipline always requires dominating our impulsive, selfish thoughts and behaviors. Excellence always involves delaying gratification. Though it depends upon how creativity is understood (discussing it would take us too far afield), mastery is impossible without creativity.

[*Sidebar quotations*:

From Master Muso Kokushi: "Those who want to get paid before they do any work, so to speak, who demand assurance of success before they make any effort, will never get anywhere, either in Buddhism or in ordinary endeavors."

From Thomas A. Edison: "Opportunity is missed by most people because it is dressed in overalls and looks like work."

From Brian Tracy: "The ability to discipline yourself to delay gratification in the short term in order to enjoy greater rewards in the long term is the indispensable prerequisite for success."]

Aesthetic experience is another good that belongs on this list. Notice that it doesn't just happen. Yes, we can be awestruck by, say, a great symphony the first time we hear it or a magnificent painting or a play. Yet aesthetic taste can and should be developed and refined. Expertise in this area is not only possible but also valuable. I wish that I better understood how to appreciate more fully the great art our predecessors have left us. However, the subject matter of aesthetic experience may also be (and this is somewhat controversial) natural objects such as mountains or seascapes. If so, enjoying the world more aesthetically is an automatic by-product of detaching from one's self-concept. A self-absorbed depressed person is incapable of enjoying a sunset.

If so, these, then, are the important abstract goods that relate to us as minds: consciousness, understanding, (theoretical) wisdom, awakening, happiness, freedom, love (including friendship), creativity, and aesthetic experience.

8.5 Perceptual

We are, in part, our perceivings. What perceptual values are important with respect to mastery?

[*Sidebar quotation* from Giordano Bruno: "out of the world we cannot fall."]

The answer may surprise you. Before you began reading this book, you may never have examined your attachment to the idea that you are a perceiving subject who is different from the objects perceived. It's normal to identify with the perceiver over here who is separated from the perceptual objects over there.

If you remain attached to such dualisms, you'll never experience unity. **Mastery requires experiencing unity.**

The conceptualization 'perceiver/perceived' is just another attachment. Ultimately, there's no difference. As the Third Zen Patriarch writes: "things are things because of mind, / as mind is mind because of things."[139]

To awaken is to go beyond the mind/thing distinction: "These two are merely relative, / and both at source are Emptiness." Ultimate reality is emptiness, a unity beyond subject and object. To fail to awaken to it, to fail to experience it directly (in other words, without conceptual mediation), is to remain stuck in duality, which exacts a high price: "Remaining in duality, / you'll never know of unity."[140]

We have a choice: awaken or fail to awaken. Those of us who remain stuck in duality, foundering in our likes and dislikes, are suffering from the mind's disease. **To awaken is to begin to master life.**

All egocentric attachments are poisons: "If you're attached to anything, / you surely will go far astray."[141] Being an intellectual, I always think of intellectual attachments, attachments to views or to enquiry itself. (It's good to understand, but attachment to gaining understanding is, of course, just another attachment.)

Thales was the first western philosopher, who was known as wise even in his lifetime—yet Plato repeats "the story about the Thracian maidservant who exercised her wit at the expense of Thales, when he was looking up to study the stars and tumbled down a well. She scoffed at him for being so eager to know what was happening in the sky that he could not see what lay at his feet."[142] Oh, how we grow so fond of our ideas and theories that we miss our lives!

Yet we don't live in the domain of being. Our lives occur in the domain of becoming. This is why the Third Patriarch warns: "do not reject the sense domain."[143] What's his point?

Think of eating a peach. Please never do it distractedly with your mind elsewhere. Look at it and enjoy its color. Heft it in your hand and enjoy touching its fuzziness. Smell it with anticipation. Sink your teeth into its skin and enjoy the burst of flavor. Masticate thoroughly and slowly while savoring the taste. That's the way to eat a peach. In general, *paying attention is the way to live well.*

Quick: right now, how's your posture? Are you alive to what you are touching? Are your senses alive or dead?[144]

We are colors, sounds, smells, tastes, tactile feelings, and so on. Rejecting them is rejecting our lives.

As long as our senses work normally, we naturally enjoy all the perceptual values appropriate to mastery *if we pay attention.*

Life is lived well or poorly right here now. Set aside attachment to conceptualizing: live. Thus!

8.6 Emotional

We are, in part, our emotions. What emotional values are important with respect to mastery?

Here again, the answer may surprise you. [I've written elsewhere about the nature of emotions.[145]]

You might expect that the answer would concern which positive emotions are most favorable to practicing. Instead, it concerns freedom.

What fosters practicing best is emotional **detachment**. Emotional detachment is not itself an emotion; it's freedom from emotional bondage. It's freedom from both negative and positive emotions. Emotional detachment fosters concentration.

Mastery requires concentration. Emotions distort concentration. Intense emotions narrow concentration; someone in a rage is aware only of being enraged. The more emotional we are, the less we are able to focus. Haven't you noticed how it's impossible to concentrate whenever you are upset?

Have you ever been stricken by intense grief? Have you ever had someone you dearly loved die or dump you? I can recall a time years ago after such an experience when I'd simply be driving down the road and suddenly burst into tears. I was unable to go to a shopping mall, because I'd see couples together and that would remind me of my loss. I was unable even to sleep for more than ninety minutes at a time. Have you suffered through similar grief? Forget focusing on practicing for more than a few minutes when you're gripped by that sort of intense emotion.

Given the infrequency with which humans achieve the emotional detachment that comes with awakening, it's not surprising that our ordinary language doesn't contain appropriate words for describing it. Instead, what we do is to borrow emotional words like 'joy', 'bliss', 'peacefulness', 'tranquility', and 'serenity' and modify with them with adjectives such as 'abiding', 'incessant', or ' lasting' to indicate that we are not talking about emotions, which are always temporary and sometimes fleeting. For example, 'abiding joy' does not denote the feeling of joy that alternates with sorrow.

[*Sidebar quotation* from Charlotte Joko Beck: "the ultimate reality—not only in our sitting, but also in our lives—is joy. By joy I don't mean happiness; they're not the same. Happiness has an opposite; joy does not. As long as we seek happiness, we're going to have unhappiness, because we always swing from one pole to the other."]

The emotional detachment of a sage is the "abiding joy" that comes from breaking the attachment to the self-concept. A fully enlightened sage would be selfless; a fully enlightened sage identifies with everything. There is no separation in the unitive experience. No separation, no dissatisfaction. No dissatisfaction, "abiding joy." The dissolution of attachment to self is, typically, the result of years of practicing detachment.

Emotions inhibit practicing detachment.

[*Sidebar quotation* from Pema Chodron: "Until we start working with our mind, we are ruled by our emotions. . . It is just as difficult to detox from emotions as it is to recover from heavy drugs or alcohol."]

It's not possible to communicate even a shallow awakening experience conceptually. Again, it is beyond joy and sorrow just as it is beyond movement and rest, like and dislike, easy and difficult, subject and object, waking and sleeping, large and small, self and other—and all other oppositions and discriminations.

If so, then, the only important abstract good that relates to us as emotional is freedom from all emotional bondage. Instead of attachment to positive emotions that we like, mastering life requires detachment from our likes and dislikes, including emotions we like.

8.7 Activity

As we've seen, acting rightly isn't easy because we are incapable of knowing how to act rightly. We are, though, in part, our activities and dispositions to activity. What values with respect to these are important with respect to mastery?

Acting rightly is the mark of a master. Masters are excellent at some activity (or life itself). Masters have (practical) **wisdom**. There are two requirements that are both necessary for practical wisdom.

[*Sidebar quotations*:

From Shantideva: "we can never take / And turn aside the outer course of things. / But only seize and discipline the mind itself, / And what is there remaining to be curbed?"

From Master Eckhardt: "There is no stopping place in this life—no, nor was there ever for any man no matter how far along his way he'd gone."

From Booker T. Washington: "The world cares very little about what a man or woman knows; it is what a man or woman is able to do that counts."

From Andrew Matthews: "It's not *what* you do, it's *how* you do it."]

Good intentions are important but insufficient. The worst criminal is always capable of rationalizing immoral acts as attempts to promote some abstract good or other. Who doesn't think of themselves as having good intentions? The terrorist thinks that killing all those infidels will promote God's kingdom on earth. The Inquisitor thinks that burning all those people at the stake gives them (the burned) their best chance for repentance. A Hitler or Stalin thinks that genocide is necessary for the good of the state.

Most people, I believe, really do have good intentions. It's normal to promote mutual understanding, friendship, peace, justice, freedom, and enjoyment.

The underlying culprit is the idea that something needs to be promoted or gained by our actions, that we make our lives meaningful by certain achievements.

We ourselves are suffering, and we notice others who suffer more. We think that by helping them we'll be helping ourselves. We think that, if we help enough other people get whatever they want, we'll get what we want. What, you ask, is so wrong with that?

It's not necessarily the action itself. When we feed the hungry or nurse the sick or house the homeless our actions are not necessarily wrong and may be right in terms of the consequences produced.

The problem concerns *how* we are acting. Whose good is being promoted? If I am feeding the hungry or nursing the sick or housing the homeless because I am motivated to make my life better, then I am merely *using* those suffering people for my own egocentric purposes. Though my actions look like loving actions, they are quite the opposite: I'm not giving but taking. Loving isn't taking; loving is giving.

On the other hand, if I am feeding the hungry or nursing the sick or housing the homeless because I am motivated by my identification with their plight, in other words, with a selfless concern for their welfare, then I am acting in a loving way. To act in a loving way is to get the *how* right.

[*Sidebar quotations*:

From Nisargadatta: "It is not what you live, but how you live that matters."

From Lama Surya Das: "For you, the seeker, what matters is how you attend to the present moment . . . This is not just about what you do but *how* you do it."]

In order to act in a loving way, it's important that my actions are guided by correct understanding. If I misunderstand the situation or if my behavior isn't skillful, my actions are not loving actions even if they are done with the right *how*. It's sometimes much more difficult than we tend to think to know what is best for someone else. (This is particularly true with respect to those less articulate such as children and nonhuman animals.) It's easy to misunderstand a situation, and it's easy to act with unskillful behavior.

This is why acting rightly isn't easy. Anyone who thinks it is easy is naïve. This is why we require counselors and physicians and teachers and many other professional helpers to have years of education. Proper professional training lessens the odds of misunderstanding a situation or treating it unskillfully.

In my experience, most people who seek proper professional training are, at least in part, motivated by the desire to help others. Still, without breaking the back of egocentricity, that desire itself may be subtly egocentric.

[*Sidebar quotation* from John Daido Loori: "Enlightenment and morality are one . . . morality functions in the world of duality . . . When morality becomes effortless, purposeless, and playful, it becomes the nonmoral morality of the Buddhas and ancestors."]

In other words, **the best way to serve others** is to have whatever professional training is appropriate and to be a sage.

I am not, of course, claiming that the acts of professionals who are not sages are always wrong. In terms of the act itself (and not its *how*), there is no reason why the acts of a nonsage cannot be as right as the acts of a sage; there's no reason why the acts of a nonsage cannot have optimific or optimizing consequences. Notice, though, that there's also no reason why the acts of a purely selfish person cannot have optimific or optimizing consequences *for others*!

Similarly, there is no reason why the acts of a sage cannot be as wrong in terms of their consequences as the acts of a nonsage. Why? The acts of a sage are not necessarily skillful; being properly motivated is insufficient.

This is why the best way to exercise our active dispositions is to become sages and, if we want to serve others, acquire appropriate professional training.

Again, this is an ancient way of thinking. For example, 2500 years ago Plato required that the rulers in his Republic not only have a high level of education but also have the right psychological motivation. By itself, being well educated isn't enough. By itself, having proper motivation isn't enough. Wasn't he right? Wouldn't you prefer political leaders who were not only well educated but also properly motivated to tend to the welfare of their citizens (instead of using the citizens to enhance their own welfare)?

If so, if you really want to help others help themselves, become a sage and also obtain the relevant professional training. Without your awakening and enlightenment, the world might well be better off if you kept working on yourself for a while longer before attempting to help others. After all, what you'll really be sharing is your experience.

[*Sidebar quotation* from Pema Chodron: "Our own experience is the only thing we have to share."]

Even then, be careful. It's not easy for anyone, even for a well-educated sage, to act well. For this reason, in practice, it's usually best to let people come to you for help. It's often counterproductive to go around trying to help people without their consent, to try to change the world when nobody is asking you to change it. If, instead, you make yourself available to those who might be interested, in my experience your odds of success will dramatically increase. It's simply not possible to help those who aren't interested in helping themselves. Like genuinely helping others, being genuinely helped by others requires commitment.

Suppose, then, that you want to educate yourself, to become a sage, or both. Suppose, in other words, that you want to master or become successful at some activity or other or that you want to master life itself. What should you actually do?

[*Sidebar quotation* from Thomas Carlyle: "Doubt, of whatever kind, can be ended by action alone."

From Woody Allen: "Nothing worth knowing can be understood with the mind."]

Chapter 9: Habits

Your self is what you make it. You are not an independent continuant substratum. Whether you realize it or not, you are inherently free.

Your self-concept, in other words, can be small or large at your discretion. If you only identify with your skin and what's inside it, you have a very limited conception of yourself—and you are a sociopath. If you were to identify also with your lover, or with your children, or with your culture, or with all mammals, you would be creating a more expansive conception of yourself.

Moral growth occurs as one expands one's self-concept. Initially, when we began to distinguish between self and other we also began to value some others (usually mother and father) as being critically important. Later, we may include siblings. Still later, playmates and schoolmates became natural objects of identification. We typically also identify with those from our towns or cities, our states or provinces, and our countries, as well as with those who share our religion and language.

Sometimes obstructions block development. In most humans, moral development slows and stalls somewhere along the way. In a few, it keeps going as far as possible. Sages identify themselves with the world. They have the most expansive self-concepts.

With respect to developing habits necessary for excellence, it's critically important that we expand our self-concepts to include more than just our minds (consciousness).

This requires habits that stretch our self-concepts. Excellence is impossible without generating beneficial habits and deleting detrimental ones.

[*Sidebar quotations*:

From George Santayana: "Habit is stronger than reason."

From Ed Foreman: "Good habits are hard to form, but easy to live with; bad habits are easy to form but hard to live with."

From Thomas Leonard: "Some people appear to be 'getting away' with wrong actions or bad habits. That's an illusion. Sometimes it might take a long while before the damage shows. But when it does, it's significant damage. And the remainder of a lifetime may not be enough to deal with the ill effects. Lung cancer is only one example. On the other hand, even if you can't see immediate results from clear-headed actions and good habits, the truth is that they're accruing like money in the bank."]

We've seen how there is nothing to consciousness except "intentionality."[146] Therefore, consciousness lacks what is required for habit formation. There's nothing at all ever habitual about consciousness. It is incessantly new, as spontaneous and endlessly upwelling as becoming. If we were only consciousness, we could never master anything. This is why it is critical for mastery to expand our self-concepts.

9.1 I's and Me's

Historically, Descartes is the philosopher in the western tradition who separated mind from body. Minds are thinking and nonspatial, while bodies are spatial and nonthinking. In the Second Meditation, he identifies himself with his mind. He writes that he is able to doubt his existence as a body but that he is unable to doubt his existence as a mind. He may or may not also be a body, but, surely, he is certain at least that he exists as a mind, a thinking thing.

Whatever Descartes's exact intentions, many come away from reading his <u>Meditations on First Philosophy</u> wondering if they are nothing but ghosts in machines. There's something radically unsettling about such a view.

In his excellent book <u>The User Illusion</u>, Tor Norretranders identifies the problem: it's not that we are primarily conscious, it's that we are primarily nonconscious![147] I am a person, not merely consciousness. I am "Me", not merely a conscious "I."

The truth that the "I" (the mind, consciousness) doesn't want to accept is that, though my life is all my experiences, in other words, everything that I perceive, think, and do, *I am more than what I am conscious of experiencing, more than what I am conscious of perceiving, thinking, or doing.* Notice how this fits with the idea that our self-concepts are prisoners created by certain shifts in the development of language[148]; in other words, since the way that we think of ourselves is a by-product of a certain kind of literacy, it's not surprising that we dislike the more inclusive understanding of ourselves.

[*Sidebar quotation* from Richard Bandler and John Grinder: "It's important for some people to have the illusion that their conscious mind controls their behavior. It's a particularly virulent form of insanity among college professors, psychiatrists, and lawyers."]

Perhaps the best way to realize this is to notice what actually happens in emergencies.[149] In an emergency, we know better than to think about what to do; what we actually do is to become spectators of our own actions. We are able to step back and watch ourselves do whatever is required, which is living fully in the present moment, if we are to survive the emergency. **Don't think—act!**

Since it is an emergency, we know better than to permit ourselves to think. When I raced my friend skating, it wasn't an emergency; he allowed himself the luxury of thinking and promptly fell to the ice.[150] In genuine emergencies, we don't allow ourselves that luxury. *It's in emergencies that we are able to attain our first taste of mastery.* If you are batting in a baseball game, you'd better not think about what to do when a fastball is coming straight at your head—you'd better just react.

[*Sidebar quotation* from Roshi Bodhin Kjolhede: "Ego simply means a sense of separation, of self-and-other . . . the basic fallacy is to believe you're somehow different in a fundamental way."]

If you are like me, you really enjoy observing other people when they are able to suspend their I's in order to allow their Me's to live fully. It's wonderful observing a great actor in the theater, a great musician or conductor in the concert hall, a great athlete in championship competition.

If you have ever had a lover and allowed your attachment to your self-concept to loosen, the best sex came (pun intended!) when you permitted your I to trust your Me.

Why does mastery require disciplined training? It's to learn to permit one's I to trust one's Me.[151] We cannot be the performance if we hold ourselves apart from it. *There cannot be unity if we stay stuck in duality.*

Mastery is the result of a balancing process. The I insists on the training, but the Me insists on letting go of the training. The I is right: there's no mastery without clear, disciplined awareness of *what* one is doing; however, the Me is also right: there's no mastery without a nonconscious (non-self-conscious) performance, which is getting the *how* right.

Which comes first? The training demanded by the I.

Without the training, there'd be no *what* to do and, so, no *what* to do automatically. It's when we persist long enough in practicing that, finally, we begin to do it automatically. Doing it automatically is getting the *how* right. At that point, the performance seems almost effortless. It is almost effortless, but it's a performance that is, usually, based on years of deliberate effort.

Understanding this makes persistent practicing *much* easier. Once you understand it, you have no reason not to let all distracting thoughts go as soon as you notice them and return your focus to your practice. For example, if you find yourself wondering whether or not you really have what it takes to be excellent in the activity you've chosen, just let that thought go as soon as you notice it in favor of returning focus to your practice.

[*Sidebar quotations*:

From Leonardo da Vinci: "Iron rusts from disuse, stagnant water loses its purity, and in cold weather becomes frozen: even so does inaction sap the vigors of the mind."

From Eddie Cantor: "It takes 20 years to become an overnight success."]

9.2 System

This is why *practicing (training, rehearsing) must be systematic.* Everything must be rehearsed over and over, and nothing must be omitted. In other words, *practicing must be comprehensive* as well as *regular*; furthermore, when different skills are involved, practicing must be *prioritized.*

Typically, an activity can be chunked down into constituent skills, usually about five to seven. Take, for example, a running back in (American) football. What does an excellent running back do? There are six discernible skills that he must have.

(1) He must know how to run well with the ball. He must know, for example, how to hold it and how to be tackled. He

must know how to feint and use a stiff-arm. He must know when to be patient and when to burst with all possible speed. He must know how to read a teammate's behavior who is blocking or setting up a block.

(2) He must know the plays and the rules. There's no point in regularly running where none of your ten teammates expects you to go, and taking foolish penalties is counterproductive.

(3) He must know how to block. When they are not running with the ball, excellent running backs block well to contribute to the play.

(4) He must know how to fake. If he isn't running with the ball, the other way to contribute to the team's effort on a play in addition to blocking is by faking a run, which often has the same effect on the defense as a good block.

(5) He must know how to catch the ball. How much more useful to the team is a running back with good hands than a running back with hands of stone? An inability to receive passes is a good way for a running back not to play.

(6) He must know how to react when plays break down. He must be drilled to tackle instinctively and properly, for example, when a player from the opposing team intercepts a pass or recovers a fumble.

Notice that none of these skills means much if his head isn't in the game. If he's worried about a cheating wife, a heavy lawsuit, or the impending death of his beloved father, he won't be congruent. Although he may be able sometimes to transform them temporarily into angry energy, attempts to compartmentalize his worries won't be effective if he's too emotionally distracted by them. This is why some means of clearing the mind, such as meditation, is very important with respect to excellence, in other words, either success or mastery.

Developing and sticking with a training program that is comprehensive is half of what makes a training program systematic. The other half is developing a training program that is prioritized.

The most practice time should be devoted to the most important skills, and, of course, skills must sometimes be mastered in an appropriate sequence. There's no point in working on an archer's release of the bowstring until the bow has been properly strung and drawn. There's no point in trying to teach a hockey player who cannot skate well how to shoot a slap shot.

So, what should a running back's training look like? The purpose of the training is to make using these skills habitual (almost automatic or instinctive). Not all of the skills are of equal value. Jim Brown was a great running back who rarely bothered to block. Obviously, a coach should construct practices so that running backs devote most of their training time to the most important skills; in other words, a coach should prioritize drills effectively.

The most important skill of a running back is how to run, so more training time should be spent on this skill than on any of the others. Since one cannot run well without being in the excellent physical condition appropriate for football, this would also include eating well; exercising well for cardiovascular fitness, muscular strength, muscular endurance, and explosive power; and developing flexibility. Though gaits are inborn, there are various drills that can improve running. Though both were great, Eric Dickerson and Barry Sanders had completely different running styles; different backs have naturally different styles. Different training protocols may be used to strengthen an athlete's strong points and to shore up his weak ones.

It's possible to break down the way that a back, for example, receives a hand-off from the quarterback and then to rehearse the correct technique so frequently that it becomes habitual. Great coaches like Vince ("Gentlemen, this is a football...") Lombardi break down mastering each skill into a simple, step-by-step process. They teach players the best way to do it and then have them rehearse and rehearse and rehearse it correctly until they are able to do it quickly and habitually without rushing.

In fact, it's possible for an excellent player to be concussed and still play effectively. It happened to Floyd Little and it has also happened to many other football players.

It happens in other sports as well as in football. One time in the middle of a playoff hockey game, Dan, who was my defense partner that season, threw one of the hardest body checks I've ever seen, and both he and the puck carrier dropped to the ice. What made that hit especially memorable was what happened afterwards. I was sitting with him in the locker room well after the game; some of our teammates had already showered and left, and I knew that his wife was waiting for him outside. However, he was still sitting there fully dressed in his hockey equipment. Then he "came to" and, as it turned out, he was unable to recall anything from that hit until the moment when he "woke up" and found me talking to him in the locker room. I was able to tell him that he had played the rest of the game very well, and he was delighted to learn that our team had won. Do I have to mention that Dan was a master defenseman? He was one of the most skilled players I ever played with. His performance for the last part of that game was habitual.

Excellence is established systematically. Any effective training system is both comprehensive and prioritized, and it should be used regularly for as long as it takes. No critical skills are neglected. All skills are learned in a proper sequence and practiced roughly in accordance with their importance. The point is to make excellent performances habitual, which is what happens only when skills are so well rehearsed that the "I" gets out of the way.

Of course, as any coach or teacher will confirm, every athlete or student is different. Even though mastery is established systematically, this doesn't entail that individuals should be plugged mindlessly into training systems. A master will individualize each disciple's training in order to make it maximally effective.

Therefore, after you have selected an activity to master, please be sure that your training system is not only both comprehensive and prioritized but also individualized for you. Doing so will also help eliminate second-guessing as well as the temptation to quit. The training *always* becomes inconvenient and difficult, which naturally generates doubts about its effectiveness. The more confidence you have in the training system before starting to train, the better.

[*Sidebar quotation* from Tor Norretranders: "The claim, then, is that the user illusion is a good metaphor for consciousness. Our consciousness is our user illusion for ourselves and the world . . . Consciousness is a user illusion for the aspect of the world that can be affected by oneself and the part of oneself than can be affected by the consciousness. / The user illusion is one's very own map of oneself and one's possibilities of intervening in the world . . . If consciousness is my user illusion of myself, it must insist that precisely this user *is* the user . . . Therefore the user illusion operates with a user by the name of *I*. / The *I* experiences that it is the *I* that acts . . . But it is the *Me* that does so. *I am my user illusion of myself* . . . Even what we actually experience is a user illusion . . . The world just *is*. It has no properties until it is experienced."]

It's interesting to note that recent advances in brain-scanning technology have shown that our brains work differently when we are learning something new from when we are operating automatically doing something familiar.[152] Compare the same behavior sequence (the same *what*) performed in different ways (with different *how*'s). Think of, for example, walking to your car, getting in it, and driving away.

The first time you did that, you were thinking about what to do. You were aware of making a sequence of decisions. In fact, you were using your prefrontal neocortex as you were weighing what to do at each step of the sequence. Your prefrontal neocortex is the grey mass of brain matter just above your eyes that works carefully and relatively slowly. It requires an effort to learn something new (as, perhaps, you realize just from reading this book).

After you performed that same sequence enough times to make so habitual or automatic that you could do it without consciously thinking about what you are doing, you were actually using your basal ganglia to control your behavior. This is an area deep within your brain whose synapses "fire" in an exact sequence. It enables you to perform familiar tasks, which are most daily tasks, without consciously thinking about them. In fact, normally you'll be conscious of other matters while you perform the sequence yet again (and you won't ordinarily ever think of them unless something goes wrong); it's effortless in the sense that you don't need to spend any mental energy on it.

What happens when, say, you buy a new car and you find it necessary to change the sequence? Suppose, say, that you go from a manual transmission to an automatic transmission.

That requires learning a new sequence. That requires thinking about the new sequence, which will involve the prefrontal neocortex. It will take an effort to learn something new.

However, if you from now on only drive a car with an automatic transmission, you'll quickly find that doing so will become habitual or automatic; you'll soon be able to do it without consciously thinking about it at all.

Understanding this enables us to understand how it is possible to change habitual behaviors. Suppose that you have habits that you want to change. Perhaps you want to free yourself from addiction to sugar or other refined (processed) carbohydrates such as bread, pasta, or bagels. Perhaps you want to free yourself from addiction to television. Perhaps you want to free yourself from addiction to smoking. What's the best way to do it?

Although alcohol addiction is an important exception and there may be others, almost always the best way to break an addiction is to quit it "cold turkey." *Consciously force yourself to engage in your new behavior and let no exceptions occur until the new behavior becomes habitual or automatic.* Doing so will be difficult for a while, but it's often just a few days or weeks.

In fact, though you can face a relatively short time that is thoroughly unpleasant, a bit of concentrated suffering is sometimes the price for freedom. Freedom is always worth it!

Once you understand the idea of changing *how* you are behaving from being under control of the prefrontal neocortex to being under control of the basal ganglia, you are able to understand the shortest and most effective way to create new habitual or automatic behaviors. That's a really useful idea.

Whatever activity you select to master will require you to develop some new habits. You now are armed with some valuable information about the best and quickest way to establish those new practices.

Without knowing your activity in advance, it's not possible to suggest any general guidelines for listing or prioritizing its requisite practices. However, by working from the fivefold system of fundamental human qualities, I have some useful, though general, suggestions on this topic to offer you in the rest of this chapter.

[*Sidebar quotation* from Florence Littauer: "It is humbling to admit we've been doing something wrong for years, but it's the first step in growing up."]

9.3 Physical

[*Sidebar quotation* from Philip J. Goscienski, M.D.: "Most people have a termite lifestyle. You can't see the damage until something collapses. . . "]

It's natural to have heroes to admire, role models to imitate. Early in my graduate training in philosophy I attended a social mixer, which was then called a "smoker," at a convention of the American Philosophical Association. There was such a high degree of intellectual energy in the room that it was exciting. My mentor happened to be chatting with a scholar whose best-known book I had read and thought excellent. Was I disappointed when I discovered that he was a fat chain-smoker. He was indeed theoretically wise when it came to the history of western philosophy, but he was also obviously deficient in practical wisdom. His life was out of balance.

[*Sidebar quotation* from Andrew Weil, M.D.: "Health is wholness and balance, an inner resilience that allows you to meet the demands of living without being overwhelmed. . . health is not static. . . The *healing system* is a functional system. . ."]

Which habit[s] will increase the odds of being alive, whole, and able to enjoy pleasure, health, and wellness?[153]

If you are not feeling good physically, if you are ill or injured, how will that affect practicing for success or mastery?

[*Sidebar quotations*:

From St. Augustine: "Care for your body as though you were going to live forever."

From D. Hutson, C. Crouch, G. Lucas: "If you don't take care of your physical body, where are you going to live?"]

With respect to developing habits beneficial for instantiating each of the five different kinds of goods, I suggest paying the most attention to people who have walked the walk instead of to people who just talk the talk. If you want to flourish physically, even though an obese drug addict who is weak and unfit may have a lot of theoretical understanding, doesn't it make a lot more sense to pay attention to someone who is also demonstrating what it takes to flourish physically?

If you are foolish enough to prefer to get financial advice from someone who is broke rather than from someone who is wealthy, go ahead. That's not my way. You'd be better off to listen to that advice and do exactly the opposite.

There's no way to know what to do to stay alive and whole. You might want to avoid obviously risky activities; you might want to avoid doing too much smoking, drinking, cliff jumping, motorcycle riding, automobile racing, horseback riding, and hang gliding.

Chronological age is less important than biological age. Health span is more important than life span. What's the way to prolong vitality and reduce disability as we age?

What's the best way to be able to keep practicing?

Eating and exercising well.

Do that and you'll enjoy physical pleasures and maintain health and wellness for as long as possible. Why not do your best with respect to eating and exercising well? How could that do anything except enhance life as well as success or mastery?

Mastery isn't what's easiest; it's what's best.

Tending your body properly (in other words, eating and exercising well) isn't what's easiest; it's what's best.

[*Sidebar quotations*:

From Barbara and Allan Pease: "Human biology is dangerously out of date."

From Deirdre Barrett: "Hunter-gatherers of the Paleolithic era ate the greatest variety of foods: fruits, berries, vegetables, nuts, roots and prey ranging from insects to animals much larger than themselves. . . Physical activity used to occur automatically. . . the human genome evolved within an environment of high physical activity. . ."]

Just think of your brain. Scientists now understand that our brains continue to create new brain cells throughout life. What is the greatest stimulus of brain growth?

Physical exercise. Fitness (aerobic) exercise and strength training.

Everyone understands that fitness exercise benefits the heart and cardiovascular system and that strength training benefits the muscles, connective tissues, and bones. Physical exercise also improves *alertness, learning, memory, and thinking*. This is hardly surprising once it's understood that brains evolved to coordinate movement.

[*Sidebar quotation* from Deirdre Barrett: "brains exist largely to coordinate movement, and they require movement to function well."]

It's easy to imagine some fat, weak, pencil-necked, chain-smoking, hard-drinking intellectual mocking emphasis on physical training. What's that got to do with mastery?

I just pointed out how tending one's body improves one's brain. From my school days I had a number of fat, weak, pencil-necked, chain-smoking, hard-drinking friends—and some of them are already dead. If you are tempted to write off those who tend their bodies seriously as health nuts, do yourself a favor and lose the attitude.

Here's the plan: *First*, start thinking well about tending your body properly. *Second*, start tending your body properly—and never stop.

I do not recommend changing your eating and exercising habits without the blessing of your physician. I do recommend consulting with your physician to figure out the best way for you to close the gap between where you are physically and where you want to be. Start with a thorough physical examination.

If you have some bad physical habits, figure out how to eliminate them and do whatever it takes. If your life doesn't depend upon it, the quality of your life does. You cannot, for example, enjoy freedom from moment to moment if you are addicted to tobacco, alcohol, or other recreational drugs. Slaves aren't free.

So, if you don't already, start reading about flourishing physically. Figure out for yourself, and then discuss with your physician, an appropriate set of habits about eating and exercising well for you as well as a training program to make them concrete.

[*Sidebar quotations*:

From Thomas Jefferson: "Not less than two hours a day should be devoted to exercise, and the weather should be little regarded. I speak this from experience, having made this arrangement of my life. If the body is feeble, the mind will not be strong."

From Kilmer S. McCully, M.D.: "We're killing ourselves with our food. . . Once you're aware of what's nutritionally good for you, it becomes harder and harder to eat what isn't."

From Philip J. Goscienski, M.D.: "All the chronic diseases of modern life are avoidable . . . most modern humans kill themselves . . . Most modern humans do not exercise as if their lives depend on it—but they do."]

Your physical training program should correlate to whatever activity you select to become successful at or master. The requirements are different for running backs and accountants. Also, if your physically flourishing has been permanently compromised, then your habits must reflect that.

Still, we all have bodies. In terms of eating and exercising well, are there general guidelines that can serve those of us who are healthy and enable us to get started on a general strategy that will puts the odds of physically flourishing in our favor?

Yes there are, and they have been well understood by researchers for over twenty years. The best overall strategy is a combination of eating well and exercising well.

[*Sidebar quotation* from Tom Venuto: "There is a big difference between knowing what to do and doing what you know. Goals are the bridges that span this gap."]

The best overall strategy is **a balanced strategy**. Just as it's possible to eat too much or too little food, it's possible to get too much or too little exercise. Once again, centered living is the mark of excellence.

EXERCISING

The best overall strategy for exercising well is based on regular (i) strength training, (ii) fitness training, and (iii) flexibility training.

[*Sidebar quotations:*

From George Patton: "An active mind cannot exist in an inactive body."

From Frank Zane: "We have a choice as we age: don't exercise and suffer the physical liability of aging against your will, or exercise and consciously choose how you suffer."

From Frank Booth: "Human cells are maladapted to an inactive lifestyle."]

You are not flourishing physically if you are too fat. At least two out of three of us are too fat. The single best way to combat fat, which is biologically inactive energy storage, is to increase lean muscle mass, which is biologically active tissue, in other words, to improve your ratio of muscle to body fat.

As we age, it becomes more difficult to flourish physically for a variety of reasons:

    a. We lose whole motor units (sets of muscles and nerves that work together) as well as fast-twitch muscle fibers.

    b. Our base metabolic rates decline, which means in practice that a typical 70-year old requires 500 fewer daily calories than a 20-year old. 500 calories is about what I use in 45 minutes of brisk uphill walking on a treadmill. Imagine how much fatter we become from age 20 to 70 unless we either dramatically reduce daily caloric consumption or do a significant amount of daily exercise.

    c. Even if we don't gain weight, our percentage of body fat typically goes up—and the distribution of that fat is an even better predictor of chronic disease and mortality.

    d. The amount of oxygen that our bodies can process declines.

e. Our ability to control blood sugar (glucose) decreases; in other words, we tend to experience creeping blood sugar intolerance.

f. While HDL-cholesterol (the "good" kind) tends to remain constant, the LDL-cholesterol (the "bad" kind) tends to increase, which increases the total cholesterol/HDL ratio. The lower that ratio, the better.

g. There's no reason why aging should increase blood pressure, but it does in this country.

h. Bone density declines.

i. Aging reduces the body's ability to regulate its internal temperature.

j. Homocysteine level rises.

Are you immune to these and other effects of aging? Of course not. You have been aging since the moment of conception. If you are under thirty, you simply may not have noticed them yet.

Are you too fat to flourish physically? Here's a quick test: Simply divide your waist measurement by your hip measurement. A result of .9 or higher for men or .85 or higher for women indicates a greater risk for heart disease. This test is for fat distribution.

One measure of overall fat is your 'Body Mass Index' [BMI]. It's easily available online.[154] Your "ideal" BMI is associated with the lowest risk of chronic disease or mortality. Here it is: *age range/male/female:* twenties/21.4/19.5; thirties/21.6/23.4; forties/22.9/23.2; fifties/25.8/25.2; sixties/26.6/27.3; and seventies/27.0/27.8.

If you are aging and getting fatter, what can you do about it? *Plenty*.

(i) If you are not already doing it, one or two times weekly do intense strength training.

If you want to flourish physically, strength training is not merely an option. We never become too old to gain muscle mass and strength.

The single best way to combat fat is to increase lean muscle mass. The best way to add muscle is to do strength training. [Consider my short book <u>Weight Lifting.</u>]

(ii) Fitness training isn't optional for most of us either. The physiological and psychological benefits of an efficient cardiovascular system are difficult to overstate. It may be that you don't find it at all fun. So? Please detach from your likes and dislikes and just find a way to do it regularly.

(iii) Flexibility training is, by far, the least important of the three. It's easy, and it feels good. An effective routine only requires 15 or 20 minutes twice a week. It's best to do it after either strength or fitness training.

Exercise is natural. Immobility and inactivity aren't. Your body is the product of millions of years of evolution. Your ancestors were not immobile or inactive. You were born to move!

What should you do if you don't know how to exercise? Find out how. Then begin. It may be a lot more fun than you imagine. Whether it is or not, if you have not been exercising properly and begin, you'll soon be feeling a lot better. It may be a lot more beneficial than you imagine. Whatever you do to practice, you'll do it better if you are fitter, stronger, trimmer, and more flexible.

If you are skeptical about the relationship between physically flourishing and being a success or master, pay closer attention. Haven't you observed Presidents exercising? How many fat CEO's do you know? Do you see lots of fat popes and Zen masters? How many fat athletes did you observe at the last Olympics? Yes, there are exceptions, but

Babe Ruth and Mickey Mantle might have had even greater baseball careers if they'd taken better care of themselves.

What, exactly, is a comprehensive, balanced approach?

1. Do intense strength training once or twice weekly.

2. After strength training or twice weekly, do stretching for 20 minutes or so, and, if you are over 55, include some simple balancing exercises.

3. Two or three times weekly do intense fitness exercise.

That's it. That's sufficient and, if you want more, do more. Individualize it to fit yourself. Get your physician's blessing in advance. Here are some additional suggestions.

Everyone should take a whole week off from strength training every two or three months.

Stretching twice a week is a minimum. It will make you feel better, so you may stretch daily if you want to. Again, especially if you are over 55, include some simple balancing exercises.

The two or three weekly fitness sessions should be intense, which means they must be short. The same goes for the strength training workouts. Intensity and duration are inversely proportional.

The **good news** isn't just that this system is effective and practical, it's that you may obtain detailed assistance about it for free 24/7 online or at various websites, including http://www.lasting-weight-loss.com/ .

My co-webmaster and I have included sections introducing both fitness and strength training that include specific guidelines for exercising safely. You'll find a list of the best exercises as well as programs for beginners and intermediates.

In case you refuse to do any physical exercise other than walking, we've even including two walking programs.

EATING

[*Sidebar quotation* from Bill Phillips: "[N]othing tastes as good as being in the greatest shape of your life feels."]

Working out the best nutritional strategy for you should not be too complicated.

It's true that there is no single ratio of macronutrients (namely, carbohydrates, proteins, and fats) that works best for everyone. However, it you focus on eating natural foods that are as fresh and unprocessed as possible, you'll be doing a lot right.

Focus on getting plenty of protein and fat from natural sources. Eat at least 4 meals daily. Spread those meals through your waking day; eat soon after arising in the morning and don't eat within 3 hours of going to bed.

The best way to measure nutrient intake is simply to focus on grams of protein consumed. Take your lean body weight in pounds and divide it by the number of daily meals (usually 4). Eat about that many grams of protein from natural sources at each meal. For example, if you lean body weight is 160 lbs., average about 40 grams of protein per meal.

If you are eating protein from natural sources, you'll almost certainly be getting sufficient fat. With respect to carbohydrates, they are not needed for excellent health. It's usually best to restrict their consumption to 25 grams of less at least six days weekly.

Drink plenty of clean water. (We have a page on water intake at http://www.lasting-weight-loss.com.)

[*Sidebar quotations*:

From Kilmer S. McCully, M.D.: "The so-called 'diseases of Western civilization'—heart disease, obesity, hypertension, diabetes, cancer, dental caries, and others—became pervasive in human populations of deveopled nations during the twentieth century primarily because of the consumption of a diet containing refined carbohydrates, especially white flour and sugar."

From Philip J. Goscienski, M.D.: "your food style and your activity style will have a more profound effect on the way you look and feel, on your life span and your health span, than your genetic makeup or anything the science of medicine has to offer. / Getting older is what nature does to us; aging is what we do to ourselves."]

The purpose for implementing a rational strategy for flourishing physically is to help you become more excellent in whatever ways you choose.

In addition to becoming a success or a master in whatever fields are most valuable to you, why not also become at least a success in terms of training yourself physically? If you do, you'll discover for yourself how it will contribute to excellence in other areas of your life.

9.4 Mental

[*Sidebar quotation* from Wayne Dyer, Ph.D.: "The state of your life is nothing more than a reflection of your state of mind."]

Which habit[s] will increase the odds of continuing to be or becoming conscious, awake, free, loving, happy, and creative with increased understanding, theoretical wisdom, and ability to enjoy aesthetic experience?[155]

If you are confused or ignorant, how will that affect your training for success or mastery? If you are unclear about what you are trying to do and the training required for those goals, how could you possibly achieve excellence in any important activity?

Our most important ability is our ability to control our minds, our ability to focus.[156]

In reading and thinking through the ideas presented in this book, you are making critically important progress with respect to your mind. You are asking for and grappling with answers to exactly the right questions. That is precisely the kind of progress required.

Improved understanding is the result of clashing ideas against each other. Please do it daily.

[*Sidebar quotations*:

From George Patton: "If everyone is thinking alike, no one is thinking."

From Gary Hoy: "Your environment educates you 24 hours a day . . . You will be a product of your environment whether you like it or not. Take control of it, or it will continue to control you."]

Furthermore, you are doing it in the right sequence, namely, from the more fundamental to the less fundamental. Most people make the mistake of trying to proceed from the less fundamental to the more fundamental. Because there's no context established for serious enquiry, that procedure never works well. It's backwards.

Thinking is questioning. Since better thinking creates better lives, better questioning creates better lives. How could less fundamental questions be answered before more fundamental questions are answered? There's no more fundamental context in terms of which to answer them.

By way of contrast, we began Part II discussing by discussing the nature of the world and your world. Then we proceeded to discuss your nature and your fundamental attitude. Though it's neither typical nor easy, that's really the best, most efficient process. Good work.

This procedure eliminates intellectual obstructions before they become serious obstacles. The paralysis caused by conflicting values need not hamper your efforts at increasing excellence. It is a slower procedure in the beginning, but the resulting congruence will enable you to proceed much more rapidly than otherwise with your training.

It's important to continue to ask questions with answers that will empower you to question even better. The process of questioning should end only when you do. I think it was Albert Einstein who reminded us that the important thing is never to stop questioning.

A life of questioning is an examined life, which is the life that all philosophers lead. They lead it because they realize that the only alternative, the unexamined life, the life of a fanatic, is far worse.

This is **good news**. It means that you and I are not alone in our quest to live more excellently, to become successful or masterful. Many philosophers have preceded us; they've left us signposts and blazed the trail. Some of them, the sages, have succeeded. It would be foolish not to listen to them, not to let them help us.

[*Sidebar quotation* from Denis Waitley: "Continuous learning is the minimum requirement for success in any field."]

If you will read in an important work by a philosopher for just 30 minutes every day, in just ten years you'll have read approximately 240 books. If you'll read for an hour each day, you'll have read nearly 500 books in the next ten years. Can you imagine reading hundreds of books about living better without coming across some ideas worth testing for yourself? Can you imagine that *all* those ideas that you test for yourself will fail? Don't be ridiculous.

Furthermore, these days, there are plenty of audio and visual programs available that may be helpful. They are, in general, more expensive than books, but, for many people, they are even more effective tools than books. Furthermore, there are also dozens of seminars and courses available that also may be helpful. They are, in general, more expensive than audio or visual programs, but, for many people, they are even more effective than such programs.

Though unfiltered and loaded with negative, misleading, and false information, the world wide web also contains a lot of good information (like my websites) that's available for free. Some free e-zines (email newsletters) are excellent. There are many helpful how-to videos on YouTube.

Furthermore, there are often opportunities online for learning offline that are also free or inexpensive. For example, often there are telephone conference calls that last for sixty or ninety minutes that contain excellent information. It's true that they typically contain pitches for products, but you may simply ignore those (although, sometimes of course, the products are valuable).

Where should you begin? It depends upon what you want to succeed at or master. There are plenty of fine general books listed in the bibliography. A good way to find books that relate to a specific field that interests you is to use do a subject search at Amazon.com.

Once you narrow down your focus to a more specific activity, it's very likely that you'll find an extensive literature about it. Why not learn from the mistakes and successes of others? Especially when you already understand the big picture, imitation is much faster, much more effective, less expensive, and less painful than trial and error.

I've benefited from reading some recent works by psychologists, and I've briefly discussed some of the tools they recommend on the website. If you are interested in improving your thinking in practical ways, including how to get each day off to the best possible start, how to adjust your attitude, the role of commitment, the purpose of goal setting and how to do it effectively, learning, visualization, self talk, the time-line technique, and improving your personal environment, then I recommend taking a few minutes to read through the pages from the 'Psycholgy & Tools' section of lasting-weight-loss.com.

The most effective techniques ever devised for living better are spiritual habits. Please don't confuse 'spiritual' with 'religious.' The English word 'spiritual' comes from the Latin '<u>spiritus</u>', which means 'a breathing' or 'a wind.' So a spiritual practice is one based on awareness of the natural process of breathing. There's nothing supernatural or religious about it. Spiritual practices are effective for atheists, agnostics, and theists alike.

Meditation is a spiritual practice. Whether you are interested in becoming successful or masterful with respect to some specific activity, I hope that you experience for yourself how much benefit comes from a daily meditation habit. With respect to mastering life itself, I do not believe that it is possible without actually mastering some meditation practice.[157]

If you develop and sustain appropriate daily habits of reading, using some psychological tools, and meditating, you will be doing what is required to take charge of your mind and to make the best use of your most important asset.

9.5 Perceptual

Which habit[s] will increase the odds of enjoying your perceptual ability?[158]

[*Sidebar quotation* from Mozart about his ideas: "*Whence* and *how* they come, I know not; nor can I force them."]

If you are living in your head and separated from the other-than-human world around you, how will that affect your practicing for success or mastery?

The key to full enjoyment of your perceptual ability is to get out of your own way. In other words, full enjoyment of the other-than-human world comes from getting out of our own heads, from teaching ourselves how to live concretely rather than abstractly.

What this means in practice is letting go of attachment to our self-concepts. The more we actively practice doing that, the more successful at it we become. The more successful at it we become, the more habitual it becomes.

Contrary to what one might expect, sages are the experts when it comes to enjoying our natural perceptual ability. Without exception, sages are masters at some spiritual practice or other. It is this mastery that frees them from the tyranny of attachment to their self-concepts.

Therefore, practicing meditation is a very clever way to enjoy life.

Since he equates practicing Buddhism with practicing meditation, Thich Nhat Hanh says: "Practicing Buddhism is a very clever way to enjoy life." It's unexpectedly clever because one might expect that the discipline required to train the mind would result in less contact with the sensuous domain around us, but it's quite the opposite. Nobody knows how to enjoy eating a peach like a sage.

Sages repeatedly mention the never-waning freshness of life after spiritual awakening and enlightenment.

Nobody experiences the more-than-human more fully than a sage. Your ancient ancestors did it quite naturally, which is why you, too, have the ability to do the same. The only question is whether or not you will teach yourself how to use that natural ability. In other words, the only question is whether or not you will master some spiritual practice or other.

9.6 Emotional

[*Sidebar quotation* from Richard Dawkins: "It is not demeaning to human emotion that we try to analyse and explain it."]

Which habit[s] will increase the odds of emotional detachment?[159]

If you are emotionally troubled, if you lack peace of mind, how will that affect your practicing for success or mastery? Surely you have experienced how, when you are emotionally distraught, it becomes impossible to do anything normally. You cannot sleep normally, eat normally, relax normally, work normally, and so on.

You may try venting (expressing) your distress, but that only intensifies it. You may try ignoring your distress, but that's impossible.

The only short-term solution is to love your emotional distress, to notice and accept it just as it is. To do anything else would be to try to reject part of your life, and rejecting yourself is impossible. Loving your distress is making it the object of meditation.

The only long-term solution is to master meditation. The reason doing that works is because meditation weakens attachment to the self-concept. Since the core of every emotion is egocentric, reducing the attachment reduces the power of the ego. Eventually, with sufficient practice, sages are able to break that attachment, which enables them to enjoy freedom from emotional bondage, which comes from the tyranny of egocentricity.

[Again, for more on this important topic, read: http://www.lasting-weight-loss.com/emotional-eating.html or my books How to Stop Emotional Eating, How to Survive College Emotionally, and Emotional Eating.]

Though it may seem initially too good to be true, **emotional suffering is an option.**

Why? Mastering emotions is a real possibility.

9.7 Activity

[*Sidebar quotations*:

From Paul "Bear" Bryant: "It's not the will to win, but the will to prepare to win that makes the difference."

From Walter M. Bortz, III: "If who you are is what you do, when you don't you aren't."]

Which habit[s] will increase the odds of practical wisdom?[160]

If you are immobile and stuck, how will that affect your practicing for success or mastery?

Since there's no practicing without getting unstuck, the real key is simply to start practicing.

Once you have selected an activity to master and come up with an action plan for making mastery concrete in your life, just begin to work the plan. It really is that simple.

The more you think about beginning, the harder it will be to get started. Since life has burned us all, it's easy for us to dwell on negative experiences and potential negative outcomes. Since it is impossible to know that beneficial consequences will follow from practicing (since it is impossible for anyone to know what tomorrow will bring), it's easy for us to decide not to risk beginning since doing so might only bring us harmful experiences.

This is bad thinking. Deciding not to practice may itself bring more harmful than beneficial consequences. "I should not do anything" does not validly follow from "I don't know what will happen."

Once you have decided what you want and accepted a plan for obtaining it, risk beginning. Find or invent some reason just to start. The fact is that being inactive is depressing. It is natural to be active, and it is unnatural to be inactive. If you are depressed and worried and timid, begin anyway. As you begin to practice for success or mastery, you'll discover sooner or later that the **practicing is its own reward**.

[*Sidebar quotation* from George Leonard: "To take the master's journey, you have to practice diligently . . . But while doing so . . . you also have to be willing to spend most of your time on a plateau, to keep practicing even when you seem to be getting nowhere . . . you practice diligently, but you practice primarily <u>for the sake of the practice itself</u>. Rather than being frustrated while on the plateau, you learn to appreciate and enjoy it just as much as you do the upward surges . . ."]

In fact, if you stay attached to the hoped-for consequences of the practicing, you'll never achieve them. Why? It's because you'll be practicing while focusing on what is not (the future consequences) rather than on what is (practicing in the present moment). In other words, *practicing well requires focusing on the practicing*. It's only when we practice well that we become excellent (successful or masterful).

Once you begin practicing, let the practice teach you. Trust the process. Adjust the way you are practicing from the feedback that you are receiving. You are an individual; nobody else is exactly like you. You may learn how to begin to practice by imitating those who are successful or masterful. You should try to find a suitable teacher or mentor. However, you'll only become excellent by teaching yourself on the basis of experience. As you practice attentively, you'll figure out what works for you and what doesn't.

This is why no book of instructions can tell you exactly what you need to do to achieve success or mastery. The instructions may be excellent as far as they go, but they won't be individualized to you. They'll be too general. Use them to get started. Consult them as you continue to practice for additional suggestions that you may not have fully absorbed when you were just getting started. However, the key to success and mastery is to become absorbed in practicing. *Success and mastery are byproducts of proper practicing.*

[*Sidebar quotation* from W. Clement Stone: "Be careful the environment you choose for it will shape you; be careful the friends you choose for you will become like them."]

9.8 Daily Habits

So what's the bottom line?

If success or mastery is your A-1 goal, begin to examine everything you do, say, and think in terms of whether it is moving you towards that goal or not. Success and mastery result from proper practicing, which is a becoming.

This whole book is designed to help you achieve one of three goals: (1) become successful at an activity of your choice, (2) master an activity of your choice, and/or (3) master life itself. Since Chapter 12 is devoted to (3), let's restrict ourselves here to (1) and (2).

What daily habits contribute to becoming successful or masterful at some activity? What daily behaviors are appropriate for anyone serious about living excellently?

There are five:
    1. meditate well,
    2. study well,
    3. exercise well,
    4. eat well,
    5. and practice well.

If you do these five every day, everything else that is also important (such as being healthy, sleeping well, loving well, and so on) will automatically tend to take care of itself.

Permit me a few explanatory comments.

It is not necessary to do any of the last four to live well. Could there be a blind, deaf, starving sage who is confined to an iron lung (in other words, unable to exercise) who is living well? Yes. Such a sage's practice would be meditation. So that sage would be a master meditator and so would be meditating and practicing well even though he or she is unable to study, exercise, or eat well. If so, this shows how critical the practice of *meditation* is.

I consider meditation in Chapter 12. I think that 30 minutes daily of formal meditation practice is a minimum. If you don't have time for 15 minutes in the morning and 15 minutes in the evening, you are lying to yourself. In fact, 30 minutes in the morning and 30 minutes in the evening would be a lot better, and I've never met anyone who valued it correctly who couldn't find an hour a day for meditation.

Reading is the least expensive and most efficient way of studying. To read well is to read with concentration in some work about living well. If you don't regularly read, please fix that. However uncomfortable, reading well for just half an hour daily will result in important and lasting improvements in your life. You may substitute listening to an audio program, watching a videotape or DVD, or attending a seminar or course; however, it would be better to do any of those in addition to reading well for thirty minutes.

Study should be balanced with practice. There's too little study and too much study. In general, study should contribute to practice. Avoid the bane of intellectuals, the trap of endlessly studying without practicing. In my experience, an hour a day is about the maximum for effective study. Not long after that, a point of diminishing returns sets in. So, I suggest not less than half an hour and not more than one hour daily.

To exercise well, follow the plan I sketch in this chapter and present on the website for regular strength training, fitness training, and flexibility (and balance) training. Of course, if you are unable to do it, if you really are confined to an iron lung, then you'll have to skip it. If you are sick or injured, you may also skip it. However, please take the best possible of yourself physically. If you don't care for yourself, how could you care for others? Though there are lots of excuses, there's simply no reason why nearly all adult North Americans and others from developed countries cannot exercise well.

To eat well, follow the guidelines I present in my other books as well as at lasting-weight-loss.com. Unfortunately, eating well may not be an option for some people. If you are in prison or impoverished in a location where economic advancement is impossible such as a war zone or an economically backward country, you may not be able to eat well. At least for nearly all North Americans, however, although there are lots of excuses, there are no reasons for not eating well.

In terms of practicing your activity well, as long as you are meditating, studying, exercising, and eating well, the general rule is that, *the more you practice properly, the more quickly you'll become a success or a master.* There's no substitute for hard work at your craft.[161] The key to working hard is to enjoy it, to make the practicing fun, to think of it as play. Think of the mental and physical trainings as enabling you to practice better.

This all comes back to thinking well. Some will whine, "I can't do this, because I can't afford to eat well" or "I can't do this, because I don't have the time to exercise well." Not. That's bad thinking. If you look for excuses, your mind will supply them. That's what minds do: supply answers to questions.

To think better is to question better. So, practice asking empowering questions. "How can I afford to eat well?" "How can I find the time to exercise well?" Let your mind work on answering those questions—and it will supply answers to them. If it doesn't, the books that you read should.

Beware of focusing too much on the *what* of a regular activity and not enough on its *how*. Installing beneficial habits is not the same as living routinely and mindlessly. This may have been Miguel de Unamuno's point: "To fall into habit is to begin to cease to be." Perhaps, but not necessarily. The only effective way to avoid this difficulty is to have an effective spiritual practice.

A final question: if you were free to do whatever you wanted to do today, what would you do?

Once you become accustomed to meditating well, studying well, exercising well, and eating well, whatever else you would choose to do would be in addition to those activities. If you don't already understand that, please deliberately investigate it for yourself.

Once you understand it, notice that it is extremely likely that you are able, today, to meditate well, study well, exercise well, eat well, and practice well. This suggests an enormously empowering idea: **living well is available in the present moment.** It's available today, right here. It is only available now. We don't have to wait until tomorrow, and we don't have to regret missing the opportunity yesterday. Let all thoughts of past and future go in favor of focusing on the present moment. Live each moment as though you were showing your children how to live.

If you let it really sink in, that thought can permanently improve your life.

Chapter 10: Techniques

What's the best, quickest, and most effective way to excellent techniques?

Practicing (rehearsing, training). Practicing is the best way to achieve excellence in whatever you do. As the saying goes, "Don't learn the tricks of the trade. Learn the trade."

[*Sidebar quotation* from Beverly Sills: "There are no shortcuts to any place worth going."]

We are tempted, though, to try to learn specific techniques before anything else. Though it doesn't work, this is normal. Observing excellent techniques is what dazzles us and initially attracts us to mastery; however, those who practice excellence can make it look so easy that, when we try it for ourselves, we get discouraged.

10.1 Behold

Fifty years ago my beautiful but poorly educated girlfriend took a job as a go-go dancer, and I took to hanging around the club where she worked. Once Henny, the owner, hired a dance troupe for the night. They were young black men and two of them in particular were mesmerizing to watch. This was many years before break dancing became all the rage, but, looking back, what they were doing was something like a form of break dancing: they were spinning, jumping, twisting and jiving with fantastic skill and virtuosity. They were so good that they made it look easy.

I remember telling myself, "Hell, if I practiced, I could learn to do as well in a couple of months." Not. My bravado undoubtedly came from youthful insecurity. In truth, I never danced at all. Even then, part of me sensed that, no matter how hard and long I practiced, I might never be able to match those fellows. Whether they'd grown up dancing or not, they'd certainly worked hard to become excellent at their craft. Of course, it would have been wonderful to dance as well as they could.

[*Sidebar quotations*:

From Satchel Paige: "Work like you don't need the money. Love like you've never been hurt. Dance like nobody's watching."

From Betty Smith: "Look at everything as though you were seeing it either for the first or last time."]

What experiences have you had watching excellence in action?

Have you ever been in a crowd when a platform speaker seized everyone's attention and soon had some of the audience literally running to the back of the room to purchase whatever product he was pitching?

Have you ever been in an audience when a stand-up comedian began to speak, quickly had everyone laughing, and kept them laughing throughout his routine?

Have you ever been to a revival meeting and been swept up with the holy (or slightly less than holy) spirit?

Have you ever seen such a great performance by an athlete on, say, a basketball court, a gridiron, or the ice that you hated for the game to end?

Have you ever seen a master glassblower create a beautiful perfect piece with apparently almost no effort?

Have you ever seen a chess master visit a chess club, play dozens of games simultaneously, and win them all?

Have you ever seen a skilled pick-up artist walk up to a beautiful woman who was a stranger and walk away with her after a few minutes' conversation as if it were the most natural occurrence in the world?

Have you ever had someone who was a master at selling lead you in a perfectly relaxed, step-by-step way from mere curiosity to purchase?

Have you ever failed to put a business deal together only to watch someone else pick up the same pieces and easily put together a win-win-win deal?

Have you ever seen an actor being given an assignment and without hesitation improvise a brilliant performance that perfectly captured the essence of the character?

Have you ever seen a successful physician briefly examine a patient with serious, confusing symptoms and then accurately pinpoint the exact cause of the malady much to the astonishment of even other physicians?

Especially after having read this book, you should be much more alert for beautiful performances like these. Please appreciate them.

10.2 Beware

On the other hand, please don't be deceived by them. Especially after having read this book, you should be much more aware of what produced those performances.

Excellence looks easy. Why? It *is* relatively easy for those who are successful or masterful.

It is very important to realize, however, that it is *never* easy for anyone to become successful or masterful. Again, the key is focused, disciplined practice of some suitable kind. Success and mastery are the results of sustained, hard work.

[*Sidebar quotation* from Sir Winston Churchill: "Never give up. Never give up. Never, never give up. . . Success is going from failure to failure without loss of enthusiasm."]

You walk successfully, right? How did that happen? Was it easy? Though you don't remember your own case, you have since observed many infants learning to walk. They observe the successful people around them who are walking, and they commit themselves to learning. Suppose your own son does that. Suppose that he falls again and again. Do you tell him, "That's alright, son. You tried your best. You may quit now. I'll love you even though you cannot walk." Of course not.

What you do instead is to keep encouraging him to walk. Why? You love him. You know it will be good for him to be able to walk. The first few unsteady steps always result in falling. So? They are still glorious. We become successful walkers only after failing and failing and failing again. Failing is how we learn to make corrections. If you are unwilling to risk failing, you are unwilling to learn how.

In recent years, many brilliant people have had an unexpectedly difficult time teaching robots to walk on two legs. It's a fascinating process. It really has been a struggle. It's a wonderful ability that we tend to take for granted, at least until we become immobilized for some reason.

You became a successful walker by practicing until you got it right. You never quit. It wasn't easy; excellent never is. What you had was *persistence*. That's the key. Quitters fail, and winners persist.

[*Sidebar quotations*:

From Leonardo da Vinci: "Every obstacle yields to stern resolve."

From Ben Stein: "It is inevitable that some defeat will enter even the most victorious life. The human spirit is never finished when it is defeated . . . it is finished when it surrenders."

From Lance Armstrong: "Pain is temporary. It may last a minute, or an hour, or a day, or a year, but eventually it will subside and something else will take its place. If I quit, however, it lasts forever."

From A. Lou Vickery: "Four short words sum up what has lifted most successful individuals above the crowd: a little bit more. They did all that was expected of them and a little bit more."

From Samuel Beckett: "No matter. Try again. Fail again. Fail better."

From John C. Maxwell: "in life, the question is not *if* you will have problems, but *how* are you going to deal with your problems. Are you going to fail forward or backward?"

From Price Pritchett: "Life tests us—sometimes with problems, on other occasions with opportunities. The first question on life's many exams, though, is always the same: 'How will you explain the situation to yourself—with a positive or negative point of view?'"]

In the next chapter we'll examine options for excellence. It's critical to *pick an activity* that is really important to you. If you don't pick a valuable activity, you'll tend to quit when the practicing gets difficult. Quitting doesn't feel good, does it? You may blame the activity when you quit, but, really, your own opinion of yourself will drop. You'll like yourself less. In effect, you'll have rehearsed failure. *To begin to practice and then quit is to practice quitting.*

This is why it's also important to pick an activity that is not only important to you but one that is based on your unique abilities. If you were tone deaf, it would be foolish for you to attempt to become excellent as a musician or a singer, wouldn't it? If you were confined to a wheelchair, you presumably have the sense to know that you'll never make it as a hockey player. Selecting an activity that suits you automatically reduces your odds of quitting.

This is also why it's important to plan a training program that will enable you to advance one step at a time. *Take baby steps; keep risks small.* We all take baby steps when we begin to walk. We should all take baby steps when we practice for excellence. We become excellent bit by bit. Excellence is built from one small success to another.

[*Sidebar quotation* from The Buddha: "Remove your own impurities / Little by little."]

Each time you *practice*, you'll either be rehearsing success or failure. You'll be training a bit more effectively or a bit less effectively. Usually, it will seem as if you are on a plateau and neither jumping forward nor falling backward. In other words, you won't realize whether you are practicing successfully or not. Really, though, if your practice is focused and appropriate, even though you don't seem to be moving forward, you will be. You may be fortunate enough to have a teacher to encourage you, but you may not.

[*Sidebar quotations*:

From Chuck Coonradt: "Feedback is the breakfast of champions."

From Thomas S. Monson: "When performance is measured, performance improves. When performance is measured and reported back, the rate of improvement accelerates."]

A good way to think of it is to think of it as programming your brain for success. Though you are not aware of your brain itself, in practicing with focus you are programming it for habitual success. That's where the appearance of magic with respect to excellence comes from. It's letting go of the "I" to let the "Me" take charge. Learn to trust the "Me."

[*Sidebar quotations*:

From Maxwell Maltz: "the so-called 'subconscious mind' is not a 'mind' at all, but a mechanism—a goal-striving, 'servo-mechanism' consisting of the brain and nervous system, which is *used by* and *directed by* the mind."

From Andrew Matthews: "Have the discipline to do little things you don't like, and you can spend your life doing the big things you do like."

From Rick Pitino: "If we are not getting better, we are getting worse. There's no staying the same."]

It is critical to keep practicing, even though we don't seem to become more excellent at a steady rate or even if we seem to slip backwards. Think about the analogy to climbing a mountain. In real life, the climb is not always steadily upwards, is it? Real mountainsides also have troughs and flat spots that must be crossed. Sometimes one has to go down in order to go up. Remember the eaglet.[162]

Excellence requires persistent practice of an appropriate kind. In order to practice persistently, focus on the practicing itself and let go of the insidious habit of evaluating the quality of the practicing. Stop worrying about whether or not your practice session today went well or poorly. Did you focus as intently as possible on your practice for at least as long as you had decided to practice? If not, resolve to do better next time and forget about it; if so, forget about it.

We all have a tendency to second-guess ourselves. We all have a tendency to compare our progress to the progress of (real or imagined) others. The truth is much simpler: you are unique. Your journey to excellence will be unique. Nobody else's journey will exactly match yours. Please focus on your journey and forget what others are doing or not doing.

[*Sidebar quotations:*

From Roshi Philip Kapleau: "what works for one person may not work for another. If what is said applies to you, use it; if it does not, discard it. There is no one way, no should's or ought's ... you must find your own way."

From Paul J. Meyer: "Ninety percent of all those who fail are not actually defeated. They simply quit."

From William D. Singleton: "Too many people, when they make a mistake, just keep stubbornly plowing ahead and end up repeating the same mistakes. I believe in the motto, 'Try and try again.' But the way I read it, it says, 'Try, then stop and think. Then try again.'"

From Josiah H. DeFrees: "There is no royal road to anything. One thing at a time, and all things in succession. That which grows slowly endures."

From John Quincy Adams: "Patience and perseverance have a magical effect before which difficulties disappear and obstacles vanish."]

Work always takes the time it takes. How long will your journey to excellence take? Nobody knows. Stop asking that question; stop worrying about it. Worry wastes energy. Put your energy into practicing well. Focus on what you control. If you were building a house, would the house get built any faster if you worried about how fast it was being built? Of course not. The time it takes to build a house is the time it takes to build a house. The time it will take for you to become excellent is the time it will take for you to become excellent.

The reason we are tempted to worry about how long excellence takes is because we realize that life is short. Even if it's true that we'll have life spans of fifty or one hundred years, we obviously don't have life spans of thousands or millions of years.

This is why it is important to select activities for excellence very carefully. Time spent practicing X is automatically not time spent doing something else. We put ourselves under this time pressure. We should discuss this more (in the following section), because in this respect we are not being like sages. Sages do not feel themselves pressured by time. This is why it is said of them that, though they are *in* time, they are not *of* time. Unlike us, sages live fully in the present moment detached from past or future.

10.3 Practicing With a Job

If you are an adult who is neither retired nor is the recipient of someone else's financial support, it's quite likely that you have a job, that you are an employee. This is normal. You were brought up and educated with the assumption that you'd one day have gainful employment, that you'd go to work, that you'd get a job. Your years of formal education trained you how to be an employee. Now you work hard to learn a living by having a job. You either work for yourself or for someone else; either way, you have a job—it's just that you or someone else may own it.

Objection: Someone might have an important objection against the whole idea of achieving excellence, namely, *where is one to obtain the time, energy and money to do the necessary practicing?*

After all, suppose that you work forty hours weekly. Then there's the time spent preparing for work, recovering from work, and, perhaps, traveling back and forth to work. If you are married, you also need time to be with your spouse. If you have children, you also need time to be with your children. You need leisure time in the evenings and on weekends to do whatever you need to do to relax. You may spend about 56 hours weekly sleeping. You need time every day for routine tasks like cleaning, shopping, cooking, and maintaining home and, perhaps, lawn and garden. So, where are you going to get the time and energy to practice?

Just think of the necessary time recommended for flourishing physically' You might squeeze in resistance training sessions of thirty minutes twice weekly and two intense fitness-training sessions of fifteen minutes each twice weekly. However, where are you going to find the time to go for a walk, listen to a symphony, or enjoy a sunrise?

Furthermore, that doesn't even begin to allow for time to practice for excellence at whatever activity you choose. If you spend just an hour daily doing that, where are you going to come up with those seven hours weekly? Shouldn't it be at least two hours a day anyway? Furthermore, where are you going to come up with the money required to purchase training materials or to pay a teacher?

In other words, even if all this sounds good in theory, it's impractical. Given the already heavy demands on your time, energy, and money, how could you possibly train for excellence in the way suggested in this book?

The underlying problem here may be that *you feel trapped and alienated by your own life*. Remember the case of the disgruntled professor.[163] If so, you are normal. There's nothing wrong with you; you are not abnormal. At least since Marx, philosophers have frequently deplored the lack of freedom that most of us have. They have disagreed about how to cure it, but they have agreed in recognizing the problem. It seems that we have to work more and more just to maintain our economic position. In fact we seem to have less free time than our ancestors 20,000 or 50,000 years ago.

This is, by far, the most common objection to practicing well. Nearly all secondary objections that people have trace back to this primary one. Therefore, it's important to take it seriously and think through its answer carefully.

Reply: The *first* point to be made is that *there is no magic cure*. Alienation never just vanishes. Many people foolishly believe that, if they were to get lucky, some "external" event such as winning the lottery or inheriting a lot of money would cure all their problems. No. The old saying is true: "A fool and his money are soon parted." If you are broke and don't know how to tend money properly, what good would it do you to become wealthy quickly without knowing how to tend money properly? You'd soon be broke again.

Here's a simple question: has the world changed much in, say, the last five years?

It hasn't, has it? Oh, some people died, but others were born. Some political leaders fell, but others arose to take their places. Some friendships may have ended, but other friendships were renewed or created. Some wars may have ended, but others have begun. More generally, the sun still rises every morning. Spring still follows winter. Evaporation still follows condensation. Whatever goes up must still come down. Whatever is born still must die.

Will the world change much in, say, the next five years? Nobody knows. My guess, though, is that it won't. Five years from now, the sun will still rise every morning. Spring will still follow winter. Evaporation will still follow condensation. Whatever goes up will still come down. Whatever lives will still die.

A much more important question for you is this: will *your* world change much in the next five years? Will your surreality be in five years about like it is now or not?

The *second* point to be made in reply to the objection is that *your surreality is solely up to you.*

You and I have little power concerning whether or not the world will change. If you don't like the sun rising every morning, you'll have to learn to live with your dissatisfaction because there simply isn't anything you can do about it. You didn't create the world; you discovered it. Your power to affect it fundamentally is nil.

In a sense, that's good: you don't have to worry about sustaining the laws of nature.

[*Sidebar quotation* from The Talmud: "The sun will set without thy assistance."]

Nevertheless, and here's the critical point, you and I have power concerning our surrealities. After all, we create them. If we don't like them, *of course* we can change them.

There's nothing magic about changing our surrealities. We do it ultimately by taking full responsibility for our identity judgments and revising them in more effective ways. That has nothing to do with luck or happenstance. It has everything to do with making the most of our most precious asset, namely, the power we have to focus the mind.

It requires no extra time to live with a focused unified mind than to live with an unfocused scattered mind.

Once you absorb this thought, you'll realize that *living well takes no more time or treasure than living less than well*. The price for excellence is focus: it is neither time nor treasure.

[*Sidebar quotations:*

From Robert T. Kioysaki: "*Today* is the word for winners and *tomorrow* is the word for losers."

From D. Hutson, C. Crouch, & G. Lucas: "to live a successful life is to get not from here to there, but from there to here. 'Here' is being in the present moment in control of their thoughts."

From Goethe: "Every moment is of infinite value; for it is the representative of eternity."

From Alexander Graham Bell: "Concentrate all your thoughts upon the work at hand. The sun's rays do not burn until brought to a focus."

From Roshi Philip Kapleau: "What the Buddha's treatment amounts to is a therapy, a practice . . . a path . . . Among other things, it means becoming *completely* absorbed in *whatever* you do. . ."

From Jack Kornfield: "Everything we do in life is a chance to awaken."

From Michael Landon: "Somebody should tell us, right at the start of our lives, that we are dying. Then we might live life to the limit, every minute of every day. Do it! I say. Whatever you want to do, do it <u>now</u>! There are only so many tomorrows."

From Steve Hagan: "Meditation is simply to be here, *now.*"]

It is false that living better is the process of improving the ratio of positive to negative experiences; rather, it's the process of living in the present moment without separation from any experience.

So whether or not you live well or poorly doesn't follow from the nature of reality. Whether or not you live well or poorly follows from the nature of your surreality. Since you have full control over your surreality, *you have full control over whether or not you live well or poorly.*

This explains why, even if you are blind, deaf, friendless, near death, and living in an iron lung, you have the power to live well. Regardless of the circumstances, everyone has the power to live well. Of course, it doesn't follow that everyone understands this. Many, perhaps most, people don't understand it. Furthermore, many of those who do understand it may not understand how to do it.

Part of the reason may be that ignorance seems easier. Most people aren't philosophers; they don't seriously seek to figure out for themselves what it takes to live well. However sad, it's a fact. If I were unaware that I am able to live well, why would I worry about living well? If I don't know what is required to live well, why would I worry about doing it? All I need to do is to focus on survival, getting through this day with the minimum amount of effort.

[*Sidebar quotations*:

From Charles Dickens: "We forge the chains we wear in life."

From Gary Koyen: "If you don't do something differently, you'll end up where you are headed."

From Ralph Waldo Emerson: "Unless you try to do something beyond what you have already mastered, you will never grow."

From Kurt Vonnegut: "The door to hell is locked from the inside."]

Again, though, since living well is easier than living less than well, the appearance that ignorance is preferable is misleading.

Furthermore, and this is the *third* point, even though our power to affect the world fundamentally is nil, it doesn't follow that we don't have any power to affect our circumstances. We may, in fact, discover that we have a lot more power than we think we do.

[*Sidebar quotation* from Julia Cameron: "We attempt to think our way into right actions rather than act our way into right thinking."]

Let's consider a minor break out and, in the next section, a major one.

Answer quickly: do you watch too much television? Don't worry about the quantity—do you spend too much of your life watching television?

[*Sidebar quotation* from Deirdre Barrett: "Animals and man are indeed often harmed by what they desire—especially when encountering new stimuli for which evolution hasn't prepared them . . . Television is another instance of the supernormal stimulus . . . Humans have a basic instinct to pay attention to any sudden or novel stimulus, usually a movement or sound . . .[164]]

The cuts, visual zooms and pans, and sudden noises of television attract us: we reflexively orient towards them. It's addictive. We don't like many of its consequences such as obesity and other weight-related health problems and aggressiveness. Even educational programs tend to be superficial and take too much time to present their content. If you are hooked, what should you do?

With most addictions, the best way to free yourself is to quit rather than to cut back. It works well for television addiction as well as for additions to sugar and other refined (processed) carbohydrates. Quit completely for one month (or, even, just a week) and see if you don't feel much better. Yes, the first several days will be hard, but your system will quickly adjust.

Don't believe me? Just do it. Unplug the idiot box and you'll be amazed in a week or two at how much extra time you suddenly have for practicing what is important to you.

10.4 One Kind of Freedom

Let's consider a major break out. Suppose that you are a normal employee financially dependent upon your job. Do you have to stay that way? If you committed to doing so, could you change your own economic circumstances within the next five years?

Why not?

How? You have to do your job to earn a living, but you'd have to work on yourself to earn your financial freedom (independence). In fact, in terms of financial freedom, it's more important to work hard on yourself than it is to work hard on your job. Ideally, you should work harder on yourself than you do on your job.

[*Sidebar quotations*:

From Robert Kiyosaki: "Take responsibility for your finances or take orders all your life. You're either a master of money or a slave to it."

From Brian Tracy: "The number one reason that people never succeed financially is because it never occurs to them that they can do it. As a result, they never try. . . If you don't set goals for yourself, you are doomed to work to achieve the goals of someone else."

From Sherry Argov: "Financial neediness is no different than emotional neediness."]

As many have pointed out, there are really two economies. Different authors have different names for them. Let's simply call them the "wage" and the "profit" economies. Financial freedom is a good because it enables those who have it to buy back their own time and energy. In other words, being financially free enables us not to have to work at a job. It's good because it expands our range of choices. In effect, it's a way to purchase back the time of our lives. It doesn't mean that we will never again work at a job; instead, it means that we will never again *have* to work at a job. It gives us a choice. To have a choice is to be free to choose. Being free to choose is better than not being free to choose.

If you were financially free, you could, if you wanted, spend all day long doing whatever you wanted to do, for example, practicing, exercising, reading, meditating, and loving. Now there's a plan for a great day.

It is possible to live well without being financially free, but it's not possible to live well without being temporally free. As Socrates says, "The free man always has time at his disposal."[165] Becoming financially free is one way to create temporal freedom for yourself (and your family).

How could you become financially free? Excellent question: the best way is by deliberately shifting from the wage to the profit economy. Instead of working for money (wages), teach yourself how to have your money (profits) work for you.

How could you do this? There are two ways: either amass a big pile of money and live off the interest it generates or actively nurture a stream, or, better, multiple streams, of income until your passive (residual) income exceeds your expenses.

The first way is the traditional idea of retirement. If your father, for example, worked for a company for forty years and saved some money from each paycheck, that savings may have grown through compound interest until it became a big pile of money. Once the pile became sufficiently large to throw off in interest payments an amount that matched or exceeded his wages from that job, your father was free to retire (or not).

The second way is to set up sufficient passive income. Write a book once and, if it sells well and keeps selling, enjoy its royalties forever. Set up a business that becomes so successful that it will run on its own, then back away from it and enjoy receiving a percentage of its profits each month. Buy some apartment buildings and use their rents to pay off their mortgages; once you own them free and clear, pay all expenses (management fees, taxes, repairs, and so on) as necessary and put the rest of the income into your pocket. If you investigate "How can I generate sufficient passive income to free myself from having to work at a job?" you'll discover that there are lots of ways to do it.

Since amassing a large pile of money can take decades, let's concentrate here on the idea of your setting up a sufficiently large passive income relatively quickly.

The big idea is simple. Understand that *others pay us when we become valuable to them*. When you become ill, will you consult your physician and then pay for the consultation? Of course. Why? Your physician is valuable to you; unless you are yourself an expert when it comes to medicine, you are willing to pay for an expert opinion. When your car engine breaks down, will you pay a mechanic to fix it? When your teenage son gets arrested, will you pay an attorney to defend him? When your house becomes too small, will you pay a builder to expand it or build you a bigger one?

Others will pay us very well when we become very valuable to them.

Is your income lower than you'd like it to be? Is it more active than you'd like it to be? If so, why don't you fix that?

In other words, why don't you make yourself more valuable to other people? If you become more valuable to them, they'll pay you more. Supposedly, Tony Robbins made himself so valuable to others that they were willing to pay him $1,000,000 for an hour's work. At that rate, might you not want to work an hour at least every few months?

The fundamental idea here is quite simple: make yourself more valuable to others and then let them know that you are now worth more to them.

How should you implement this idea if you want to? There are five steps to the process, which begins with demand.

(1) Find out what they want. They don't want just one thing; people want lots of different kinds of goods and services.

(2) From that list, which one would you be best at supplying? Which one best matches your talents? Which one could you supply better than it's being supplied now? Once you decide, commit to it.

(3) Do whatever it takes to become excellent at it.

(4) Once you are more valuable in that way, let others know that you are now more valuable to them. Market your new ability.

(5) When they invite you to help them, serve them well.

If you implement this process, your income will automatically rise. If you serve them really well, you could make ten or a hundred times the income you now earn as an employee. In this sense, the market is quite fair; your income accurately reflects the assessment of others concerning your value to them.

Please don't misunderstand: I'm *not* arguing that you should work to become financially free. Yes, it's a good, but that doesn't automatically mean that it's one that you should select as an activity to master. Maybe you should, maybe you shouldn't. It's perfectly possible to live well without being financially free.

My point is that there's an extremely good response to the objection. If nothing is preventing you from becoming financially free and if you think you should become financially free, then why don't you? If you are living in solitary confinement, it's not an option for you at this time. However, at least for most adults in developed countries, it is a genuine option. The only thing stopping you is you.

Of course, many people stop themselves. That's because they are fanatics attached to living inside their own conceptual boxes. Instead, I suggest becoming a philosopher relentlessly searching for a better way to live.

[*Sidebar quotation* from a saying: "Tell me who you hang out with and I'll tell you who you are."]

It you live freely in a developed country and are an economic failure, it's not because the marketplace doesn't work properly. It's simply because you haven't yet done what you need to do to improve yourself to make yourself valuable to others. If you teach yourself how to give people what they want in an ethical and legal way, you'll get whatever you want. It's a calculated way of doing what is best for you by doing what is best for others.

[*Sidebar quotation* from Napoleon Hill: "It is literally true that you can succeed best and quickest by helping others to succeed."]

If you really don't have the time required to practice sufficiently to become excellent in your chosen field, why not become at least successful financially? If you are presently a wage-slave and worked well to free yourself financially for the next sixty months, could you? Why not? If you don't try, failure is guaranteed. Opportunities abound.

There are many thousands of your neighbors who have already freed themselves financially. They purchased back the time of their lives. Why not investigate how they've done it and emulate them?

Especially if you are young and aren't sure what activity to select, why not initially select one that will free you to become excellent in other domains? Financial freedom passes that test.

Furthermore, doing it has a great hidden benefit: it will force you to focus on others. You more quickly and thoroughly you focus on helping others, the more quickly you'll become financially free. It decreases self-centered thinking.

In other words, it's true that you cannot guarantee yourself a financially bright future. Nobody can do that. Nobody has any idea what tomorrow will be like. The past is history, and the future is mystery. However, suppose you build a company, free yourself financially by stepping away from it while taking a percentage of the profits regularly, and it eventually fails through no fault of your own? Guess what? You already know how to build another one. Your income can be taken away, but nobody will ever be able to take away your ability to serve others, right?

[*Sidebar quotation* from Abraham Lincoln: "The only security a man can ever have is the ability to do a job uncommonly well."

From Douglas MacArthur: "There is no security on this earth; there is only opportunity."

From Wayne Dyer, Ph.D.: "Only the insecure strive for security."]

Practical education and character development are the chief benefits of financial freedom. Ample passive income is what attracts many to financial freedom. In fact, financial freedom might still be attractive even if all you did was improve yourself and you never made a penny. How? The education involved should teach you how to serve others more effectively, in other words, how to become less egocentric. What's more valuable than reducing egocentricity?

The people with lots of money didn't gain it because they were selfish. It's true that their motivations may have been selfish; their motivations may have been pure self-interest. It doesn't follow, however, that they gained their wealth by being selfish. In fact, they gained their wealth by becoming valuable to others (and, so, it turned out to be in their self-interest to become valuable to others).

It's important not to confuse wealth with value. As I have stated, I believe that we are all infinitely valuable. Obviously, some of us are wealthy and others aren't. In other words, being valuable in the marketplace is not the same as being valuable.

As a rule, sages are not wealthy people. In practice, as Aristotle points out, "philosophers can easily be rich if they like."[166] I'm not sure about the "easily" part, but some philosophers have certainly done it. For example, Thales, who is traditionally regarded as the first western philosopher, did it by cornering the wine harvest one year. Many, though, have lacked that kind of ambition.

In theory, however, there's really no correlation. There's no reason why sages couldn't be wealthy, and some have been.[167] The only theoretical point is that it's impossible for a sage to be attached to being wealthy. In other words, though wealth itself is not an evil, because all attachments are poisons, any attachment to wealth is a poison. Wealth is a good, but attachments to goods are not themselves goods.

In other words, it's not money that is bad: it's the love of money that's bad. The truth is that money itself is neither good nor bad; it's neutral. In terms of practicing, it can help or hinder.

What should you do if you genuinely think that it might help you? I happen to believe that the best way to become financially free is to own a business system. A business system is like a money tree.

What's the best way to provide yourself with fruit indefinitely? If you are like most people, you'll go to the grocery store and buy some, and you'll keep repeating that process whenever you want fruit.

There's a better way: own a fruit tree. If you'll go to the one-time trouble and expense of buying, planting, and nurturing a fruit tree, year after year it will yield fruit with little or no additional bother. If you want lots of fruit, plant and nurture a whole orchard. Why rely on only one tree for fruit?

Lesson: by doing today what most people won't, you'll be able to live tomorrow as most people can't.

Why not grow a money tree to enjoy financial freedom? A business system is a money tree. Once you have created and nurtured it, it will continue to provide you with money with little or no additional bother. Doing so would provide you with all the time freedom required for practicing well.

Here's an important point: if you want something, give it away.

If you want a punch in the nose, give one away. If you want a friend, give friendship away. If you want more time and money, give them away. This is simply a law of causation.

[*Sidebar quotations:*

From Saint Francis of Assisi: "It is in giving that we receive."

From Ralph Waldo Emerson: "The only gift is a portion of thyself."

From Ken Keyes, Jr.: "Service is love in work clothes."

From Lao-tzu: "The sage does not take to hoarding. . . The more he gives the more he abounds."]

If you want to own a money tree that enables you to enjoy ample time and money, first give away time (your laboring activity, your sweat equity) and money (whatever it costs for your education and business start-up). Once others in the marketplace learn that you are able to improve their lives by giving them time and money (in whatever way of the many possible ways to do that you have chosen), they'll give you in return lots of time and money. Of course, just as different kinds of seeds are available for growing fruit trees, there are different kinds of seeds available for growing money trees. The kinds of seeds that will work best for you depend, of course, on your particular circumstances.

You don't have to plant a fruit tree or a money tree. Neither is necessary for living well. If, though, one might benefit you, why not educate yourself more about the possibility?

Perhaps you'd like financial freedom and the practical options it provides, especially freeing up large chunks of time for formally practicing the techniques appropriate to excellence in your chosen field. Selecting an activity to master is the topic of the next chapter. As a transition to that topic, permit me to encourage you to think about the answer to a question related to financial freedom.

10.5 Reaction

How did you react to the idea of your becoming financially free? If you were already familiar with that idea, how did you react to it when you first learned about it?

I ask because your reaction may indicate something important about you. It may be an indication of your openness to change and willingness to grow.

[*Sidebar quotation* from Bob Burg: "Presented with a chance to break out of mediocrity, reclaim their lives, provide better for their family, give more back to the planet, and live a life of freedom . . . most people will just say no."

From S. Orman: "The road to financial freedom . . . begins with your thoughts . . . When it comes to money, freedom starts to happen when what you *do, think*, and *say* are one."

From Stuart Wilde: "Money doesn't give you real strength; it just keeps you comfortable while you experience your dysfunction."

From Earl Nightingale: "[M]oney is like good health, in that we are concerned about it to the extent that we don't have it."]

I discovered how stimulating an idea it was when I taught a course in ethics for business majors some years ago. Many people (not just undergraduates), of course, do as little thinking as possible. Instead of trying to break out of the conceptual boxes in which they live, they try to prevent damage to any of the ideas to which they attach themselves. It's sad.

At first, people may be skeptical that anyone could be financially free. Alternatively, they'll assume that financial freedom is always based on luck, such as receiving a large inheritance or some genetically based characteristics. It's easy, however, to provide them with many specific examples that undermine that idea. Usually one or two students in a class will have a relative who is financially free. Once the fact that many people are financially free because of their own efforts sinks in, it becomes impossible for anyone to cling to the belief that financial freedom isn't really possible.

The remaining question is: "Is it possible for me to become financially free?" There are really only two answers: "yes" or "no."

Those who answer "no" simply build financial dependence into their surrealities. Of course, unless they change their thinking, they never become financially free. It's a self-fulfilling prophecy. Even if their world permits others to be financially free, there's no room in it to think of themselves as financially free. Typically, there's some rationalization against it such as thinking that all wealthy people are crooks.

Why would anyone think this way? It seems easier. Once financial freedom is recognized to be a genuine option, it requires a good reason not to pursue it since it's an important good. After all, one need not desire financial freedom for oneself. Why not have plenty of money to help one's family and friends? Does an aging relative need help with medical or surgical costs? Could a friend use some money for counseling for a troubled child? Could you pay off the mortgage on your parents' house? Does an impoverished relative need a down payment for a house? Could you find a youngster with the aptitude but no money for college? Could your favorite charity better enable people to help themselves if they had more income?

How does my laziness or inconvenience rank with respect to important benefits like those? This is the problem: once we admit that it's not only possible but also beneficial, then we have to decide whether or not to pursue it. If we decide against pursuing it, we need a good reason. Since it could help us give time and money to others, I'll think that either my reason for not doing it is simply selfish or I am pursuing an even more important way of helping others.

Those who answer "yes" can get so enthusiastic that they rush out and embrace the first opportunity that presents itself. When they do that, the results are predictable. Lacking a genuine understanding of what success or mastery requires, they fail. They want to fix others rather than fix themselves. That's not the right path. Then, once they fail, they feel guilty for failing and may permanently retire to lick their wounds.

Yes, the idea of personal financial freedom is a stimulating idea. How did you react to it? What does that say about you?

Let's think more carefully about the way you are and the way you might be.

Part III: Making Mastery Concrete

Part II

Chapter 11: Selecting An Activity To Master

[*Sidebar quotation* from Swami Ajaya: "Some of us would like to leave the restlessness and confusion of the world behind. We would like to go on a permanent holiday, somewhere in the mountains or in the country where we can enjoy peace and tranquility. We think 'If only I were in a more serene environment, then I could work on myself, I could calm myself down and begin to feel good.' But we don't realize that our most intimate environment is our own mind and that we take this with us wherever we go, in whatever we do. We have to learn to relate to this internal environment, and once this is achieved we can be comfortable in any surroundings in which we may find ourselves . . ."]

"Know thyself" was inscribed over the entrance to the ancient Greek temple at Delphi. The concept of self is the most important and fascinating concept. Nothing is closer to us than ourselves, but how can our self-concepts be so malleable? Nothing is more natural than to divide the world into self and other, yet, since we were not born with self-concepts, how can this be?

We have seen[168] that a self is a cluster of five qualities. If you lacked any one of them, you wouldn't be what you are. Each is necessary, but none by itself is sufficient. Since an object without qualities cannot be thought, it's impossible to think of your self as an independent substratum.

Your self is an object in the dynamic domain of becoming; it is not an object in the static domain of being.

Decisions create uniqueness. Who is the decision maker? Again, it's impossible to think of a qualityless entity somehow "behind" the decisions. If it had a quality, it could be conceptualized; because it lacks all qualities, it cannot be conceptualized. If so, there are experiences without a self who has those experiences.

We've also seen that much of what we do in our daily lives is habitual or automatic; it does not require conscious thinking.[169] In fact, conscious thinking can inhibit automatic, appropriate behavior in, for example, an emergency.

Thinking cannot go farther here. This may seem surprising, even shocking. However, it's not. Someone acting masterfully is acting beautifully without incongruent parts working against each other. To think is to conceptualize, and to conceptualize is to separate. To think nonseparation or unity is obviously impossible.

[*Sidebar quotation* from Jianzhi Sengcan: "To seek Great Mind with thinking mind / is certainly a grave mistake."]

However, there is direct experience of unity, which is the home of mastery. Maslow calls masterful experiences "peak" experiences; Csikszentmihalyi calls them "optimal" experiences. Many call them "flow" experiences.

11.1 Flow

A masterful or flow experience occurs whenever there is direct experience of unity.[170] 'Direct' here means 'nonconceptual.' In a flow experience, there is no separation, even just separation in thought. In a flow experience, one is not separated from whatever one is doing. One may be washing dishes or wielding a sword in combat or arranging flowers or writing a symphony. If one is doing well, there is no separation between oneself and the doing: one is the doing. There is no remainder, no ontological surd. There is no ego.

This is the profound truth behind Aristotle's idea that ordinary things are what they are because of their work.[171] The work of a tree, for example, is the work of growth and reproduction. It's not that a tree is separated from its work: a tree is its work. To be is to be at work. There are different kinds of things because there are different kinds of work.

Are trees happy? That's an odd question. We don't usually think of trees as the kinds of entities that are either happy or unhappy. Try this: would a tree be unhappy if, while it was doing its work, it was thinking about something else? If a tree could be separated in that way, then it would be unhappy. Separation causes dissatisfaction.

Sit perfectly still for twenty minutes and observe how your mind jumps around. Your body is still, but your mind is anything but still. It seems utterly chaotic, doesn't it? Two classic analogies are that our thoughts are scattered like a troupe of monkeys jumping around in the forest canopy or like beads of water in a cascading waterfall. It seems natural for consciousness to be restless and incessantly active. It seems natural for mind to be disordered. Uncontrolled, it naturally seems to drift towards entropy.

Your ultimate purpose in reading this book is to understand how to live better. Since your life is your experiences, *your experiences must improve for your life to improve.*

Experiences can be broken down into *what* and *how*. They can be described in terms of *what* is happening and *how* it is happening. If you are doing something, the activity itself is *what* you are doing and the way that you are doing it is *how* it is happening.

Both the *what* and the *how* are important when we evaluate experiences. In masterful experience, both the *what* and the *how* are correct. However, the *what* is less important than is usually thought and the *how* is more important than is usually thought.

In effect, someone who masters life, a sage, masters getting the *how* consistently right so that it matters little *what* is being done, whether the sage is walking or eating or talking or whatever. **A fully enlightened sage is always enjoying a masterful experience, which is what it means to live in abiding joy.** Sages live without separation from their doings. They live without ego. They are fully present. They directly experience unity.

In this chapter let's focus on getting the *what* right and in the next chapter let's focus on getting the *how* right. To anticipate, getting the *how* right means acting wholly without ego and with detachment from the outcome. To get the *how* right is to act without separation.

[*Sidebar quotation* from Sylvia Boorstein: "attachment to being somewhere other than here creates suffering in the mind right now."]

Doing without attachment is easier for some *whats*, some kinds of activities, than for others. The purpose of this chapter is to help you select an activity to become excellent at performing, preferably to master (and not merely to become successful at doing).

[*Sidebar quotation* from Andre Gide: "One doesn't discover new lands without consenting to lose sight of the shore for a very long time."]

Since you are unique, there's no general rule for making a selection, no recipe that will work for everyone. However, there are some important, useful guidelines.

Here's the plan for the rest of this chapter: Let's begin considering you and then proceed to the guidelines.

11.2 Heritage

We've seen how we each have natural preferences concerning what naturally energizes us, what kinds of information we naturally remember and notice, how we naturally make decisions, and how we prefer to organize our surrealities.[172] This provides us with a useful tool for understanding the similarities and differences between others and ourselves..

It would be foolish not to take these preferences into consideration when selecting an activity to master. There is an analogy between this task and vocational counseling. A "sensor" might more naturally enjoy, say, work as a police officer, nurse, elementary school teacher, or real estate agent, whereas an "intuitive" might more naturally enjoy work as a lawyer, psychologist, researcher, or computer programmer.

However, please don't take this analogy too far. Some *whats* may come more naturally to you than others, but it's more important to focus on the *how*. Personality type is *not* a critical factor in selecting an activity to master. On the other hand, why ignore it?

By way of contrast, at least with respect to ruling out certain kinds of physical activities, your physical heritage is a critical factor. Let's briefly consider your brain, your sex, and your birth order.

Given its well-protected location, it's very difficult to study the *brain*. Perhaps its most amazing feature is that, unlike other organs, it seems to grow backwards. Synapses are the connections between brain cells (neurons) that enable them to communicate with each other. All our thoughts and behaviors depend upon the formation of appropriate synaptic connections among neurons.

Here are two facts that, taken together, are puzzling. *First*, your brain got big very quickly. Your body created your first neuron about 42 days after conception and just 120 or so days later your brain had one hundred billion neurons. Some 60 days prior to birth, your neurons started trying to communicate with each other by literally reaching out (on strands known as 'axons') to each other. Each successful connection formed a synapse. By the time you were three years old, *each* of your hundred billion neurons had formed 15,000 connections. This extensive and intricate pattern was unique to you. *Second*, your brain then shrank into adulthood. Many of the connections were not used and, so, disintegrated. By the time you hit your 16th birthday, half of your connections had permanently disappeared.

As your brain became smaller, you became smarter. Why? Billions of connections were closed down to enable you to exploit more fully those that remained.

Now, as an adult, you are thinking about how to improve your life. How can you best continue to learn how to improve?

There are only three ways: strengthen your remaining synaptic connections, lose more of your extraneous synaptic connections, or develop more synaptic connections. Since it takes a relatively large amount of energy to create the biological infrastructure to develop new connections, this is the least efficient of the three ways. So your best strategy for improving your life is to focus on the other two ways.

How can you strengthen your remaining synaptic connections and lose more of your extraneous synaptic connections?

It's by figuring out what you are best at and concentrating on becoming excellent at an activity related to that. That will maximize your abilities by strengthening your favored synaptic connections and, since you'll be focusing on what you do well instead of on what you do poorly, that will automatically weaken your extraneous synaptic connections.

So the best strategy is *to maximize what you do well (your abilities or talents) and to minimize what you do poorly (your disabilities)*. This strategy is rooted in the physiology of your brain. It's the critical strategy for living more excellently. [See the next section.]

Your *sex* is also an important part of your physical heritage.

Whatever works tends to persist; whatever doesn't work tends not to persist.

As an individual, this insight explains why your most important clues concerning your talents come from examining your habits. [See section 5 below.] When you were a child, like the rest of us, it was natural for you to keep doing whatever you did well and for you to avoid doing whatever you did poorly. In this way, you developed habits based on your talents. Control of how you did them moved from your prefrontal neocortex to your basal ganglia. As you practiced them more, you became better at them, which reinforced those behaviors.

To uncover your talents, then, simply examine your habitual behaviors. Of course, external influences such as parental, peer, and cultural pressures led you in certain directions rather than others, but try to discount those when thinking about your talents.

Think hard about what you were good at growing up.

(This also explains one reason why it is sometimes extremely difficult to let go of old habits and to develop new ones. The old habits may be based on talents whereas the new ones may not be.)

As a group, this insight grounds evolution. Evolution is the idea of descent with cumulative genetic modification. Organisms evolve initially due to various random processes. However, the process itself is intelligible; in many organisms, including humans, it is based on two fundamental factors, namely, natural selection, which adapts species to their environments, and sexual selection, which shapes each sex in relation to the other sex. We evolved to have brains that predispose us to survive and mate (in other words, engage in courting, sexual, and parenting behaviors).

So the results of recent research in evolutionary biology and psychology should not be ignored as we engage in the ongoing process of trying to understand ourselves. They offer explanations of many important behaviors. It's often very important to keep in mind our natural dispositions to survive and mate. With respect to our topic of living more excellently, excellence does require survival, but it doesn't require mating. In fact, like celibacy, mating has disadvantages as well as advantages.

There are significant differences between male and female brains. Since it's obvious that there are significant differences between male and female bodies, this is hardly surprising. These differences have evolved from the different roles males and females play with respect to mating. Do these differences relate to selecting an activity to master?

Yes, of course. Why do you think there are no female running backs in the National Football League? Like most males, females lack the necessary physical attributes for that work. (Given the nearly 100% injury rate, even if they could do it, women might have the good sense to choose not to do it anyway.) The point is only that your sex may rule out certain activities as being suitable for you to master.

Your *birth order* is another important part of your heritage.

Why did your synaptic connections develop as they did? Nobody yet has anything like a detailed explanation. However, in recent decades there has been some very interesting work that yields important clues, such as birth order. First-borns are influenced by their birth order in different ways than children born later.

If this topic interests you, I recommend Frank Sulloway's <u>Born To Rebel</u>, in which he applies evolutionary theory to birth order. If you have siblings, it may explain some of the similarities and differences between you and your siblings.

It would be irresponsible for me not to mention taking heritage into account. It may provide some useful clues. Still, such clues as it provides are weak and negative. Except to rule out some activities, there's not much valuable guidance here. Perhaps there will be some day. For now, let's expand the strategy already mentioned.

11.3 Strategy

As unique human beings, we each find ourselves with strengths and weaknesses. Is it a better strategy to maximize strengths or to shore up weaknesses? Consult your own experience.

Have you ever mastered anything unusual? If so, what did you do? Did you develop strength into mastery or did you develop weakness into mastery?

[*Sidebar quotation* from Martin Seligman, Ph.D.: "The keystone of high achievement and happiness is exercising your strengths, not correcting your weaknesses."]

Even if it were possible to turn weakness into mastery, why bother? Life is limited: why not spend less time and energy turning strength into mastery?

It's not possible to turn weakness into genuine strength anyway. Consider an analogy.

What would your strategy be if you were crippled, physically handicapped? Would you, for example, spend your days somehow trying to run so that you could play running back in the National Football League? Of course not! That would be idiotic. If you were crippled physically, you'd do damage control with respect to your limited physical abilities and concentrate on developing other talents. You'd be wise to identify nonphysical talents and hone them into strengths.

Well, *we are all handicapped in the sense that we all have weaknesses*. When it's necessary or important to develop weaknesses, it is often possible to increase our understanding and skills and to become competent in a naturally weak area. However, it's hard work, and natural weaknesses never become areas of consistent excellence. We never really feel good about them. That's not the way to excellence.

According to Benjamin Franklin's analogy, undeveloped talents are like "sundials in the shade." Why hide your sundials in the shade?

[*Sidebar quotation* from M. Buckingham & D. Clifton: "The real tragedy of life is not that each of us doesn't have enough strengths, it's that we fail to use the ones we have."]

Just as we all have weaknesses, so *we all have talents* (aptitudes, strengths). (I discuss in the next chapter your most important talent.) Everyone may become excellent at something. To select an activity for you to excel at, identify your talents and develop them into strengths, important skills. (See sections 5, 6, and 7 below.)

11.4 Entrapment

Before discussing how to do that, it's important to point out an important virtue of the procedure adopted in this book. The procedure in Part II involves growing from the more fundamental to the less fundamental.

This, though, goes against the normal procedure, which is to move from the less fundamental to the more fundamental. For example, we become mesmerized by someone's display of excellent techniques, which we may then try to emulate—only to discover that isolated techniques or skills don't work well. To work well, they need to be thoroughly integrated on solid fundamentals. Once we realize this, we either quit or have to begin to work on getting all the fundamentals right.

Someone who has done insufficient work on the more important levels of the mastery monument is blocked from using the strategy of building on ability. The blockage comes from being conceptually trapped. It comes from having so far failed to break the bonds of our own concepts. In other words, we often entrap ourselves. As Joanna Macy points out[173], this happens in two primary ways.

One way this happens is when someone attaches to the idea that the world is a battlefield. Life is understood to be a constant struggle. Life is war. It's a war between the forces of good and evil, the forces of light and darkness. The ancient Zoroastrians and Manichaeans have many descendents today. These are people who excel at feeling threatened. They whip themselves up by arousing courage, anger, and hatred. They become attached to their worldview, convinced that their surrealities are reality. They often become self-righteous, militant fanatics. Living excellently is understood by them as a life of constantly struggling to vanquish their unbelieving foes.

[*Sidebar quotation* from the Buddha: "People with opinions just go around bothering one another."]

A milder version of this is that the world is a classroom. The purpose of life is to pass the tests that life provides as challenges. If you fail a test, you get to repeat it; you have to keep repeating it until you learn its lesson. If you pass a test, you get to go on to the next test. The more tests you pass, the more moral you become. This view leads to a kind of contagious fundamentalism that is particularly popular with fanatics who are stuck in monotheistic religions.[174] Living excellently is understood by them as a life of constantly struggling to become morally superior.

The other way this happens is when someone attaches to the idea that the world is a trap. The purpose of life is to escape from the trap. We may escape from the trap only by freeing ourselves from our lower physical nature and emphasizing our higher mental or spiritual nature. We naturally have physical desires to gain what we like and to avoid what we don't like. We need to break free from these desires by dissolving them. This is why, for example, many take the path of asceticism, in other words, physical renunciation and denial. They understand living excellently as a life beyond the entrapment of the physical domain.[175]

Is reality either a battlefield or a trap? As we have seen, reality itself, unconceptualized reality, is beyond either conceptualization. It is neither a battlefield nor not a battlefield; it is neither a trap nor not a trap.

It is perfectly possible to live one's whole life with the genuine, fundamental conviction that the world is a battlefield. It is also perfectly possible to live one's whole life with the genuine, fundamental conviction that the world is a trap. These are very popular alternatives that provide certainty for many people. Even if what's available is only delusional, many have a high need for security. If fear is the ultimate explanation for this need for security, that would explain why these fanaticisms are so common. They are, like all egocentric attachments, poisons.

Of course, *if* the world is a battlefield, *I* am on the side of the forces of goodness! Of course, *if* the world is a trap, *I* am on the side of the wise who are freeing themselves from it. Put this way, it's not difficult to see that these are *egocentric* attachments, attachments designed to benefit ourselves. These attempts conquer fear are attempts to raise self-esteem. After all, if I'm fighting the battle on the side of the good guys or if I'm getting out of the trap that otherwise catches all those other foolish people, obviously I'm doing better than they are. I am superior to them.

Once I adopt the fanatic's point of view, it's easy to come up with "evidence" that supports it. If I'm a fanatic, then people who disagree with me are, obviously, too ignorant to be either with the forces of goodness as I am or to be with those of us who are getting out of the great trap. In other words, all fanatics adopt an interpretation of reality and then interpret their experiences in light of the way that they have already decided to interpret them.

It's a bit like a classic Freudian psychoanalyst interpreting a dream. He has decided in advance that all dreams are about wish fulfillment (often with a sexual content). When he then is exposed to a dream to examine, he keeps interpreting it until he finds an interpretation of it as being about wish fulfillment. Since dreams have no meaning until they are interpreted, he simply interprets the dream to fit his theory. If he never alters his procedure, he never takes seriously any other interpretation.

Life is an abstract good. Insofar as it's an instance of that good, a particular life is good.[176] However, it doesn't follow that it is unqualifiedly good. A particular life may also be an instance of an important abstract evil. So a particular life is intrinsically neither good nor evil.

Life has no meaning until it is interpreted, and to interpret it before examining it is senseless. Meaning is a concept. Ultimate reality is beyond both the concept of meaning and the concept of meaninglessness. So, for example, selfless service is not the meaning of life. A life of selfless service may be the consequence of living excellently; it is not, however, the meaning of life itself.

The whole method of fanatics is alien to philosophers. Ideally, philosophers have experiences and then honestly try to interpret them. It's true that it's very difficult to get back to the experiences themselves, to free ourselves from incessant conceptualizing, but it's also critically important to keep trying to let go of our prejudices and preconceptions. It turns out that there really is a way to do it that is discussed in the next chapter. It's critically important to keep striving to break free of our conceptual attachments.

Why? Again, it's because *fanaticism prevents living well*. It prevents us from enjoying abiding joy.

Perhaps this will become clearer if I share two real stories.

The first story is about my father. My father was a clinical internist. He loved the intellectual challenge of figuring out why patients were hurting and then helping them to do whatever was medically possible to regain their health. He made a very good living, but he didn't go into medicine to become wealthy. He enjoyed being a respected professional, but it wasn't as if he needed the confidence boost that provided. He simply loved doing his work. He had a good sense of humor (apparently inherited from his Irish mother), told wonderful jokes and stories, and loved dealing with people. He practiced for decades without ever missing a single day of work. He'd go out every morning with a smile on his face; he'd often actually say, "I'm off to save some lives." He spent his (often twelve-hour) days working to help his patients become healthier and, frequently enough, saving lives. He found his niche and he loved it. You've probably known people like that, and perhaps you are one yourself.

Now, let's step back and think about this. Imagine that you happened to be one of his patients. Would you want him to be attached to a diagnosis before examining you? Would you want him to have in mind the cure and prognosis before even hearing your complaint? Of course not. You'd want him to examine you with an open mind and then apply all his expert understanding to figure out an effective treatment.

Doesn't it make sense, similarly, to treat examining life itself as a physician examining a patient? The physician begins by examining the patient. Doesn't it make sense to examine life with as open a mind as possible? Doesn't it make sense to examine it honestly before deciding what to do about it?

The second story is about me. My father went to Blair Academy. He spent three (instead of the normal four) years in high school. He always greatly valued the experience, and he wanted its benefits for his offspring. As the eldest surviving son, guess who received a strong parental push to attend Blair?

I went to public high school for three years and spent my fourth year of high school at Blair. Though it proved to be a positive turning point in my life, there wasn't a lot about it I didn't hate. Unlike today, when it is once again co-ed and has a hockey team, in those days there were no girls and no hockey. Of course, my friends from public high school weren't there, either; when I went off to Blair, I didn't know a single student there. I was separated from my family and familiar surroundings by hundreds of miles. We attended classes six days a week, and chapel attendance on the seventh day was mandatory. There was no access to cars or beer. We also had to wear jackets and ties every day. All things considered, it was rather like living in prison.

I signed up to play football. I hadn't played football in a couple of years, and I'd never been a quarterback. However, I went to Blair early for preseason football and told them that I was a quarterback. I don't think I fooled anyone but, nevertheless, I actually became a quarterback. (I even lettered, for the simple reason that I was second-string and the first-string quarterback got injured falling on a fumble and missed over half the season.)

The reason was that I had a good arm. In fact, I could pass even better than the first string quarterback. I was able to throw the ball from one goal line and have it land at the far thirty-five yard line; being able to throw 65 yards is good (but not great) for a high school kid. I could throw short passes of, say, 15 to 30 yards straight, hard, and accurately. Unfortunately for the team, I was also inexperienced, which meant that I took weeks just to get the footwork straight, and I was a poor sprinter, so poor that I was facetiously called the "running quarterback" in the yearbook since the only time I ran was on a busted play.

Now, let's step back and think more about this. Please imagine yourself in my position. I was trying hard to learn how to be a quarterback. I had to learn a whole new playbook and how to execute the plays. I had some athletic ability, like a good arm, but I also had some physical disabilities, like having a slow start as a runner.

Imagine this: imagine the coach asking me to throw left-handed. (I'm naturally right handed.) Suppose he had attached himself to the position that quarterbacks should work on improving their weaknesses rather than on improving their strengths. Well, if he had, I'd have tried.

Do you think I ever could have thrown a football sixty-five yards left-handed? Of course not. I probably couldn't have ever thrown it thirty yards left-handed. Furthermore, I couldn't have ever thrown it accurately or hard even at short distances. It would have been an incessant struggle. I never would have done it well and, so, I'd have never felt good about what I was doing.

Similarly, what would have happened if he had insisted that I work on my sprinting? Instead of spending limited practice time on passing and ball-handling drills, imagine that I would have instead spent that time working on sprinting drills. What would have been the result? I'd still never have become good at sprinting. My ability to sprint might have slightly improved, but it's impossible to take someone who is unable to sprint well and make that person an excellent sprinter. There are natural limitations on how well that particular ability can be improved. Excellence requires *ability* plus proper practice. Furthermore, I'd have failed to develop the other skills necessary for a quarterback.

Fortunately, our coach wasn't a fool. Actually, that would be more like idiocy than foolishness. Any football coach stuck on the idea that players should work on improving their weaknesses rather than improving their strengths wouldn't last very long as a coach.

However, that's just what people do who get attached to either the idea that the world is a battlefield or that it's a trap. If they aren't struggling hard, doing poorly, and feeling bad about themselves, they think something is wrong.

Where is it written that life must always be a struggle, that we cannot be excellent, and that we must feel bad about ourselves?

If you have a tendency to think that way, please stop. Whatever the advantages of thinking that way, they are far outweighed by its disadvantages. The good news is that you have the ability to prove this for yourself.

If you have not straightened out your fundamentals first, you will never master anything. In effect, you'd be unwittingly blocking yourself from living excellently. This is why the procedure in Part II is the best procedure. First, get what is more fundamental straight, then work on what is less fundamental.

[*Sidebar quotation* from Brian Tracy: "Lack of planning is the cause of all failures. . . Long term thinking dramatically *improves* short-term decision-making."]

Even if it were possible to master something using the normal backwards procedure, why do it that way? It would be exceedingly more difficult. Please make sure the ice on the lake is sufficiently thick before going skating. Sufficient preparation can reduce the time and effort spent mastering techniques by 90%.

[*Sidebar quotation* from Sir John M. Templeton: "Only one thing is more important than learning from experience, and that is not learning from experience."]

If some attachment is blocking you from maximizing your abilities, let it go. Simply practice releasing it until doing so becomes habitual. If you only read Part II and have never worked on yourself enough to get what is fundamental straight, I invite you to begin to do it now.

[*Sidebar quotation* from The Bible (Proverbs 13:20): "Walk with the wise and be wise; / mix with the stupid and be misled."]

Then figure out what your talents are and turn them into strengths.

11.5 Identifying Talents

Once you adopt the strategy of developing your strengths maximally, doing damage control with respect to your weaknesses, and removing any fundamental conceptual obstructions, the first step to excellence is to identify your talents, your potential strengths. There are three ways to do this, and they complement each other.

(i) The best way is through introspection and memory. Your brain organizes experiences in certain ways. *Introspect and notice how you naturally react.* Instead of focusing on major decisions that are atypical and cause intellectual agony, think of the hundreds and hundreds of smaller ones you make automatically every day. How, for example, do you naturally react to interruptions? How do you greet people? How do you react to having to wait? How do you react in traffic? And so on.

In doing this, you are identifying your everyday habits. Not everyone shares these same habits. Your habits initially came from your talents. As a child, you found some ways of behaving more congenial than others. You tended to persist in the ones you found natural and valuable (and you probably thought that everyone else was the same way until you learned differently) and you tended to avoid those you didn't.

[*Sidebar quotations*:

From B. F. Schumacher: "But what is wisdom? Where can it be found? Here we come to the crux of the matter: it can be read about in numerous publications but it can be *found* only inside oneself. To be able to find it, one has first to liberate oneself from such masters as greed and envy."

From Lama Surya Das: "whatever we are looking for, *it* is always right here. *We are usually elsewhere.* That's the problem."]

Over and over again, your brain guides you down familiar paths, paths of least resistance, paths that reflect your underlying talents. This reveals how frequently and well you do something. Talents that are potential strengths will be ones that you use consistently and that make you feel better, more energized.

Sit down in a quiet place with some paper, a pen, and a calm mind. Ask yourself this question: "What are my best habits?" In other words, ask yourself about yourself. Write out your answers. Don't stop until you come up with at least six. If you have ten or fifteen, that's fine—but six is a minimum. For example, perhaps you have noticed that you are extremely good at not letting other people get you down, that you are usually able to maintain a good mood even when others around you provide reasons for anger or disappointment or fear. If you don't let other people pull your strings, good for you. Write it down—and come up with at least five more good habits.

(ii) Ask your spouse or close friends and family members to help you identify your best habits. Talents can seem so natural that we overlook them. If something comes easily to us, we may assume that it must also come easily to others—but that's not necessarily true. If you ask different people who know you well, *patterns* in the answers you receive may prove quite useful. We can be too close to our own talents to identify them easily. *Ask for help.*

If you do this, it's important to ask in the right way. Explain why you are asking, and listen carefully to any answers you are fortunate enough to receive. Do not get defensive or argue. Genuinely thank the person helping you. Furthermore, it's important to help others identify their strengths. I've found two excellent resources to help with these tasks. (1) <u>Unique Ability</u> by Catherine Nomura, Julia Waller, and Shannon Waller. If you don't want to purchase it, why not borrow it for free from a library? It's based on ideas developed by Dan Sullivan and explained by him in (2) his excellent audio program "Pure Genius." [Both are listed in the bibliography.]

You'll ask them to identify your best habits. Since you are not asking them to say something negative about you, they shouldn't be reluctant to give you a one-sided evaluation (although, when I did it, I received back some less than flattering evaluations'). You can explain to them briefly why you are doing it, which might stimulate them to ask you to assist them.

Allow others to help you and return the favor. Not a bad idea'

(iii) *Take a good test.* I'll mention two that Dan Sullivan recommends and uses routinely. There are probably other good ones, but these work well.

First, if you are willing to purchase a new book, here's what I recommend. Purchase a new copy of Marcus Buckingham & Donald O. Clifton, Ph.D., Now, Discover Your Strengths. (My copy cost less than $20.) On the inside of the dust jacket is a code. Go to the Gallup Organization's website, register using that code, and take the StrengthsFinder test (at no additional cost) online. It will identify five characteristics (out of thirty-four) where you have the greatest potential to develop a strength.

[Mine happen to be: "intellection," "command," "learner," "strategic," and "input." Though they are common words, they have technical uses with respect to this test.]

Once you have clearly identified your most important talents, it's time to develop a plan to transform them into strengths by gaining the appropriate understanding and mastering the relevant skills.

Second, if you are willing to spend about fifty dollars, I recommend discovering your "conative" profile using a test that was developed by Kathy Kolbe.

Your "striving instincts" are the way that you naturally go about getting things done. They are an important factor in your behavior. They are constant throughout adult life. They are a kind of extra perspective that many of us tend to overlook.

We overlook them at our peril. When we link our striving instincts with our tasks, we become more energized. On the other hand, when our striving instincts and our tasks are mismatched, our energy level wanes.

If you want the task of transforming your talents into strengths to be energy increasing rather than energy draining, consider how you naturally accomplish tasks.

The Kolbe A Index measures your instinctive method of operation. The idea is to get a more accurate picture of your striving instincts, your natural mode of operation.

[My natural advantage according to the test is as a "Strategic Planner. You have an outstanding knack for designing complex systems and thoroughly researching methodologies. Classifying evidence and coordinating details is your forte. You can be counted on to compile all available data and place it into an efficient format. With an innate ability to sort through complexities, you are adept at handling logistics." It's not an accident that that is exactly what I'm trying to do for you in this book.]

To take it, go to: www.kolbe.com .

The test itself is not likely to reveal a lot about yourself that you didn't already either realize or suspect. Rather, what's likely to happen is that its results will provide you with peace of mind. "Of course," you'll think, "that really is what I'm like." Taking into account the way that you naturally complete tasks is an important factor in deciding on an activity for excellence.

11.6 Selecting a Talent

If you didn't merely read the previous section but worked through it, you now have a list of your talents. The next task is to select your most important ability to master.

Are there any common elements in your list? Are there overlapping or closely related abilities? Is there a way to reduce the list of separate abilities down to a common core?

If there is, state it in writing. Try condensing what you have written into one sentence. You are looking for a distillation of your abilities to develop into a strength.

I have seven other suggestions concerning your decision that may be helpful. The first two are methodological, and the other five are guidelines for making your selection.

(1) It's important that you realize that there's no way to know in advance how to do this perfectly. Take that pressure off yourself. You may pick something that you think will work and be wrong. So? You won't have failed: you'll simply have learned what didn't work for you.

Make a decision about which talent is most important for you to turn into a strength. Commit yourself wholeheartedly to doing whatever it takes to become successful or to master it. Figure out how to practice its development. Begin training by taking regular baby steps. Examine the feedback you receive, and adjust your training accordingly. Persist in practicing.

Please avoid two common mistakes: (i) demanding a guarantee of excellence in advance and (ii) waiting to begin until every possible training condition is satisfactory. Just begin by following the method mentioned in the previous paragraph. Start immediately; do something today as soon as you finish reading this chapter.

(2) It's also important to remove financial considerations from the selection process. Ask yourself this way: "If I had ample time and money to do whatever I wanted, which talent would I choose to master?"

If you don't do this, a lack of money may distort your judgment. This I know from experience.

As a professor at a state college, I never thought of myself as having an ample amount of money. In fact, though, I didn't care or think much about money at all. Over thirty years ago, I was living alone in a small apartment with, except for my books and my Harley, few valued possessions. I had a tenured job teaching philosophy. I was regularly playing amateur hockey. I had a lovely girlfriend. I was healthy. I had no financial debts. Life was terrific.

My best friend at the time sat me down and told me that I was a fool. Fortunately for me, he was one of the few people in the world I would have listened to after such a beginning. His argument was that I was paying the government far too much in taxes; he recommended at least buying a house as a primary residence to enjoy some standard tax deductions. He was right. I was wasting too much money in taxes. I soon thereafter purchased a cottage that came with the apartment building I had been living in.

Since I had then become a real estate investor, I eventually wondered if investing in real estate might work well for me financially. I knew that I could develop some of my related some my abilities, for example, my ability to learn how to analyze potential real estate deals. Could real estate investing become a source of serious income?

What happened? Well, I did learn a lot. I may have spent around $20,000 in books, audio programs, and seminars, but

I also probably made more than that as an investor. It was actually unexpectedly fun trying to put together win-win-win real estate deals, in other words, deals in which the seller would benefit, the buyer would benefit, and I would benefit. Unfortunately, there was a big downside that I had failed to anticipate: my phone kept ringing.

Being a successful real estate investor requires breaking down the whole process into its sequential parts and setting up a system to handle each of the parts. The problem was that, for example, potential sellers and buyers would, naturally, have to contact me. Time was of the essence: if I didn't respond quickly, they would go to another investor. That meant that I had to pay attention to interruptions. That meant that I wasn't able to read, write, or meditate properly. So, I quit trying to expand my real estate empire.

I didn't quit because I was unable to do it well. I learned a lot; if I had to, I have no doubt that I could make more money annually as a real estate investor than as a professor. It's good to have that as a fallback position; it creates peace of mind. However, I quit because it didn't fit with my most important priorities. It was incongruous for me.

Perhaps I would have anticipated that downside if I hadn't also been influenced by a desire to do better financially. So, I encourage you to set aside any desire to do better financially.

The truth is that, if you make yourself excellent at following your heart, you will benefit other people. If you benefit enough other people well enough, they will enable you to gain whatever you want to gain financially. So, don't go after the money, go after the best way for you to be excellent; that will be of service—and the money will follow anyway. In this respect, life is quite fair.

(3) A talent or ability is something that you are unusually good at doing. It's something that you can become very skillful at doing. It's not just something that you like doing.

For example, I loved playing hockey. I learned as a boy that skates are a great equalizer: one doesn't have to be big or strong (like football players) to do well in hockey and one doesn't have to be tall (like basketball players) to do well in hockey. It's great fun to fly around the ice surface while playing a competitive game. Some boys are so good at it that they eventually grow up and are able to get paid to do it.

Well, I was never a potential player for the Montreal Canadiens. I loved playing, but I simply wasn't that good. (For starters, I lacked the sprint speed.) I did my best to maximize my abilities and I played for many years even as an adult, but that probably said more about my character than my abilities on the ice.

The talent you pick should be a superior talent, something you are really quite naturally gifted at doing. If you cannot hit a curve ball as a boy, don't train for years believing that you'll eventually make it as a major league hitter.

The purpose of education is to test for and develop abilities. Recall the kinds of activities that you tended to do naturally and well when you were a child in school. They are key clues to identifying your talents.

(4) Furthermore, the talent you select should be something that you feel good about using, something that creates rather than drains energy.

At the end of hockey games, for example, I was exhausted. I tried to leave everything on the ice; I never tried to save anything or hold back or protect myself. Even so, despite being exhausted, I was always energized. I would feel terrific. Knowing what I would feel like, I never had any difficulty whatsoever getting up for a hockey game. (In fact, I would usually get so "up" just before a game that I routinely had to take medication to control an upset stomach.)

Similarly, when I go on a seven-day Zen retreat, I anticipate it for weeks in advance. I look forward to the challenge. Even though one is physically tired at the end of the week, even though one may have only managed an average of four or five hours of sleep per night (or less), there is a post-retreat state that lasts for days afterwards. The energy created by many hours of daily practice (called 'joriki' or 'samadhi power') easily overwhelms one's being physically tired. (This may explain why sages may need less sleep than the rest of us.)

If you don't feel really good, positively charged, when you use a particular ability, that's not an ability that you want to select to develop into an important skill.

(5) Avoid playing too small. Don't pick something that is too easy for you to become successful at; instead, select an ability that will enable you to enjoy a lifelong journey of increasing excellence. Play chess instead of checkers; play go instead of hearts.

In other words, pick something that permits indefinite improvement. Academic domains and martial arts are good examples.

According to Dan Sullivan who coaches them, many successful entrepreneurs find themselves trapped. They have taken ability, strengthened it, marketed it successfully, and are reaping the financial rewards. The problem is that they have lost interest in it—but they cannot give it up without undermining their financial success. They are like the disgruntled professor mentioned earlier.

If the pond you select to swim in is too small, sooner or later you'll lose interest in swimming in it. Avoid trapping yourself swimming in a pond that is too small for you. Better to swim in a large lake or an ocean.

(6) Pick an ability to maximize that doesn't essentially rely on other people. Once you become excellent at it, could you do it successfully alone if you were stranded on a desert island for the rest of your life? If not, be wary of selecting it.

For example, suppose you have a talent for history or mathematics and discover that you really enjoy teaching it. You get a teaching certificate and begin teaching in a high school. The problem is that you don't own your work. At any moment, the school board could fire you. (Never forget what Mark Twain said about school board members: "They were what God made when he was practicing to make idiots.") There is a kind of chronic insecurity built in. Despite a tenure system, your having a teaching position is not wholly up to you. Even if your evaluations are good, sometimes schools close.

For financial purposes, you may choose to disregard this criterion, which is fine. All things considered, for you being a teacher might be your calling. You know going in that it won't (one hopes) last until you die, that you'll have to quit teaching long before you die. Your being a teacher does not depend solely on you. Still, you are excellent at it, you love history or mathematics, and you get paid to help youngsters expose themselves to it. Despite the long hours, poor pay, and a lot of stress, it can be a wonderful job. Teaching may be the noblest profession, but enter it and similar lines of work, if you do, with eyes open about your future lack of independence.

(7) The final criterion is the most important, but it's also the most difficult to express. Pick an ability that is such that, when you use it, you feel as though you are at home, right where you belong.

Officially, I'm recognized as a master of only one domain, namely, academic philosophy. It happens to suit me well. (Distinguish being a philosopher from being a professor of philosophy; essentially, I'm a philosopher—not a professor.) I was a freshman in college when I genuinely discovered philosophy. I instantly had the sense that, if it hadn't existed and I was bright enough, I'd have invented it. It seemed perfectly suited to me. I knew immediately that I had found a home.

I had a similar experience many years later. I was in my forties when I discovered Zen meditation. I had read about it as an undergraduate, but reading isn't doing. The very first time I begin to "sit" I wondered where this practice had been for the last thirty years. I "knew" I was exactly where I was supposed to be.

Have you had similar experiences? If so, please don't discount them. Life was trying to tell you something important.

Such experiences are quite different from ordinary experiences in which we often second-guess ourselves. There's something missing from these extraordinary experiences: worry. Should I really be doing this now? Is there a more effective use of my time? There's no need to worry about being home.

When you settle on an ability that is right for you, it will feel exactly right for you. When you execute this ability, whatever it happens to be, you'll have the sense that this is perfect for you, that doing exactly this is how you want to spend the rest of your life.

If you haven't had such experiences, then keep educating yourself. Keep opening to different kinds of activities. Sooner or later, you'll find one that feels just right.

Please don't get impatient, either. Remember, if the quest takes longer than you'd like, you are benefiting as you proceed because you'll be learning what doesn't work for you. If you don't wait for that gut feeling, you may prematurely commit to a destination that isn't right for you and waste a lot of money and time going in a direction that's wrong for you.

[*Sidebar quotaiton from* Mohandas Gandhi: "Man often becomes what he believes himself to be. If I keep on saying to myself that I cannot do a certain thing, it is possible that I may end by really becoming incapable of doing it. On the contrary, if I shall have the belief that I can do it, I shall surely acquire the capacity to do it, even if I may not have it at the beginning."]

11.7 Strengths

The training program you adopt should be suited to your abilities and to the talent(s) you select. Because there are different practices relevant to different talents, it's impossible here to provide any specific guidance for the talent(s) you have selected.

[*Sidebar quotation* from Richard Bandler and John Grinder: "All generalizations are lies."]

However, typically you'll be able to find some good books that will get you started. Go to amazon.com, type in your subject, see what books are available, and read some of the reviews. Look for books that aid beginners to your activity, and read a few to increase your understanding.

Look for a mentor, a master who is willing to help you practice. Your first mentor may be an author. Read that person's books, listen to any audio programs available, and take any seminars offered. If you are lucky and know someone who is a master who is willing to help you personally, terrific. Make it very easy for that person to help you; ensure that he or she benefits, too, from associating with you.

[*Sidebar quotation* from Andrew Matthews: "You get excited about doing things *after* you start . . . The secret is to *make a start.* / Another thing about starting things . . . you will never ever be absolutely *ready* for anything! . . . *start without all the answers and without any* guarantees. / You get motivated by *doing* things, not thinking about them . . . Only commit to something if you know you will follow through . . . *whatever you say you'll do, do it* . . . 'Being comfortable' is overrated . . . If you follow any kind of dream you'll sometimes be uncomfortable . . ."]

Furthermore, there are some general guidelines that apply. These guidelines, as you might expect, follow from material that has already been covered. For example, everyone who isn't already at least successful at it can benefit greatly from the practice described in the next chapter.

Just like the example of the running back, whatever activity you select may be broken down into about six separate tasks. It's astounding but there always seem to be five to seven components. List them on a sheet of paper in the order in which they need to be mastered. Your reading should help with this.

Understand that becoming excellent is a process. Therefore, do not try to master each element simultaneously. Similarly, do not try to master some of the first, then some of the second, and so on. Instead, become successful at each element in sequence. There's no point worrying about releasing the arrow until you have strung the bow.

Focusing on step one, does it have components that must be mastered? If so, list and prioritize them. Either begin with step one, or begin with the first component of step one.

What could you do to master it? If you already have a clear idea, fine. If you don't, sit down, again with a calm mind (preferably the first thing in the morning), a pen, and some paper, and write out twenty possible ways of mastering it. It's very important not to quit until you have twenty—not eight or fifteen. Twenty. Don't evaluate them: just write down twenty possibilities as quickly as possible. (This is Earl Nightingale's "mindstorming" technique.) If you think of more possibilities later, add them.

Evaluate your list the following day. Pick one of the twenty elements that seems as though it might work best for you and start there. How will you recognize when you are successful at it? What is the relevant test? Begin practicing, and practice daily (although, occasionally, some activities such as serious strength training cannot be practiced productively so frequently). If it yields positive feedback, keep using that to practice. If it doesn't, try another one from the list. When you have satisfied your criterion, do the same for the next step. Keep going until you have had success at all the components. When you look up, you may be amazed to find yourself already successful at that activity. Then proceed to become successful at the next activity.

It's important to understand that, initially, you may have to force yourself to practice every day. Deal with it. Just do it.

It typically will take at least three and typically more like twelve weeks for an activity to become thoroughly habitual. So?

Plan your practice for the next ninety days. It may be necessary to adjust your practice schedule well before then, but begin with a 90-day plan. Experience has shown that our lives can get better in 90-day chunks. The plan doesn't have to be written in stone, but it should be written.

Pick an auspicious time to begin. If your birthday or the New Year is rapidly approaching, use that. Doing some mental preparation in advance can help increase your momentum. If you have some psychological tricks that have worked for you before, use them. Be shameless. It doesn't matter what you think to begin practicing; what matters is the practicing, not to hold yourself separate from the practicing. There are helpful books by psychologists on how to change listed in the bibliography; why not read one or two?

When you have begun to practice, except for serious illness or injury, let no exceptions occur for ninety days (about twelve weeks). That should be sufficient to incorporate the new habit into your life. Zero exceptions. If your plan calls for you to practice daily, then practice daily with no excuses.

The key to becoming successful is to master your mind. You may need to think about future benefits to practice today, but, insofar as it is possible, *concentrate your efforts on the present moment*. Focus as fully as possible on practicing and try to detach from the benefits of practicing simply by not thinking about them. Remember: the goal is to become the practicing.

[*Sidebar quotation* from Saint Anthony the Great: "The prayer of the monk is not perfect until he no longer realizes himself or the fact that he is praying."]

Since our brains do not seem to grasp negative, keep thinking about your practicing in a positive way. Instead of thinking, for example, "I want to lose fat" or "I do not want to be so fat", think "I want to be trim" or "I want to be fit." *We attract what we think about.* If you think loving thoughts, you'll attract love into your life. This general principle fails, however, when we think negative thoughts; it's as if our brains cannot process "not." If you think, for example, "I do not want to be afraid," all you'll succeed in doing is attracting more fear into your life. So focus on what you want; do not focus on what you don't want.

We all have the ability to rationalize. Use that power to practice well. If you are practicing to be a running back, keep telling yourself that if you don't become a better running back your girlfriend will dump you (even though that's false). When you go to sleep every night, remind yourself that you must practice intensely the next day lest you slip back into the horror of living without your girlfriend. This seems ridiculous, but it works. Why?

Our brains cannot distinguish the real from the unreal.

Suppose, to echo a famous example from Kant, you have a one hundred dollar bill in your pocket. Now, imagine seeing a one hundred dollar bill on the table; really imagine it in detail, its colors, shape, images, and so on. Now: what's the difference between the real one in your pocket and the imaginary one on the table?

Aren't both rectangular? Don't they have the same colors? Don't they have the same images? And so on.

Reality is not a phenomenal quality. As we have seen[177], reality is inexhaustibility, which is not a phenomenal quality. It's impossible to perceive an object's reality in the same way that it's possible to perceive its color or shape.

Of course, as we have seen, there is a difference: real objects are multiply noticeable whereas unreal objects are not. You will be able to touch the dollar bill in your pocket as well as see it, but that won't be true for the imaginary one on the table. (Couldn't you, however, dream that you are both seeing and touching it?) The point is that a judgment about identity, such as "the bill that I'm touching is the same as the bill that I'm seeing," is quite different from merely noticing something.

The mind is our biggest asset. The very best method for practicing well is to use the mind well in favor of practicing. You may think of this as rationalization or in any other way. How you think of it doesn't matter. Just use it. It works because you are not a fixed continuant substratum. You are inherently free.

In other words, use the mind to create a better surreality for yourself.

[*Sidebar quotations*:

From Publilius Syrus: "A wise man will be Master of His Mind / A Fool will be Its Slave."

From Tao-Hsin: "There is nothing lacking in you, and you yourself are no different from the Buddha. Be boundless and absolutely free from all conditions. Be free to go in any direction you like."

From Maxwell Maltz: "use 'experiencing' as a direct and controlled method of changing the self image . . . the human nervous system cannot tell the difference between an 'actual' experience and an experience *imagined vividly and in detail* . . . you will 'act like' the sort of person you conceive yourself to be . . . the self image can be changed . . . one is never too young nor too old to change his self image and thereby start to live a new life."]

Humor helps. Especially as an awkward beginner, there will be times when the best procedure is simply to laugh at yourself. Use your sense of humor. When events are incongruous or ridiculous, enjoy them! Have fun with practicing. **Mastery, when work becomes play, is really fun.** You can make that true in your surreality.

[*Sidebar quotation* from Melvin Helitzer: "Humor must come out of reality."]

In the end, however, it comes down to doing it, to practicing doggedly and properly. Remember: it's not practicing that creates excellence; *perfect practicing creates excellence*.

Practice each time as if it will be during this practice session that you'll breakthrough to the next level of excellence.

Do whatever it takes to practice perfectly. That means getting both the *what* and the *how* right. *What* you are doing will depend upon the activity you have selected. Perhaps surprisingly, however, *how* you practice well is actually the same in all cases.

As our final topic, then, let's turn to an examination of getting the *how* right.

Chapter 12: The Most Important Activity

The most life-enhancing idea of all time is the idea that it is possible always to get the *how* right. Excellence need not only characterize an activity, a part of life; it can characterize the whole of life. **Living excellently (wisely, well) is possible**. The opportunity is here, now.

12.1 Sages

The evidence for this is that sages are real. Even if it's true that there is no such thing as a fully enlightened sage, it's nevertheless true that there are sages. If you have ever met one or, better, if you have become one, you already realize this.

Sages are human beings who live excellently. They are not gods. They get hungry and sick. They grow old and die. They feel pain and experience disappointments. Some are married with children, and some live alone. Some are illiterate, and some are well educated. They sleep, eat, and exercise like the rest of us. Some have ordinary occupations; some don't.

Sages are successful philosophers. They are no longer seeking how to live excellently; they doing it.

[*Sidebar quotation* from Martin Seligman, Ph.D.: "Meditation works by blocking thoughts that produce anxiety. It complements relaxation, which blocks the motor components of anxiety but leaves the anxious thoughts untouched."

In terms of *what* they do, they are largely indistinguishable from everyone else. "Largely" but not "entirely." Often they are recognized as masters of the art of love. Almost always, they have a formal spiritual practice of some kind.

The point is that **sages are spiritual masters.** Like all other kinds of mastery, spiritual mastery is neither accidental nor the result of luck or happenstance. Spiritual mastery is always the result of persistently practicing an effective spiritual discipline.

[*Sidebar quotations:*

From Arnold Toynbee: "The coming of Buddhism to the West may well prove to be the most important event of the Twentieth Century."

From Albert Einstein: "The religion of the future will be a cosmic religion. It should transcend personal God and avoid dogma and theology. Covering both the natural and the spiritual, it should be based on a religious sense arising from the experience of all things natural and spiritual as a meaningful unity. Buddhism answers this description."

From Mahatma Gandhi on being asked what he thought of Western civilization: "I think it would be a good idea."]

Unfortunately, there is no consistent terminology here. So it's important to define some terms. This should help to avoid confusions such as the common belief that a spiritual practice must be a religious practice.

The English word 'religion' comes from the Latin 'religio', which means 'obligation, bond, reverence.' Although today the word 'religion' is usually used to refer to a belief or creed (set of beliefs) about the supernatural or worshipping some supernatural god or gods, etymologically at least, what is central to religion is not something divine but rebinding, overcoming separation, atonement (at-one-ment).

In his valuable The World's Religions, Huston Smith identifies six characteristics that religions are commonly thought to have.[178] (1) One is authority. In addition to supposed divine authority, there are humans considered to be authorities in the sense that their decisions carry weight. (2)

Another is ritual. There were probably religious dances that arose from collective expressions of both celebration and bereavement even before there were religious creeds. (3) Another is speculative answers to the existential questions such as: "Where did we come from?", "Why are we here?", and "What will happen to us?" (4) Another constant is traditions that are passed down to us from previous generations. (5) Also, typically, religions promise grace, which is the idea that, ultimately at least, the world is on our side. (6) Finally, there is mystery, the idea of the infinite that is beyond the reach of our finite intellects.

Of these, it seems to me that only #3 and #6 are natural. It is natural for us to wonder, to try to set our lives in a larger context. It is also natural for us to recognize our limitations, to have the sense that we are part of a larger mystery that is beyond our comprehension. Haven't these characterized humans for as long as there have been humans?

If so, what is natural relates religion to spirituality. Nothing is more natural than breathing. Again, the English word 'spiritua' comes from the Latin word '<u>spiritus</u>', which means 'a breathing.' A **spiritual practice** is an activity based on awareness of the natural physical process of breathing. Therefore, there is neither anything supernatural or religious about it, nor is there anything conceptual about it. It's a deliberate reuniting of mind and body, a healing of mind/body separation.

So, a spiritual practice is not necessarily a religious practice at all. Some spiritual practices are religious practices, for example, prayer. Other spiritual practices such as Zen meditation [<u>zazen</u>] are not religious practices (see the next section}. Sages are masters of a spiritual practice; they are not necessarily religious at all.

[*Sidebar quotation* from St. John of the Cross: "A man, then, is decidedly hindered from the attainment of this high state of union with God when he is attached to any understanding, feeling, imagining, opinion, desire, or way of his own, or to any other of his works or affairs, and knows not how to detach and denude himself of these impediments. His goal transcends all of this, even the loftiest object that can be known—or experienced. Consequently, he must pass beyond everything to unknowing."]

Not all kinds of prayer are spiritual practices. The absolute prayer of mystics clearly is a spiritual practice. On the other hand, common prayer that petitions the divine for something is not a spiritual practice. In terms of ego reduction, it is actually counterproductive. "Please, God, give me what *I* want!" merely reinforces egoistic attachments. (Furthermore, it also is blasphemous, as if the believer has the <u>hubris</u> to give God directions. Isn't the Divine supposed to know what is happening and to direct things for the best anyway?)

[*Sidebar quotation* from Stuart Wilde: "What is normally considered to be power is not real power at all. Chasing money, glamour, sex; wanting control over others—political and military power—are all manifestations of the ego . . . Many people are victimized by their egos . . . Because the ego is insecure, its fears need to be quelled, so it dominates our psychology, firing off endless demands . . . controlling the ego through discipline is a lot simpler than trying to satisfy it all the time."

From Karen Armstrong: "Yoga can be described as the systematic dismantling of the egoism which distorts our view of the world and impedes our spiritual progress . . . The disciplines of yoga were designed to destroy the unconscious impediments to enlightenment and to decondition the human personality."]

Like 'yoga,' 'meditation' is just another word for spiritual practice. Let's agree to reserve its use for nonreligious spiritual practices. As there are different kinds of prayer, so there are different kinds of meditation. I am not suggesting that nonreligious spiritual practices are better than religious spiritual practices; instead, I am trying to separate out the topic of religion from the topic of spirituality.

A personal reason for doing this is that my own spiritual practice is not a religious one. I may understand very little about nonreligious spirituality, but I certainly understand less about religious spirituality. Whether you are religious or not, I know that you are spiritual because I know that you breathe.

[*Sidebar quotation* from Joseph Campbell: "You can't teach Buddhism. You can't teach illumination. You *can* give different clues to how to get it. But if a person isn't willing to paddle his own canoe he's not going to get across the river."]

I am not myself excellent at any spiritual practice, but I do daily practice one and have for about twenty years. Since I need an example anyway, I'll write about the one most familiar to me. Please do not think that I am implicitly suggesting that it is the best one. Again, there are many spiritual practices. It's impossible to know in advance which one will work the best for you.

If you want to master meditation, you should apprentice yourself to a meditation master and persistently practice doing well whatever that master recommends. Even if you already understand what kind of meditation you would like to master, there's no guarantee that you will be able to find a suitable master willing and able to instruct you. How would it be possible for you to tell in advance which meditation practice would be best for you? The truth is: you can't.

If you are serious about becoming a sage and don't already have an effective spiritual practice, your task is to find one that will work for you.

[*Sidebar quotations*:

From Teilhard de Chardin: "We are not human beings having a spiritual experience. We are spiritual beings having a human experience."

From Roshi Bodhin Kjolhede: "In spiritual practice, unlike a lottery, everyone wins just by playing—if one is sincere and keeps at it long enough."]

12.2 Zen Buddhism

As my teacher[179] never tires of stressing, Zen Buddhism is a practice[180] I practice zazen, which is the practice of Zen Buddhists.

[*Sidebar quotations*:

From Roshi Shunryu Suzuki: "Unless you know how to practice zazen, no one can help you."

From David Chadwick: "It's been said, in Zen practice, that your first enlightenment experience is why you decide to practice. It's the first turning."

From M. Scott Peck: "The process of spiritual growth is an effortful and difficult one. This is because it is conducted against a natural resistance, against a natural inclination to keep things the way they were, to cling to the old maps and old ways of doing things, to take the easy path."

From John Daishin Buksbazen: "In a way, zazen is the opposite of addiction; it is the way of freedom from clinging, the freedom to experience each moment unvarnished and complete in itself."

From Mark Epstein, Ph.D.: "The spiritual path means making a path rather than following one. It is a very personal process, unique to each individual."

From Karen Armstrong: "Enlightenment is never easy. It is frightening to leave our old selves behind, because they are the only way we know how to live."]

Many people assume that Zen Buddhism is a religion. Is it?

The answer depends upon the meaning of 'religion.' If a practice must have the six features identified above to count as a religion, then it's not the case that Zen Buddhism is a religion. Let's consider them in turn.

In the first place, with respect to divine authority, there is no belief in Zen Buddhism in anything supernatural whatsoever. With respect to human authorities, although one (like me) may be fortunate enough to have a sage as one's teacher, really one is one's own teacher. A teacher just points the way and encourages. There is nothing to teach (in the sense of putting thoughts into a student's mind).

[*Sidebar quotation* from The Buddha: "Make the practice your teacher."]

Second, in a sangha (a community of practitioners) there are common rules that keep community life functioning smoothly so that one is as free as possible to concentrate on one's practice, but these are hardly sacred rituals. They are subject to change whenever other rules would be more useful.

Third, there is nothing speculative about Zen. It is as concrete as one's breathing and posture. Thinking distracts from spiritual training.

Fourth, there are traditions about, for example, Zen practice, which is called 'zazen,' but no practitioner thinks there's anything sacred about them; instead, they are merely fruitful practices that have been developed by one's predecessors.

Fifth, the focus is on an individual's intense, disciplined, sustained <u>zazen</u> to come to awakening and enlightenment. Global beliefs are irrelevant.

Finally, it's true that awakening and enlightenment cannot be conceptualized, but it is experienced by every sage and, so, is within the compass of the human mind.

As Huston Smith argues, (early) Buddhism, similarly, does not have the six features characteristic of a religion. Some followers of the Buddha did develop religions, but Zen Buddhism, like the practices advocated by the Buddha, is not a religion. If so, this shows that the Zen school of Buddhism is closer to early Buddhism than the other schools of Buddhism.

This is what Smith has to say on these six points:

First, "Buddha preached a religion devoid of authority . . . Contrasting his own openness with the guild secrecy of the *brahmins*. . . Buddha challenged each individual to do his own religious seeking . . .

[Second] Buddha preached a religion devoid of ritual . . . They were trappings—irrelevant to the hard, demanding job of ego-reduction . . .

[Third] Buddha preached a religion that skirted speculation . . . he maintained his 'noble silence.' His reason was simple. On questions of this sort, 'greed for views . . . tends not to edification.' His practical program was exacting . . .

[Fourth] Buddha preached a religion devoid of tradition . . .

[Fifth] Buddha preached a religion of intense self-effort . . . 'Buddhas only point the way. Work out your salvation with diligence.' . . . you can make it in this lifetime . . .

[Sixth] Buddha preached a religion devoid of the supernatural . . . [he stressed] the hard, practical task of self-advance . . . As a consequence, original Buddhism presents us with a version of religion that is unique."[181]

Instead of claiming that it is a unique religion, Smith would have been clearer if he had concluded that it isn't a religion at all. Instead of being a religion, it's a spiritual practice, a way of life, a lived philosophy.

Smith cites seven qualities that characterize this unique spiritual practice:

"1. . . . empirical . . . On every question personal experience was the final test of truth. . .

2. . . . scientific. It made the quality of lived experience its final test, and directed its attention to discovering cause-and-effect relationships that affected that experience . . .

3. . . . pragmatic. . . Buddha kept his attention riveted on predicaments that demanded solution. . .

4. . . . therapeutic . . . 'One thing I teach,' said the Buddha, 'suffering and the end of suffering' . . .

5. . . . psychological . . . in contrast to metaphysical. Instead of beginning with the universe and moving to the place of human beings within it, the Buddha invariably began with the human lot, its problems, and the dynamics of coping with them.

6. . . . egalitarian . . . he broke caste, opening his order to all regardless of social status. . .

7. . . . directed to individuals . . . in the end his appeal was to the individual, that each should proceed toward enlightenment through confronting his or her individual situation and predicaments."[182]

According to one well-known authority, then, the practice of Zen Buddhism is **empirical, scientific, pragmatic, therapeutic, psychological, egalitarian, and individualistic**. He's quite right about that.[183] If that's the kind of spiritual training that would appeal to you, please investigate it further for yourself. If not, select another kind. Different spiritual practices are like different paths to the summit of ego reduction.

12.3 Ego Reduction

[*Sidebar quotations*:

From the Buddha: "Nothing is to be clung to as I, me, or mine."

From Daniel Goleman: "Flow is a state of self-forgetfulness . . . moments of flow are egoless . . . a highly concentrated state is the essence of flow . . . it occurs only within reach of the summit of ability where skills are well-rehearsed and neural circuits are most efficient . . . mastery is a craft or skill is spurred on by the experience of flow . . . 'Creative achievements depend on single-minded immersion'

. . .Being able to enter flow is emotional intelligence at its best."]

Though we have forgotten it, nothing is more natural than ego reduction. **Living excellently is our natural way.**

Except for the relatively few sages, we have all lost sight of this. Consider: wouldn't hundreds of thousands of years of evolution have produced naturally excellent humans? It's true that our success depends upon our adaptations and they will only be effective in certain kinds of environments. Still, the environment hasn't changed that much in the last few million years. Why wouldn't living excellently be natural?

As natural as ego attachment is for us, as comfortable as we have become with ego inflation, it's become unnatural. Again[184], it's part of the price we have paid for our advanced kind of literacy. The natural mind is peaceful; the addled mind is disturbed.

This is why experiences of breaking through (awakening) are often said to reveal nothing special. In fact, it's even possible to have a shallow breakthrough experience without realizing it. Spontaneous breakthrough experiences do occur occasionally. (The problem with them is that, since they did not come about as the result of spiritual training, no additional training can enlarge and deepen them, which means that they have no lasting effect on the quality of life.) For example, the most recent description of a breakthrough experience I have read, and I've read quite a few, recounted years of difficulty practicing zazen and then, "suddenly, there it was. It was nothing spectacular, just a startled 'Oh . . . Duh!!!'"[185]

Once the mind is emptied of conceptual attachments, living excellently becomes no big deal. It's natural. Many sages have said just this.

If you haven't realized this already, why not find out for yourself?

[*Sidebar quotations*:

From Thoreau: "Only that day dawns to which we are awake."

From Lisa Takeuchi Cullen: "with the aid of advanced brain-scanning technology, researchers are beginning to show that meditation directly affects the function and structure of the brain, changing it in ways that appear to increase attention span, sharpen focus, and improve memory."

From Andrew Weil, M.D.: "Because aging reminds us of our mortality, it can be a primary stimulus to awakening and growth."

From Marcus Aurelius: ". . . do every act of your life as if it were the last."

From Jon Kabat-Zinn: "meditation . . . is just about paying attention in your life as if it really mattered. . . We have made absorption in the future and in the past such an overriding habit that, most of the time, we have no awareness of the present moment at all. As a consequence, we may feel we have very little, if any, control over the ups and downs of our own lives or our own minds."

From the Center for Mindfulness in Medicine, Health Care, and Society: "Meditation is not for the faint-hearted nor for those who routinely avoid the whispered longings of their own hearts."]

I strongly encourage you to read my <u>The Three Things The Rest of Us Should Know about Zen Training</u>. In part, here's what you'll find in it:

1. a list of the chief benefits of meditation
2. what spiritual training is and why zazen is a good example
3. how it is possible that sages are always meditating
4. how to start with momentum
5. exactly how to still the body
6. two initial exercises for stilling the mind
7. the key to practicing well
8. answers to common questions
9. suggestions for further reading

There are even better books, such as the much longer <u>The Three Pillars of Zen</u>, listed in the Bibliography.

[*Sidebar quotation* from Thich Nhat Hanh: "[I]f one doesn't know how to die, one can hardly know how to live—because death is a part of life."]

12.4 The Greatest Advantage

Everyone understands that being successful at some activity is better than merely doing it.

I've argued that mastery with respect to some activity is better than just becoming successful at it.

Why, though, even consider spiritual mastery? What advantage does it have over mastery with respect to activities such as the ones listed in the Preface? Isn't, for example, mastering, say, a martial art as good as spiritual mastery?

No, it's not. The reason is simple.

What good does a master of a martial art enjoy when he or she is not engaged in that martial art? Similarly, what good does a master of any activity enjoy when detached from the activity in question?

None.

In other words, with one exception, all activities are part-time. It's great to be a master archer, but it's only great when one is engaged in archery. Similarly, it's great to be a master of basketball, but it's only great when one is playing basketball. And so on.

The one exception is to be a master of the mind. There's nothing part-time about having a mind. Think of a spiritual master as someone who is a master of the mind.

Since one is always with one's mind, this is the greatest advantage of spiritual mastery.

12.5 A Natural Koan

In my inexpensive The Meditative Approach to Philosophy I provide you with two initial spiritual exercises that involved counting the breath. It's easy to read about them; they are quite simple. Doing them well, however, is not easy. They may take you months of practicing before you can do them well—and that's if you are enthusiastic and diligent.

My hope for you is that you find yourself a master willing to help you. That's really the best way to learn. It's important, too, to keep reading.

Still, what should you do if you don't have a master after your concentration has improved to the point where you are ripe to go beyond the two initial spiritual exercises?

If you happen to be unable to find a master to coach you, this is an important question. I have a suggestion.

One way to think about what you are attempting to do is that you are trying **to empty the mind** of all conceptual attachments—especially attachment to the self-concept. This is a very difficult task. Whether we want them to or not, thoughts (judgments, conceptualizations) just keep welling up unbidden.

It seems hopeless to try to notice and obliterate thoughts as quickly as they arise. What's the answer?

[Sidebar quotations:

From Harada-roshi: "Self-realization is not a matter of step-by-step progress but the result of a leap. Until your mind is pure you cannot make this leap . . ['pure' means] Empty of all thoughts."

From Yasutani-roshi: "For enlightenment you must have deep faith. . .Do zazen with zeal and Self-realization will take care of itself . . . Zen . . . is not easy, but its rewards are in proportion to its difficulties . . . Everything valuable has a high price."

From Suzuki Roshi: "Strictly speaking, there is no such thing as an enlightened person. There is only enlightened activity."]

The answer is to deputize a koan to do the work of emptying for us. A koan is a tool designed to shorten the learning curve to awakening. By training our focus on a koan, we are able to let go of all the other thoughts that keep appearing. It's as if the koan, as long as we don't separate from it, dissolves all thoughts it contacts. It's a magical conceptual solvent.

[*Sidebar quotation* from Master Shibayama: "the role of the koan is . . . to make us lose our way and drive us to despair."]

It takes a while for the koan to do the emptying. What's critical is to stay with the koan until it has completed its work. The training is not to separate from the koan even for an instant. The practice, then, is one of nonseparation. If to live excellently is to live without separation, this is exactly what one should expect of an effective spiritual practice.

Awakening occurs when the koan's work is complete; awakening occurs at that very instant. It only takes one moment of directly experiencing Emptiness to awaken![186]

It may take years of training to get to that moment, but, once anyone begins practicing seriously, it's impossible to predict when awaking will occur (or how thorough it will be when it occurs). Until it occurs, the training is a bit like being in a fog. Notice that, when you are in a fog, there's no way to tell when it will lift. Worrying about it is useless. It's like that with spiritual training: there's no way to tell when awakening will occur.

However, there's an important dissimilarity between being in a fog and beginning to practice with a koan. If you are in a fog and worry about it, the worry, though useless, will have no effect on how quickly the fog will lift. On the other hand, if you are practicing with a koan and worrying about when awakening will occur, that worry will *prevent* awakening from occurring. Why? **Meditating is not thinking.** If you are thinking about future awakening, obviously you are not fully engaged with the koan in the present moment.

So forget doing better tomorrow. The only time to awaken is now.

[*Sidebar quotation* from Shantideva: "The absolute is not within the reach of intellect, / For intellect is grounded in the relative."]

So, as a third spiritual exercise, I suggest practicing being fully with a koan in the present moment.

If you have any familiarity at all with the tradition of koan training, you already understand that koans are conceptual knots that cannot be untied by thinking. Thinking about a koan is useless. This is why it's impossible to think your way to living well. It's impossible to solve a koan by thinking about it, and it's frustrating to try. You could think about a koan for, say, the next thirty years and, afterwards, you will have achieved exactly nothing!

Koans are not fit objects for conceptualization. Koans are objects for meditation.

If you are ready for a koan and don't have a master, are there any natural koans that might work for you?

Yes there are. Of them, this is the best: "Who am I?"

That's it. I hope that it seems natural to you by now: I mentioned it in the first paragraph of the first chapter of this book.

I also have explained why it is not a question to be answered by thinking. To think is to conceptualize, which is to separate using qualities. Since qualities are commonalities and since you are unique, how could thinking of qualities capture your uniqueness? When it's put that way, it's obvious that it couldn't.

So the koan is not an object for thought, for your head. The koan is an object for meditation, for your gut. If the mind provides you with an answer, just ignore it.

You'll try to think about it anyway. Eventually, though, you'll figure out for yourself that that won't work. That's when the koan has begun the migration from your head to your gut.

Shorten it to just: "**Who?**" With every breath, focus on "Who?" Practicing well is that simple.

Focus on it as if your life depends upon answering it. Focus on it in an interrogative way; you are enquiring "who?"

rather than stating "who." If you don't permit yourself to separate from "Who?", the intensity will eventually grow. The pressure will eventually cause an explosion of emptiness: "All the illusory ideas and delusive thoughts accumulated up to the present will be exterminated, and when the time comes, internal and external will be spontaneously united . . . all of a sudden an explosive conversion will occur, and you will astonish the heavens and shake the earth."[187]

At each breathe, you have a choice whether to separate from "Who?" or not. It doesn't matter what else you are doing: whether you are walking or washing or raking or driving or even listening or talking. **To practice without separation is to practice-enlightenment.**

(This is what happens on a Zen retreat: from the moment you arise in the morning until the moment when you fall asleep at night, your day is organized in such a way that it makes it as easy as possible not to separate from your koan. Whether it lasts a day or a week, the hope is to take the training from that retreat and incorporate it into everyday life.)

The more you practice, the more you don't permit separation from your koan, the better.

There is, of course, much more to be said about spiritual training. My intention here, though, is just to open the possibility for you. What's it really like? What's the key to it?

12.5 Falling In Love

It's really like falling in love. Did you ever fall in love? I am referring to the good old head-over-heels falling in love that usually strikes first during one's teenage years. If you ever have, you'll never forget its intensity.

[*Sidebar quotation* from Margaret Anderson: "In real love you want the other person's good. In romantic love you want the other person."

From Jon Kabat-Zinn: "mindfulness practice is really a love affair."]

Falling in love and being in love are quite different from loving. Falling in love is frequently called "falling in lust": you intensely desire your beloved. Your whole focus is on that object. You dream about your beloved when you are asleep. You are thinking about your beloved when you wake up in the morning; you are eager for the first communication between you. You think about your beloved with every breath all day long. You dream of the moments of togetherness. You imagine an infinitely sweet future as a couple. Everything unrelated to your beloved is a distraction. Everything you value, even life itself, is united in the object of your adoration.

Falling in love and being in love are forms of insanity, paradigmatic cases of being out of balance. Instead of being centered, anyone in love is as uncentered as it's possible to be.

Did your beloved create your falling in love, or did you do it to yourself? Of course, unless you give it away, nobody (and no thing) has any emotional power over you whatsoever. Nobody has the power to make you fall in love. Therefore, you did it to yourself.

Why did you do it? You did it because you thought you'd be better off. The desire to be in love, the desire to give emotional control to another, is an egocentric desire. We falsely believe that we'll be better off by being in love than by not being in love.

This explains why falling in love and being in love are states characteristic of the immature. It's true that middle-aged and elderly people also occasionally fall in love, but what they are doing is trying to recapture the lost intensity of their youth, which makes it a sad spectacle to witness. In other words, being immature is not necessarily limited to a certain chronological age.

It's sad because it's based on the delusion that there is something to be achieved by falling in love. How could that be? When we fall in love, all we are doing is attempting to use another person to make our lives better. How could that work?

Bradford's Law of Conditioned Life is that **G + L = 0**, where 'G' stands for the satisfaction that comes from gaining whatever is desired and 'L' stands for the dissatisfaction that comes from its loss. This is why all unbalanced living doesn't yield living well.

[*Sidebar quotation* from Ralph Waldo Emerson: "For everything you have missed, you have gained something else; and for everything you gain, you lose something else."]

To live well is to live a balanced (centered) life. There is nothing to gain. There's nothing to gain that could create a well-lived life. Though we nonsages have yet to realize it, we already have everything necessary for living well.

This explains why spiritual trainees are also not living well. Since they are trying to gain something, wisdom, they are living with a lack of balance. Sages, the only masters of life, realize that there's nothing to gain, because there's nothing that is lacking. In other words, *the only thing to be gained is the realization that there is nothing to be gained.*

[*Sidebar quotation* from George Lucas: "You have to find something that you love enough to be able to take risks, jump over the hurdles and break through the brick walls that are always going to be placed in front of you. If you don't have that kind of feeling for what it is you are doing, you'll stop at the first giant hurdle."]

Good spiritual trainees are *like* those who are in love. Their faith is that there is something, namely, awakening and then enlightenment, that will make their lives better. Sages need no such faith; sages have realized that there is nothing else necessary to make their lives go well. Trainees need the confidence of faith, whereas sages don't.

Of what use is this? If you want to be a good spiritual trainee, fall in love with 'Who?"

This is not easy to do. By way of contrast, I know from experience that it's very easy to fall in love with a woman. It seems utterly natural. In fact, there's no greater distraction. How, though, could I fall in love with a koan? That seems utterly artificial, doesn't it?

The differences are not as great as they may initially seem.

How is my falling in love with, say, Anna different from your falling in love with 'Who?'?

It seems that yours is not at all natural. Would any prehistoric human have done it? Did any prehistoric males fall in love with any prehistoric females? Isn't there a lot that is artificial about falling in love with another person? After all, the ancient Greeks, for example, didn't do it. Would I have ever fallen in love with Anna if I'd never learned about the idea of romantic love? I might have lusted after her, but would I have fallen in love with her without having picked up the idea of romantic love from popular culture?

If I fall in love with Anna, am I not responsible for that? After all, Anna had no power to make me fall in love with her. Similarly, if you fall in love with a koan, are you not responsible for that? How could a koan have the power to make you fall in love with it?

Do I dream about Anna during the night? Do you dream about 'Who?' during the night?

Do I awake thinking about Anna? Do you awake thinking about 'Who?'?

Do I think about Anna with every breath throughout the day? Do you think about 'Who?' with every breath throughout the day?

Am I crazy about Anna? Are you crazy about your koan?

The more I think about Anna, the more obsessed I get. The more you become absorbed in your koan, the more obsessed you get.

In other words, there are a lot more similarities between the two cases than it initially appears.

Still, however fascinating and mysterious, a koan is not a person. As with any analogy, there are also dissimilarities. For sure, for example, it's more difficult to fall in love with a koan than it is to fall in love with another person.

The rewards, though, of falling in love with a koan are much greater than the rewards of falling in love with another person. There are no sexual rewards, of course, but what greater blessing is there than awakening and enlightenment?

Would you like to master life? Would you like to become a sage?

If you are serious about mastering life, I recommend falling in love with a koan. If a master hasn't assigned you one and you are confident that you are ready, start with 'Who?'

Endnotes

Preface
1. In Chapter 11.
2. In Chapter 12.

Chapter 1: Where We Are
3. Plato 155d.
4. G. W. F. Hegel, Phenomenology of Spirit (Oxford: Clarendon Press, 1977; A. V. Miller, tr.), p. 45. By the end of this book I shall have explained how it is possible to forget oneself.
5. See Chapter 7, section 5.
6. Julia Annas, The Morality of Happiness (N.Y.: Oxford University Press, 1993), p. 29.
7. The Morality of Happiness, p. 29.
8. I return to this in Chapters 4, 5, and 6.
9. See Chapter 6.
10. See Chapter 11, section 1.
11. Aristotle 1097B24ff.

Chapter 2: The Way of the World
12. Motivational Classics (Mechanicsburg, PA: Life Management, 1983), p. 109.
13. I explain this is Part III.
14. Motivational Classics, p. 105.
15. See Chapter 9.
16. See Chapter 4.
17. See Chapter 4.
18. See Chapter 5.
19. See Chapter 6.
20. See Chapter 1, section 1.
21. Brian Tracy, Something For Nothing (Mechanicsburg, PA: Executive, 2004), Chapter One.

22. Something For Nothing, p. 28.

23. See The Vimalakirti Sutra (N.Y.: Columbia University Press, 1997; Burton Watson, tr.).

Chapter 3: Success and Mastery

24. David Abram, The Spell of the Sensuous: Perception and Language in a More-Than-Human-World (N.Y.: Vintage, 1996).

25. The Spell of the Sensuous, pp. 100-101.

26. The Spell of the Sensuous, p. 252.

27. See Chapter 6.

28. See, for example, his Phaedrus and Sophist.

29. See his Theaetetus.

30. See Chapter 8.

31. If you would like some free additional help on this exercise, go to:

    http://www.lasting-weight-loss.com/goals.html .

Here's how: if you are reading this on a computer monitor that is connected to the internet, just click on the link to go there. Alternatively, you may copy and paste that URL to search window in your browser. (If you don't know how to copy and paste, just type it in that window exactly.) Once it is in the window, click on the search button and you'll go right to the relevant page.

32. Aristotle, Nicomachean Ethics 1100a6 and 1098a20, T. Irwin translation.

33. The Buddha, The Dhammapada (Tomales, California: Nilgiri, 1985; E. Easwaran,
    tr.), p. 105.

34. Our Appointment with Life (Berkeley, California: Parallax, 1990; Thich Nhat Hanh, tr.), p. 5.

35. One translation of the Vajracchedika Prajnaparamita Sutra with commentaries is Thich Nhat Hanh, The Diamond

<u>That Cuts Through Illusion</u> (Berkeley, California: Parallax, 1992).

36. See Chapter 2, section 3.

37. Peter Coveney and Roger Highfield, <u>The Arrow of Time</u> (N.Y.: Fawcett, 1990), p. 26.

38. <u>The Spell of the Sensuous</u>, p. 183.

39. See Chapter 12.

40. <u>The Spell of the Sensuous</u>, p. 187.

41. I return to this in Chapter 6.

42. <u>The Upanishads</u> (Tomales, California: Nilgiri, 1987; E. Easwaran, tr.), p. 45.

43. See Chapter 7, section 1.

44. Some philosophers disagree. They take the critical question to be: "What should I be?" I explain in Chapter 6 why this approach is the wrong one.

45. See Chapter 6, section 4, and Chapter 7, section 1.

46. Many thinkers have pointed out this typically underappreciated point. An excellent discussion of it is in Chapter 8 of Panayot Butchvarov, <u>Skepticism in Ethics</u> (Bloomington: Indiana University Press, 1989).

Chapter 4: What-Is

47. This refers to a story told by the Buddha. A man being chased by a tiger went over the side of a cliff and hung there grasping a strawberry bush. There was another tiger at the bottom of the cliff, and two mice, one black and one white, were circling around the trunk of the bush while nibbling it. There was a strawberry near the man's face, so he put it into his mouth. It was delicious!

48. The reason fanaticism is discussed in Chapter 2 is because it's important.

49. See Chapter 7, section 5.

50. Even if you are not interested in lasting weight loss, you will find these pages useful. That website is about much more than lasting weight loss.

51. <u>The Spell of the Sensuous</u>, p. 42.

52. <u>The Spell of the Sensuous</u>, p. 50.

53. Compare Kant's <u>Critique of Pure Reason</u>, B129ff.

54. I am here considering, as foundational, perceivings that are expressed by statements of the form "Someone perceives x"--as opposed to "Someone perceives x as F". ('x' stands for objects; it's a variable that ranges over objects such as tables. 'F' stands for concepts; it's a variable that ranges over concepts such as the concept of being a table.) The reason is simple: we are able to perceive objects that we may not know how to conceptualize. Presumably, we used to do that all the time as infants. We may be able to perceive x without being able to classify x as F. As adults, our perceivings are typically contaminated by our concepts; however, it's the perceivings that are foundational.

55. The best book I've read on this is Panayot Butchvarov, <u>Skepticism About the External World</u> (N.Y.: Oxford University Press, 1998). It's densely argued, but it's excellent.

56. <u>Skepticism About the External World</u>, p. 26.

57. Its lessons may be reconstructed as follows. Though not necessarily wholly, our knowledge of material objects ultimately rests on perception. However, the senses may deceive us, for example, when an object is too small or too distant. Sometimes we can correct for distortions and sometimes, perhaps even during a hallucination, we may withhold making any judgments. However, we are unable to do this when dreaming. Any correction of a perceptual judgment made during a dream would be itself part of the dream and therefore worthless. Where 'p' stands for some

perceptual judgment, if I am dreaming then I neither know that p nor have any evidence that p. When they occur in dreams, perceptions are worthless with respect to apprehending real material objects. This is true even if those perceptions happen to be as coherent and colorful and systematic as veridical perceptions. Compare Butchvarov, <u>Skepticism About the External World</u>, p. 66.

58. I return to this in the next chapter.

59. I discuss this in more detail in chapters 3-5 in my <u>The Fundamental Ideas</u>. For a more thorough discussion, see Butchvarov's <u>Being Qua Being</u> and chapter 5 of his <u>Skepticism About the External World</u>.

60. Merely remembering an object doesn't count as noticing it in a different way.

61. Technically, existential judgments are "material identity" judgments, which are judgments of the logical form "x is y" (as opposed to "formal identity" judgments, which are judgments of the form "x is x"). A material identity judgment is one in which, if it is true, it is about one object that is noticed in two ways, whereas, if it is false, it is about two different objects. Existential judgments are "positive" if they mean that an object or category of objects is real; they are "negative" if they mean that an object or category of objects is unreal. How can there be negative existential judgments? It's because such judgments, as Meinong shows, are about unreal objects. The fact is that, sometimes, we may experience such objects (for example, in a dream or a hallucination). Although myths and stories are real, their characters may not be. For example, didn't you learn as a youngster that Santa Claus didn't exist? You did learn something, namely, how to classify Santa Claus correctly. However sad it made you, you put old Saint Nick into the unreal bin.

62. See Chapter 12.

63. For more on this topic of what-is as being beyond conceptualization, see the "The Conditioned and the Unconditioned" section in my <u>The Three Things the Rest of Us Should Know about Zen Training</u>.

64. At least there will always be more to master if the notion of a fully enlightened sage is only an ideal.

Chapter 5: Creating Your Reality

65. See Chapter 9.

66. See Chapter 3, section 1, as well as the section "The Conditioned and the Unconditioned" in my <u>The Three Things the Rest of Us Should Know about Zen Training</u>. Following Plato, it's traditional to say that they inhabit the domain of *being* rather than the domain of *becoming*. The domain of being is the domain of pure thought. It is perfectly static, lifeless, dead. There's nothing wrong with abstract objects. They can be fascinating, alluring, and even beautiful. However, their relations are always necessarily one way rather than another (for example, it's necessarily true that 3 is greater than 2 and necessarily false that 2 is greater than 3). Since immutability is irrelevant to mastery, we may set abstractions aside. Compare my <u>Getting Things Done</u>.

67. See Chapter 12 and my <u>The Meditative Approach to Philosophy</u>.

68. See my "Beyond Skepticism in Ethics" in Larry Lee Blackman, ed., <u>The Philosophy of Panayot Butchvarov</u> (Lewiston, N.Y.: Mellen, 2005), p. 308ff.

69. This is the term Thich Nhat Hanh uses, and it's a good one. He also is good at explaining it, and my explanation that follows has benefited from his in, for example, <u>The Heart of Understanding</u> (Berkeley, California: Parallax, 1988), pp. 3-5, and <u>The Miracle of Mindfulness</u> (Boston: Beacon, 1975), pp. 47-8.

70. Quoted from Thich Nhat Hanh, <u>The Heart of The Buddha's Teaching</u> (Berkeley, California: Parallax, 1998), p. 206. See also Chapter 3 of <u>Early Buddhist Discourses</u> (Indianapolis: Hackett, 2006; John J. Holder, tr.).

71. Compare Thich Nhat Hanh, <u>Zen Keys</u> (N.Y.: Doubleday, 1974), p. 112.

Chapter 6: Understanding Yourself

72. James Joyce. <u>A Portrait of the Artist as a Young Man</u> (N.Y.: Viking, 1964), p. 15.

73. For more, see Butchvarov's <u>Being Qua Being</u> and <u>Skepticism About the External World.</u>

74. The arguments are readily available elsewhere, for example, in the two books mentioned in the previous note.

75. See Chapter 3, section 1.

76. See Chapter 12.

77. Without substrata, what clusters the qualities of an individual together? For my answer, see my <u>The Fundamental Ideas</u>, pp. 146-9, or Butchvarov's <u>Being Qua Being</u>, chapter 8. This problem, too, goes far beyond the scope of this book on mastery.

78. Chapter 2, section 5.

79. I return to awareness in the next section.

80. If the topic of emotions particularly interests you, I suggest my book <u>Emotional Eating</u>, which has little directly to do with eating.

81. See, for example, <u>Early Buddhist Discourses</u>, pp. 83-86.

82. Chapter 3, section 1.

83. See Chapter 4, section 4, and my <u>The Fundamental Ideas</u>, Chapter 7.

84. See Chapter 11.

85. Mastering life itself is the topic of Chapter 12.

86. Eugene Herrigel, Zen in the Art of Archery (N.Y.: Vintage, 1953; R. F. C. Hull, tr), p. 45.

87. Zen in the Art of Archery, p. 52.

88. Zen in the Art of Archery, p. 49.

89. Zen in the Art of Archery, p. 56.

90. Zen in the Art of Archery, p. 61.

91. Zen in the Art of Archery, p. 56.

92. Zen in the Art of Archery, p. 65.

93. Zen in the Art of Archery, p. 76.

94. Zen in the Art of Archery, p. 77.

Chapter 7: Adjusting Your Attitude

95. Quoted from Richard N. Bosley & Martin M. Tweedale, eds., Basic Issues in Medieval Philosophy (Orchard Park, N.Y.: Broadview, 1997), pp. 646-649.

96. Basic Issues in Medieval Philosophy, p. 650.

97. See Chapter 3, sections 4 and 5.

98. Compare my Love and Respect.

99. See also my Love and Respect.

100. See Chapter 12.

101. See Chapter 12 and my The Meditative Approach to Philosophy and The Three Things the Rest of Us Should Know about Zen Training.

102. Compare Hanh, The Miracle of Mindfulness, p. 94.

103. Robert C. Solomon, The Passions (Indianapolis: Hackett, 1993), p. 258.

104. Basic Issues in Medieval Philosophy, p. 583.

105. Basic Issues in Medieval Philosophy, p. 587.

106. Basic Issues in Medieval Philosophy, p. 588.

107. Compare Wayne Dyer, Ph.D., "How To Be A No-Limit Person" audio program.

108. Quote from Steven M. Cahn, Classics of Western Philosophy (Indianapolis:Hackett, 1999; 5th edition), p. 289.

109. <u>Classics of Western Philosophy</u>, p. 279. The next quote is from the same source.

110. If Hume had done nothing else, his analysis of causation by itself would have marked him as a major philosopher.

111. <u>Nicomachean Ethics</u>, Book II.

112. I obtained the idea for this formula from Andrew Weil, M.D.

113. Quoted in Thich Nhat Hanh, <u>Teachings on Love</u> (Berkeley, California: Parallax,
    1997), p. 12.

114. Chapter 4, section 4.

115. <u>Teachings on Love</u>, p. 42.

116. <u>Teachings on Love</u>, pp. 77 & 86.

117. His Holiness the Dalai Lama and Howard C. Cutler, M.D., <u>The Art of Happiness</u>
    (N.Y.: Riverhead, 1998), p. 114.

118. <u>Teachings on Love</u>, p. 37.

119. <u>The Dhammapada</u>, p. 195.

120. <u>The Dhammapada</u>, p. 198.

121. <u>The Dhammapada</u>, pp. 199 & 193.

122. <u>The Dhammapada</u>, p. 199.

123. For more information on one good way for beginners to make an offering available online, simply go to: <u>http://www.lasting-weight-loss.com/</u> and click the rectangular box at the bottom of any page that reads "Powered by Site Build It." It is an affiliate link.

124. <u>The Dhammapada</u>, p. 167.

125. The concept of self is discussed in Chapters 6 and 12; the concept of a good is discussed in Chapter 8.

126. Compare Butchvarov, <u>Skepticism in Ethics</u>, Chapter 6.

127. William Faulkner: "the 'Ode on a Grecian Urn' is worth any number of old ladies.'"

Chapter 8: Organizing Your Values

128. See Chapter 12.

129. See, for example, the Buddha's <u>Sutra on the Four Establishments of Mindfulness.</u>

130. See Chapter 4.

131. See Chapter 5.

132. See Chapter 6.

133. If you want to read more about this, I recommend the Tiegers' <u>The Art of Speedreading People</u>. (Incidentally, I'm an introverted, intuitive, thinking Judger.)

134. Compare Gary Chapman, <u>The Five Love Languages</u>.

135. See Chapter 11.

136. This specific method I learned from the Style Interview in David DeAngelo's "Interviews With Dating Gurus" series (2005).

137. Chapter 6, section 2.

138. See Chapter 12.

139. Quoted from <u>Chants & Recitations</u> (Rochester, N.Y.: The Rochester Zen Center, 2005), p. 27. Compare Berkeley's Identity Principle many centuries later: it is impossible "to separate, even in thought," the things we see and feel, in other words, the objects of sense perception, from perception. George Berkeley. <u>Of the Principles of Human Knowledge</u>, Part I, section 5.

140. <u>Chants & Recitations</u>, p. 26.

141. <u>Chants & Recitations</u>, p. 28.

142. Plato, 174a, Cornford translation.

143. <u>Chants & Recitations</u>, p. 28.

144. See Chapter 3, section 1.

145. Cf. my <u>Emotional Eating, Compulsive Overeating Help</u>, and <u>How to Stop Emotional Eating</u>.

Chapter 9: Habits

146. Chapter 4, section 4.
147. Tor Norretranders, <u>The User Illusion</u> (N.Y.: Penguin, 1991; J. Sydenham, tr.), p. 259.
148. Chapter 3, section 1.
149. <u>The User Illusion</u>, p. 262.
150. See Chapter 5, section 4.
151. <u>The User Illusion</u>, p. 264.
152. Deirdre Barrett, <u>Waistland</u> (N.Y.: Norton, 2007), p. 167.
153. See Chapter 8, section 3.
154. For example, from http://nhlbisupport.com/bmi
155. See Chapter 8, section 4.
156. See Chapter 12.
157. See Chapter 12 and my <u>The Three Things the Rest of Us Should Know About Zen Training</u> and <u>The Meditative Approach to Philosophy</u>.
158. See Chapter 8, section 5.
159. See Chapter 8, section 6.
160. See Chapter 8, section 7.
161. Cf. my <u>The Meditative Approach to Philosophy</u>. If you'd like greater business success, see my <u>How to Become Happily Published</u> and <u>12 Publicity Mistakes that Keep Marketers Poor</u>.

Chapter 10: Techniques

162. Chapter 1, section 2.
163. Chapter 6, section 4.
164. Compare Chapter 5 in Deirdre Barrett's <u>Waistland</u> (N.Y.: Norton, 2007).
165. <u>Theaetetus</u> 172d, Cornford, tr.
166. 1259a6.

167. For example, Plato and Aristotle didn't have jobs (except for the fact that Aristotle was a tutor and both Plato and Aristotle founded schools), and, in the east, Vimalakirti was a wealthy sage.

Chapter 11: Selecting an Activity to Master

168. Chapter 6.

169. See Chapter 9, section 2.

170. See Chapter 12.

171. 1028a20-25. Strictly speaking for Aristotle, only humans among substances act (1222b19).

172. Chapter 8, section 1.

173. Joanna Macy, <u>World As Lover, World As Self</u> (Berkeley, California: Parallax, 1991.)

174. As Nietzsche famously announced, God is dead, in other words, the reality or unreality of God is irrelevant.

175. In fact, extreme asceticism doesn't work for living well. It only yields premature death.

176. This is why, considered in abstraction from its consequences, deliberate killing, taking a life, is always wrong; however, since actions do have consequences, it does not follow that killing is always wrong.

177. Chapter 5.

Chapter 12: The Most Important Activity

178. Huston Smith, <u>The World's Religions</u> (San Francisco: HarperCollins, 1991), p. 92ff.

179. The Venerable Bodhin Kjolhede, Roshi.

180. The practice arose in China and later spread to Japan, Korea, and Viet Nam. The Chinese practice is called '<u>ch'an</u>' or '<u>chan</u>.' The Korean practice is called '<u>son</u>.'

181. <u>The World's Religions</u>, pp. 94-7.

182. <u>The World's Religions</u>, pp. 98-99.

183. In fact, the chapter in his book on Buddhism is so good that I wasn't able to understand how someone who

didn't regularly practice <u>zazen</u> could have written it. Buried in the footnotes, I found the answer: in addition to personal contact with D. T. Suzuki, friendship with Philip Kapleau, and extensive reading, he spent six weeks practicing Zen Buddhism in Kyoto with Zen master Goto Roshi. Someone who had not practiced <u>zazen</u> so extensively could not have written that chapter.

184. See Chapter 3, section 1.

185. *ZenBow*, xxix, #2, p. 15.

186. I capitalize 'Emptiness' to denote that it is beyond the ordinary concepts of emptiness and fullness.

187. Katsuki Sekida, ed. & tr., <u>Two Zen Classics</u> (N.Y.: Weatherhill, 1977), p. 28.

<u>Cover photo</u>: The photo on the cover is one that I took of a photo that a friend gave me years ago. I don't know who took the original photo. Its subject is the somewhat smaller than life size Miroku Bosatsu in the seated Hanka pose. It was carved of camphor wood in the 7th century by an unknown Korean artist. It was given to Japan, and it's housed in the Koryuji temple in Kyoto. (One of my few wishes before I die is to see it in person.)

I've a **favor** to ask you: Please go to amazon.com, find this book (by entering either its title or my name into the search box) and leave some feedback about it, which may help others if not me. Thank you in advance. I wish you peace.

Selected Bibliography

Abe, Masao, and LaFleur, William R. Zen and Western Thought. Honolulu: University of Hawaii Press, 1985.

Abram, David. The Spell of the Sensuous. N.Y.: Vintage, 1996.

Aitken, Robert. Taking the Path of Zen. N.Y.: Farrar, Straus, and Giroux, 1982.

Allan, Christian B., and Lutz, Wolfgang. Life Without Bread. Los Angeles: Keats, 2000.

Anonymous. Chants & Recitations. Rochester, N.Y.: Rochester Zen Center, 2005.

Anonymous. The Bhagavad Gita. N.Y.: Random House, 1985. E. Easwaran, tr.

Anonymous. The New English Bible. Oxford and Cambridge: University Press, 1970. 2nd ed.

Anonymous. The Upanishads. Tomales, California: Nilgiri, 1987. E. Easwaran, tr.

Aristotle. The Complete Works of Aristotle. Princeton, N.J.: Princeton University Press, 1984. Jonathan Barnes, ed.

-----.Nicomachean Ethics. Indianapolis: Hackett, 1985. T. Irwin, tr.

Armstrong, Karen. Buddha. N.Y.: Penguin, 2001.

Audette, Ray, and Gilchrist, Troy. Neanderthin. N.Y.: St. Martin's, 1999.

Baker, Robin. Sperm Wars. N.Y.: Thunder's Mouth, 1996.

Bandler, Richard. Using Your Brain—for a Change. Moab, Utah: Real People,1985.

----- and Grinder, John. Frogs into Princes. Moab, Utah: Real People, 1979.

Barrett, Deirdre. <u>Waistland</u>. N.Y.: Norton, 2007.
Batchelor, Stephen. <u>Buddhism Without Beliefs</u>. N.Y.: Riverhead, 1997.
Beck, Charlotte Joko. <u>Everyday Zen</u>. San Francisco: HarperCollins, 1989.
-----. <u>Nothing Special</u>. San Francisco: HarperCollins, 1993.
Bennett, William J., ed. <u>The Book of Virtues</u>. N.Y.: Simon & Schuster, 1993.
Benson, Herbert. <u>The Relaxation Response</u>. N.Y.: Avon, 1975.
Berkeley, George. <u>Principles, Dialogues, and Philosophical Correspondence</u>. Indianapolis: Bobbs-Merrill, 1965. C. M. Turbayne, ed.
Blackman, Larry Lee, ed. <u>Classics of Analytical Metaphysics</u>. Lanham, M.D.: University Press of America, 1984.
-----, ed. The Philosophy of Panayot Butchvarov. Lewiston, N.Y.: Edwin Mellen, 2005.
Blanton, Brad. <u>Radical Honesty</u>. N.Y.: Dell, 1994.
Bodian, Stephan. <u>Meditation For Dummies</u>. N.Y.: Wiley, 1999.
Boorstein, Sylvia. <u>Don't Just Do Something, Sit There</u>. San Francisco: HarperCollins, 1996.
Borg, Marcus, ed. <u>Jesus and Buddha: The Parallel Sayings</u>. Berkeley, California: Ulysses, 1997.
Bosley, Richard N., and Tweedale, Martin, eds. <u>Basic Issues in Medieval Philosophy</u>. Orchard Park, N.Y.: Broadview, 1997.
Bradford, Dennis. <u>Compulsive Overeating Help</u>. Las Vegas: Ironox. 2013.
-----. <u>Emotional Eating</u>.. Las Vegas: Ironox. 2013.
-----. <u>Getting Things Done</u>.. Las Vegas: Ironox, 2013.
-----. <u>It's Not Just About the Money!</u>. Las Vegas: Ironox,,

  2013.

-----. <u>The Meditative Approach to Philosophy.</u> Las Vegas: Ironox, 2012.

-----. <u>The Three Things the Rest of Us Should Know About Zen Training.</u> Las Vegas: Ironox, 2013.

-----. "Beyond Skepticism in Ethics" in Larry Lee Blackman, ed., <u>The Philosophy of Panayot Butchvarov.</u>

Bradley, F. H. <u>Appearance and Reality.</u> Oxford: Clarendon Press, 1897. 2nd ed.

-----. "My Station and Its Duties" in <u>Ethical Studies.</u> Oxford: Clarendon Press, 1927. 2nd. ed.

Braly, James, and Hoggan, Ron. <u>Dangerous Grains.</u> N.Y.: Avery, 2002.

Brentano, Franz. <u>Psychology from an Empirical Standpoint.</u> N.Y.: Humanities, 1973. A. C. Rancurello, D. B. Terrell, and L. L. McAlister, trs.

Bronowski, J., and Mazlish, Bruce. <u>The Western Intellectual Tradition.</u> N.Y.: Dorset, 1960.

Buddha, The. <u>Basic Teachings of the Buddha.</u> N.Y.: Random House, 2007. Glenn Wallis, ed.

-----. <u>In the Buddha's Words.</u> Boston: Wisdom, 2005. Bhikkhu Bodhi, ed.

-----. <u>The Dhammapada.</u> Eknath Easwaran, tr. Berkeley, California: Nilgiri, 1985.

-----. <u>Dhammapada.</u> Thomas Byrom, tr. Boston: Shambhala, 1976.

-----. <u>Dhammapada.</u> Thomas Cleary, tr. N.Y.: Bantam, 1994.

-----. <u>Early Buddhist Discourses.</u> Indianapolis: Hackett, 2006. John J. Holder, ed.

Buksbazen, John Daishin. <u>Zen Meditation in Plain English.</u>

Boston: Wisdom, 2002.
Buss, David M. The Evolution of Desire. N.Y.: Basic, 2003. Rev. ed.
Butler, Gillian, and Hope, Tony. Managing Your Mind. N.Y.: Oxford University Press,1995.
Butchvarov, Panayot. Anthropocentrism in Philosophy. Unpublished manuscript (but available online.)
-----. Being Qua Being. Bloomington, Indiana: Indiana University Press, 1979.
-----. The Concept of Knowledge. Evanston, Illinois: Northwestern University Press, 1970.
-----. Resemblance and Identity. Bloomington, Indiana: Indiana University Press, 1966.
-----. Skepticism about the External World. N.Y.: Oxford University Press, 1998.
-----. Skepticism in Ethics. Bloomington, Indiana: Indiana University Press, 1989.
Campbell, Joseph. The Hero's Journey. Novato, California: Novato, 1990.
Cahn, Steven M., ed. Classics of Western Philosophy. Indianapolis: Hackett, 1999. 5th ed.
Chadwick, David. Crooked Cucumber: The Life and Zen Teachings of Shunryu Suzuki. N.Y.: Broadway, 1999.
Chodron, Pema. No Time To Lose. Boston: Shambhala, 2005.
Christensen, Clayton M. The Innovator's Dilemma. Boston: Harvard Business School, 1997.
Chung Tzu. The Essential Chuan Tzu. Boston: Shambhala, 1999. S. Hamill and J. P.Seaton, trs.
Cleary, Thomas. Kensho: The Heart of Zen. Boston: Shambhala, 1997.
-----. Rational Zen: The Mind of Dogen Zenji. Boston: Shambhala, 1995.

Coleman, Ronnie. Hardcore. Woodland Hills, California: Weider, 2004.
Confucius. The Analects. N.Y.: Dover, 1995. W. E. Soothill, tr.
Cordain, Loren. The Paleo Diet. Hoboken, N.J.: John Wiley & Sons, 2002.
Cordain, Loren, and Friel, Joe. The Paleo Diet for Athletes. U.S.A.: Rodale, 2005.
Coveney, Peter, and Highfield, Roger. The Arrow of Time. N.Y.: FawcettColumbine, 1990.
Crane, Paul. The Ultimate Fat Burning Diet Primer! E-book.
Csikszentmihalyi, Mihaly. Flow. N.Y.: Harper, 1990.
Dalai Lama, The. The Art of Happiness. N.Y.: Riverhead, 1998.
Das, Lama Surya. Awakening The Buddha Within. N.Y.: Broadway, 1997.
Dawkins, Richard. Unweaving the Rainbow. Boston: Houghton Mifflin, 1998.
-----. The Selfish Gene. N.Y.: Oxford University Press, 1989.
DeAngelo, David [aka 'Eben Pagan']. Mastery With Women & Dating. Audio set from Double Your Dating.
Descartes, Rene. The Philosophical Writings of Descartes. N.Y.: Cambridge University Press, 1985. J. Cottingham, R. Stoothoff, and D. Murdoch, trs.
Diamond, Jared. Collapse. N.Y.: Penguin, 2005
-----. Guns, Germs, and Steel. N.Y.: Norton, 1997.
Dilts, Robert; Hallbom, Tim; and Smith, Suzi. Beliefs. Portland, Oregon: Metamorphous, 1990.
Dimnet, Ernest. The Art of Thinking. Greenwich, Conneticut: Fawcett, 1928.

Dogen. Moon in a Dewdrop: Writings of Zen Master
    Dogen. K. Tanahashi, ed. N.Y.: Farrar, Strauss and Giroux, 1985.
----. Shobogenzo. 4 vols. G. Nishijima & C. Cross, trs.
    London: Windbell, 1994, 1996, 1997, 1999.
Dyer, Wayne. "How to be a No-Limit Person." Audio set
    from Nightingale-Conant.
Easwaran, Eknath. Meditation. Tomales, California:
    Nilgiri, 1978.
Epstein, Mark. Going To Pieces Without Falling Apart.
    N.Y.: Broadway, 1998.
-----. Thoughts Without A Thinker. N.Y.: Basic, 1995.
Evans, William; Rosenberg, Irwin H.; Thompson, J.
    Biomarkers. N.Y.: Fireside, 1991.
Feigl, H., and Sellars, W., eds. Readings in Philosophical
    Analysis. N.Y.: Appleton-Century-Crofts, 1949.
Feigl, H., Sellars, W., and Lehrer, K. eds. New Readings in
    Philosophical Analysis. N.Y.: Appleton-Century-Crofts, 1972.
Ferguson, Andy. Zen's Chinese Heritage. Boston:
    Wisdom, 2000.
Fisher, Bruce, and Alberti, Robert. Rebuilding When Your
    Relationship Ends. Atascadero, California: Impact, 2000. 3rd. ed.
Fontana, David. The Meditator's Handbook. Rockport,
    Massachusetts: Element, 1992.
Foster, Nelson, and Shoemaker, Jack, eds. The Roaring
    Stream: A New Zen Reader. Hopewell, New Jersey: Ecco, 1996.
Frankena, William K. Ethics. Englewood Cliffs, N.J.:
    Prentice-Hall, 1973. 2nd ed.
Frankl, Viktor E. Man's Search for Meaning. N.Y.:
    Simon and Schuster, 1984. 3rd ed.

Fraser, J. T. Time. Amherst, Massachusetts: University of Massachusetts Press, 1987.
Friedman, Thomas L. The World Is Flat. Farrar, Straus, and Giroux, 2006.
Fromm, Erich. The Art of Loving. N.Y.: Harper and Row, 1956.
Fumerton, Richard A. Reason and Morality. Ithaca, N.Y.: Cornell University Press, 1990.
Goleman, Daniel. Emotional Intelligence. N.Y.: Bantam, 1995.
Goscienski, Philip J. Health Secrets of the Stone Age. Oceanside, California: Goscienski, 2005.
Gould, Stephen Jay. The Structure of Evolutionary Theory. Cambridge, Massachusetts: Harvard University Press, 2002.
Graff, Cynthia Stamper, and Holderman, Jerry. Lean for Life. Costa Mesa, California: Lindora, 2001.
Graham, A. C. Disputers of the Tao. LaSalle, Illinois: Open Court, 1989.
Gregory, Peter N. Traditions of Meditation in Chinese Buddhism. Honolulu: University Of Hawaii Press, 1986.
Groves, Barry. Natural Health & Weight Loss. London: Hammersmith, 2007.
Gunaratana, Venerable Henepola. Mindfulness in Plain English. Boston: Wisdom, 1991.
Hagan, Steve. Buddhism Plain & Simple. N.Y.: Broadway, 1997.
Hakuin. The Zen Master Hakuin: Selected Writings. P. Yampolsky, tr. N.Y.: Columbia University Press, 1971.
Hamer, Dean, & Copeland, Peter. Living with Our Genes. N.Y.: Doubelday, 1998.
Hazo, Robert G. The Idea of Love. N.Y.: Praeger, 1967.

Haney, Lee, and Rosenthal, Jim. <u>Lee Haney's Ultimate Body-Building</u>. N.Y.: St. Martin's, 1993.
Hanh, Thich Nhat. <u>Being Peace</u>. Berkeley, California: Parallax, 1987.
-----. <u>The Blooming of a Lotus</u>. Boston: Beacon, 1993.
-----. <u>Breathe! You Are Alive</u>. Berkeley, California: Parallax, 1996.
-----. <u>The Diamond That Cuts Through Illusion</u>. Berkeley, California: Parallax, 1992.
-----. <u>The Heart of The Buddha's Teaching</u>. Berkeley, California: Parallax, 1998.
-----. <u>The Heart of Understanding</u>. Berkeley, California: Parallax, 1988.
-----. <u>Interbeing</u>. Berkeley, California: Parallax, 1998. 3rd. ed.
-----. <u>The Miracle of Mindfulness</u>. Boston: Beacon, 1975.
-----. <u>Old Path White Clouds</u>. Berkeley, California: Parallax, 1991.
-----. <u>Our Appointment with Life</u>. Berkeley, California: Parallax, 1990.
-----. <u>Present Moment Wonderful Moment</u>. Berkeley, California: Parallax, 1990.
-----. <u>Teachings on Love</u>. Berkeley, California: Parallax, 1997.
-----. <u>Thundering Silence</u>. Berkeley, California: Parallax, 1993.
-----. <u>Transformation & Healing</u>. Berkeley, California: Parallax, 1990.
-----. <u>Zen Keys</u>. N.Y.: Doubleday, 1974.
Happold, F. C. <u>Mysticism</u>. Baltimore: Penguin, 1963.
Heidegger, Martin. <u>Being and Time</u>. N.Y.: Harper & Row, 1962. J. Macquarrie & E. Robinson, trs.
Heine, Steven. <u>Opening a Mountain</u>. N.Y.: Oxford

University Press, 2002.
Heine, Steven, and Prebish, Charles S., eds. Buddhism in the Modern World. N.Y.: Oxford University Press, 2003.
Heine, Steven, and Wright, Dale S., eds. The Koan. N.Y.: Oxford University Press, 2000.
Hegel, G. W. F. Phenomenology of Spirit. Oxford: Clarendon Press, 1977. A. V. Miller, tr.
Helmstetter, Shad. What To Say When You Talk To Your Self. N.Y.: Pockett, 1982.
Heraclitus. Heraclitus. N.Y.: Atheneum, 1964. P. Wheelwright, tr.
Herrigel, Eugene. Zen in the Art of Archery. N.Y.: Vintage, 1953. R. F. C. Hull, tr.
Hochsmann, Hyun, and Guorong, Yang. Zhuangzi. N.Y.: Person, 2007.
Holman, Steve, and Lawson, Jonathan. The Ultimate Mass Workout. E-book: Homebody, 2004.
-----. X-Treme Lean. E-book: Homebody, 2005.
Hui-Neng. The Sutra of Hui-Neng. T. Cleary, tr. Boston: Shambhala, 1998.
Hume, David. A Treatise of Human Nature. Oxford: Clarendon Press, 1978. P. H. Nidditch, ed. 2nd ed.
Husserl, Edmund. Ideas. First Book. Boston: Martinus Nijhoff, 1983. F. Kersten, tr.
James, William. The Varieties of Religious Experience. N.Y.: Modern Library, 1902.
Jeffers, Susan. Feel the Fear and Do It Anyway. N.Y.: Ballantine, 1987.
Kabat-Zinn, Jon. Wherever You Go There You Are. N.Y.: Hyperion, 1994.
Kant, Immanuel. Critique of Pure Reason. N.Y.: St. Martin's, 1968. N. K. Smith, tr.

Kapleau, Roshi Philip. Awakening to Zen. N.Y.: Scribner, 1997. Polly Young- Eisendrath and Rafe Martin, eds.

-----. Straight to the Heart of Zen. Boston: Shambhala, 2001.

-----. The Three Pillars of Zen. N.Y.: Anchor, 1989.

-----. The Zen of Living and Dying. Boston: Shambhala, 1998.

-----. To Cherish All Life. Rochester, N.Y.: The Zen Center, 1986.

-----. Zen: Merging of East and West. N.Y.: Anchor, 1980.

Kasulis, T. P. Zen Action Zen Person.. Honolulu: The University of Hawaii Press, 1981.

Kennedy, Paul. The Rise and Fall of the Great Powers. N.Y.: Random House, 1987.

Kierkegaard, Soren. The Concept of Dread. Princeton, N.J.: Princeton University Press, 1957. 2nd ed. W. Lowrie, tr.

-----. Fear and Trembling and The Sickness Unto Death. Garden City, N.Y.: Doubleday, 1954.

King, Ian, and Schuler, Lou. The Book of Muscle. U.S.A.: Rodale, 2003.

Kirk, G. S., and Raven, J. E. The Presocratic Philosophers. Cambridge: University Press, 1957.

Kiyosaki, Robert T., and Lechter, Sharon L. Rich Dad Poor Dad. N.Y.: TimeWarner, 1997.

-----. The Cashflow Quadrant. N.Y.: TimeWarner, 1998.

Koch, Philip. Solitude. LaSalle, Illinois: Open Court, 1994.

Kokushi, Muso. Dream Conversations. T. Cleary, tr. Boston: Shambhala, 1996.

Kornfield, Jack. A Path With Heart. N.Y.: Bantam, 1993

Kraft, Kenneth, ed. Zen Teaching, Zen Practice. N.Y.: Weatherhill, 2000.
Kraft, Kenneth, ed. Zen: Tradition and Transition. N.Y.: Grove, 1988.
Kubik, Brooks D. Dinosaur Training. Louisville, Kentucky: Kubik, 1996.
Landes, David S. Revolution in Time. Cambridge: Harvard, 1983. Rev. ed.
Lao-Tzu. Tao Te Ching. Indianapolis: Hackett, 1993. Stephen Addiss & Stanley Lombardo, trs.
-----. Tao Te Ching. N.Y.: Putnam, 2001. J. Starr, tr.
Larson, Joan Mathews. Depression-Free, Naturally. N.Y.: Ballantine, 1999.
-----. Seven Weeks to Sobriety. N.Y.: Random House, 1992.
Lawrence, T. E. Seven Pillars of Wisdom. Garden City, N.Y.: Doubleday, 1936.
Leonard, George. Mastery. N.Y.: Penguin, 1991.
LeShan, Lawrence. How To Meditate. N.Y.: Little, Brown & Co., 1974.
Levitt, Steven D., and Dubner, Stephen J. Freakonomics. N.Y.: William Morrow, 2005.
Loori, John Daido. The Eight Gates of Zen. Mt. Tremper, N.Y.: Dharma, 1992.
-----. Invoking Reality. Mr. Tremper, N.Y.: Dharma, 1998.
-----. Riding the Ox Home. Boston: Shambhala, 2002.
-----, ed. Sitting with Koans. Boston: Wisdom, 2006.
Macy, Joanna. World As Lover, World As Self. Berkeley, California: Parallax, 1991.
Macy, Joanna, and Brown, Molly Young. Coming Back To Life. Gabriola Island, British Columbia: New Society, 1998.

Maltz, Maxwell. Psycho-Cybernetics. N.Y.: Prentice-Hall, 1960.
Mandelbaum, Maurice. History, Man, & Reason. Baltimore: John Hopkins, 1971.
Mann, Charles C. 1491. N.Y.: Knopf, 2005.
Mann, Robert, & Youd, Rose. Buddhist Character Analysis. Bradford on Avon, U.K.: Aukana, 1992.
Margen, Sheldon, ed. The Wellness Encyclopedia of Food and Nutrition. N.Y.: Rebus, 1992.
-----, ed. Wellness Foods A to Z. N.Y.: Rebus, 2002.
Matthews, Andrew. Follow Your Heart. Queensland, Australia: Seashell, 1997.
Martin, Rafe. The Hungry Tigress. Cambridge, MA: Yellow Moon, 1999.
Marx, Karl. The Marx-Engels Reader. N.Y.: Norton, 1978. 2nd. ed. R. Tucker, ed.
Mayeroff, Milton. On Caring. N.Y.: HarperCollins, 1971.
McCully, Kilmer S., and McCully, Martha. The Heart Revolution. N.Y.: HarperCollins, 1999.
McDonald, Kathleen. How To Meditate. Boston: Wisdom, 1984.
McGill, V. J. The Idea of Happiness. N.Y.: Praeger, 1967.
McLaughlin, Brian P., and Rorty, Amelie Oksenberg, eds. Perspectives on Self-Deception. Berkeley: University of California Press, 1988.
McRobert, Stuart. The Insider's Tell-All Handbook on Weight-Training Technique. Nicosia, Cyprus: CS, 1996.
-----. Build Muscle Lose Fat Look Great. Nicosia, Cyprus: CS, 2006.
McWilliams, John-Roger, and McWilliams, Peter. You

Can't Afford the Luxury of A Negative Thought. Los Angeles: Prelude, 1988.
Miller, Geoffrey. The Mating Mind. N.Y.: Anchor, 2000.
Millman, Dan. Body Mind Mastery. Novato, California: New World, 1999.
-----. Way of the Peaceful Warrior. Tiburon, California: New World, 2000. Revised edition.
Moore, G. E. Principia Ethica. Cambridge: University Press, 1903.
Murphy, Michael, and Donovan, Steven. The Physical and Psychological Effects of Meditation. San Rafael, California: Esalen, 1988.
Murray, Michael, and Pizzorno, Joseph. Encyclopedia of Natural Medicine. U.S.A.: Prima, 1998. 2nd ed.
Murti, T.R.V. The Central Philosophy of Buddhism. New Delhi: Munshiram Manoharlal, 2006.
Nagarjuna. Nagarguna and the Philosophy of Openness. N.Y.: Rowman &Littlefield, 1997. Nancy McCagney, ed.
Nagarjuna. The Fundamental Wisdom of the Middle Way. J. Garfield, tr. N.Y.: Oxford University Press, 1995.
Nietzsche, Friedrich. Basic Writings of Nietzsche. N.Y.: Modern Library, 1966. W. Kaufmann, ed. & tr.
-----. The Portable Nietzsche. N.Y.: Viking, 1954. W. Kaufmann, ed. & tr.
Nightingale, Earl. "Lead the Field." Audio set from Nightingale-Conant.
Nisargadatta Maharaj, Sri. I Am That. Durham, North Carolina: Acorn, 1973.
Norretranders, Tor. The User Illusion. N.Y.: Penguin, 1991. J. Sydonham, tr.
Novak, John. How To Meditate. Nevada City, California: Crystal Clarity, 1989.

Oech, Roger von. A Whack on the Side of the Head. N.Y.: Warner, 1998. 3rd ed.

Ogilvy, James. Living Without a Goal. N.Y.: Doubleday, 1995.

Olinsky, Frank. Buddha Book. San Francisco: Chronicle, 1997.

Pakaluk, Michael, ed. Other Selves. Indianapolis: Hackett, 1991.

Pascal, Blaise. Pensees and Other Writings. N.Y.: Oxford University Press, 1995. H. Levi, tr.

Passmore, John. A Hundred Years of Philosophy. Baltimore.: Penguin 1966. 2nd ed.

Patanjali. How to Know God. Hollywood, California: Vedanta Press, 1981.

Peace Pilgrim. Peace Pilgrim. Santa Fe, New Mexico: Ocean Tree, 1982.

Perry, John, ed. Personal Identity. Berkeley, California: University of California Press, 1975.

Pink, Daniel H. A Whole New Mind. N.Y.: Riverhead, 2005.

Pitino, Rick, and Reynolds, Bill. Success Is A Choice. N.Y.: Broadway, 1997.

Plato. The Collected Dialogues of Plato. Princeton, N.J.: Princeton University Press, 1961. E. Hamilton and H. Cairns, eds.

Plotinus. The Enneads. London: Faber and Faber, 1956. 3rd ed. S. MacKenna, tr.

Pollan, Michael. The Omnivore's Dilemma. N.Y.: Penguin, 2006.

Pratt, Steven G., and Matthews, Kathy. SuperFoods HealthStyle. N.Y.: William Morrow, 2006.

Pritchett, Price. Hard Optimism. Dallas, Texas: Pritchett.

-----. The Quantum Leap Strategy. Dallas, Texas: .

Prochaska, James O.; Norcross, John C.; and Diclemente, Carlo C. Changing for Good. N.Y.: Avon, 1994.
Rahula, Walpola. What The Buddha Taught. N.Y.: Grove, 1974. 2nd. ed.
Reps, Paul, and Sensaki, Nyogen, eds., Zen Flesh, Zen Bones. Boston: Shambala, 1994.
Ridley, Matt. The Red Queen. N.Y.: HarperCollins, 1993.
Robbins, Anthony. Awaken the Giant Within. N.Y.: Fireside, 1991.
Rorty, Amelie Oksenberg, ed. The Identities of Persons. Berkeley, California: University of California Press, 1976.
Rosenberg, Larry. Breath by Breath. Boston: Shambhala, 1999.
Ross, Julia. The Diet Cure. N.Y.: Viking, 1999.
-----. The Mood Cure. N.Y.: Viking, 2002.
Ross, Nancy Wilson. Buddhism. N.Y.: Vintage, 1980.
Ruiz, Don Miguel. The Four Agreements. San Rafael, California: Amber-Allen, 1997.
Salzberg, Sharon. Loving-Kindness. Boston: Shambhala, 1997.
Sangharakshita. The Three Jewels. Glasgow: Windhorse, 1967.
Santorelli, Saki. Heal Thy Self. N.Y.: Bell Tower, 1999.
Sartre, Jean-Paul. Being and Nothingness. N.Y.: Citadel, 1965. H. Barnes, tr.
-----. The Psychology of Imagination. Westport, Connecticut: Greenwood, 1948.
-----. The Transcendence of the Ego. N.Y.: Farrar, Straus and Giroux, 1957. F. Williams and R. Kirkpatrick, trs.
Sekida, Katsuki. Zen Training. N.Y.: Weatherhill, 1985.
Sekida, Katsuki, tr. Two Zen Classics. N.Y.: Weatherhill, 1977.

Seligman, Martin E. Learned Optimism. N.Y.: Random House, 1990.
-----. What You Can Change . . . And What You Can't. N.Y.: Fawcett, 1993.
Shantideva. The Way of the Bodhisattva. Boston: Shambhala, 2003.
Sheng-yen. Complete Enlightenment. Boston: Shambhala, 1999.
Shibayama, Zenkei. The Gateless Barrier. Boston: Shambhala, 2000.
Singer, Irving. The Nature of Love. Chicago: University of Chicago Press, 1987. 3 vols.
Simpsons, C. Alexander, and Simpkins, Annellen. Simple Taoism. Boston: Tuttle, 1999.
Smith, Huston. The World's Religions. San Francisco: Harper, 1991.
Smith, Jean, ed. Breath Sweeps Mind. N.Y.: Riverhead, 1998.
Smith, Melissa Diana. Going Against the Grain. N.Y. Contemporary, 2002.
Solomon, Robert C. "No Excuses." Audio set from The Teaching Company.
-----. The Passions. Indianapolis: Hackett, 1993.
Stambaugh, Joan. Impermanence is Buddha-nature. Honolulu: University of Hawaii Press, 1990.
Stanford, Craig B. The Hunting Apes. Princeton, N.J.: Princeton University Press, 1999.
Stevenson, Leslie, and Haberman, David L. Ten Theories of Human Nature. N.Y.: Oxford University Press, 1998.
Sullivan, Dan. "Pure Genius." Audio set from Nightingale-Conant.
Sulloway, Frank J. Born to Rebel. N.Y.: Random House,

1997.
Sumedho, Ajahn. The Way It Is. Hertfordshire, England: Amaravati, 1991.
Suzuki, D. T. Essays in Zen Buddhism. N.Y.: Grove, 1949.
-----. An Introduction to Zen Buddhism. N.Y.: Grove, 1964.
-----. Zen Buddhism: Selected Writings of D. T. Suzuki. N.Y.: Doubleday, 1956. William Barrett, ed.
Suzuki, Roshi Shunryu. Zen Mind, Beginner's Mind. N.Y.: Weatherhill, 1970.
-----. Not Always So. N.Y.: HarperCollins, 2002.
Tanahashi, Kasuaki, and Schneider, Tensho David. Essential Zen. Edison, N.J.: Castle, 1996.
Thorp, Gary. Sweeping Changes. N.Y.: Walker, 2000.
Tolle, Eckhart. A New Earth. N.Y.: Plume 2005.
-----. The Power of Now. Novato, California: New World, 1999.
Tracy, Brian. Something For Nothing. Mechanicsburg, PA: Executive, 2004.
Venuto, Tom. Burn the Fat Feed the Muscle. E-book: Fitness Renaissance, 2003.
----- and Benson, Jon. Fit Over 40. E-book: Venuto, 2005.
Waitley, Denis. Seeds of Greatness. N.Y.: Pocket, 1983.
Watts, Alan W. This Is It. N.Y.: Macmillan, 1958.
Weil, Andrew. Healthy Aging. N.Y.: Knopf, 2005.
-----. Natural Health, Natural Medicine. Boston: Houghton Mifflin, 2004.
Wu, John C. H. The Golden Age of Zen. N.Y.: Doubleday, 1996.
Yates, Dorian, and Wolff, Bob. Blood and Guts. Woodland Hills, California: YB Small, 1993.
Zane, Frank. Fabulously Fit Forever—Expanded. Palm

Springs, California: Zananda, 1993.

Zweig, Connie, and Abrams, Jeremiah, eds. <u>Meeting the Shadow</u>. N.Y.: Putnam, 1991.

About the Author

Dennis E. Bradford grew up in Toledo, Ohio, and graduated from Blair Academy in 1964. He graduated from Syracuse University in 1968. After two years in the U.S Army as a lieutenant with overseas duty in Korea, he entered The University of Iowa where he obtained an M.A. in 1974 and a Ph.D. in 1977. Panayot Butchvarov was his dissertation director.

He taught philosophy and humanities at SUNY Geneseo from 1977 until 2009. In 2004 he founded the Ironox Works, Inc., publishing company [http://ironoxworks.com]. He's the author of over 20 books, which are available at amazon.com.

He's a former member of MENSA and The American Philosophical Association. He played hockey for many years in the Rochester Metro Hockey League. He enjoys vacationing in Algonquin Park and the northern Muskoka district of Ontario. He regularly does strength training as well as fitness exercise. His health is good. He lives peacefully and happily in solitude on the shore of the westernmost of the Finger Lakes in upstate New York.

There are two brief autobiographical sketches available online. One is at his Author Central page: http://www.amazon.com/-/e/B0047EI11A and the other at http://consultingphilosopher.com.

You may connect with him on LinkedIn: http://www.linkedin.com/pub/dennis-e-bradford/1a/a2a/524/ There is contact information available there.

He writes a blog on wisdom and well-being: http://dennis-bradford.com . Its posts are grouped in terms of six kinds of well-being (in no particular order) on the sidebar, namely, financial, moral (inter-personal), intellectual, physical, emotional, and spiritual. Begin with whatever interests you most.

If you are interested in finding out more information about getting his help with your own book, go to: http://ironoxworks.com/.

If you are interested in more information about his national media citation service, go to: http://ironoxworks.com/media-authority-publicity-icons/ .

If you interested in more information about consulting with him one-on-one, go to http://consultingphilosopher.com/

www.ingramcontent.com/pod-product-compliance
Lightning Source LLC
Chambersburg PA
CBHW051938090426
42741CB00008B/1188